WEYERHAEUSER ENVIRONMENTAL CLASSICS

Paul S. Sutter, Editor

WEYERHAEUSER ENVIRONMENTAL CLASSICS

Paul S. Sutter, Editor

WEYERHAEUSER ENVIRONMENTAL CLASSICS are reprinted editions of key works that explore human relationships with natural environments in all their variety and complexity. Drawn from many disciplines, they examine how natural systems affect human communities, how people affect the environments of which they are a part, and how different cultural conceptions of nature powerfully shape our sense of the world around us. These are books about the environment that continue to offer profound insights about the human place in nature.

Debating Malthus: A Documentary Reader on Population, Resources, and the Environment, edited and introduced by Robert J. Mayhew

Environmental Justice in Postwar America: A Documentary Reader, edited by Christopher W. Wells

Making Climate Change History: Documents from Global Warming's Past, edited by Joshua P. Howe

Nuclear Reactions: Documenting American Encounters with Nuclear Energy, edited by James W. Feldman

The Wilderness Writings of Howard Zahniser, edited by Mark Harvey

The Environmental Moment: 1968–1972, edited by David Stradling

Reel Nature: America's Romance with Wildlife on Film, by Gregg Mitman

DDT, Silent Spring, and the Rise of Environmentalism, edited by Thomas R. Dunlap

Conservation in the Progressive Era: Classic Texts, edited by David Stradling

Man and Nature: Or, Physical Geography as Modified by Human Action, by George Perkins Marsh

A Symbol of Wilderness: Echo Park and the American Conservation Movement, by Mark W. T. Harvey

Tutira: The Story of a New Zealand Sheep Station, by Herbert Guthrie-Smith

Mountain Gloom and Mountain Glory: The Development of the Aesthetics of the Infinite, by Marjorie Hope Nicolson

The Great Columbia Plain: A Historical Geography, 1805–1910, by Donald W. Meinig

WEYERHAEUSER ENVIRONMENTAL CLASSICS is a subseries within Weyerhaeuser Environmental Books, under the general editorship of Paul S. Sutter. A complete listing of the series appears at the end of this book.

DEBATING MALTHUS

A Documentary Reader on Population, Resources, and the Environment

EDITED AND INTRODUCED BY
ROBERT J. MAYHEW

UNIVERSITY OF WASHINGTON PRESS
Seattle

Debating Malthus: A Documentary Reader on Population, Resources, and the Environment is published with the assistance of a grant from the Weyerhaeuser Environmental Books Endowment, established by the Weyerhaeuser Company Foundation, members of the Weyerhaeuser family, and Janet and Jack Creighton.

Copyright © 2022 by the University of Washington Press

Composed in Minion Pro, typeface designed by Robert Slimbach

26 25 24 23 22   5 4 3 2 1

Printed and bound in the United States of America

All rights reserved. No part of this publication may be reproduced or transmitted in any form or by any means, electronic or mechanical, including photocopy, recording, or any information storage or retrieval system, without permission in writing from the publisher.

UNIVERSITY OF WASHINGTON PRESS
uwapress.uw.edu

LIBRARY OF CONGRESS CATALOGING-IN-PUBLICATION DATA

Names: Mayhew, Robert J. (Robert John), 1971- editor.
Title: Debating Malthus : a documentary reader on population, resources, and the environment / edited and introduced by Robert J. Mayhew.
Description: Seattle : University of Washington Press, [2022] | Series: Weyerhaeuser environmental classics | Includes bibliographical references and index.
Identifiers: LCCN 2021029669 (print) | LCCN 2021029670 (ebook) |
    ISBN 9780295749891 (hardcover) | ISBN 9780295749907 (paperback) |
    ISBN 9780295749914 (ebook)
Subjects: LCSH: Malthus, T. R. (Thomas Robert), 1766-1834. | Population—Environmental aspects. | Malthusianism.
Classification: LCC HB863 .D44 2021 (print) | LCC HB863 (ebook) |
    DDC 330.15/3—dc23
LC record available at https://lccn.loc.gov/2021029669
LC ebook record available at https://lccn.loc.gov/2021029670

♾ This paper meets the requirements of ANSI/NISO Z39.48-1992 (Permanence of Paper).

CONTENTS

Foreword: The Many Moments of Malthusianism, by Paul S. Sutter ix
Acknowledgments xv
A Note Regarding Texts and Usage xvii

INTRODUCTION: On an Overgrown Path—Linking Population and Environmental History 1

PART 1: BEFORE MALTHUS

FROM Anon., *Certayne Causes Gathered Together, Wherin Is Shewed the Decaye of England* (1552) 17

FROM Giovanni Botero, *The Cause of the Greatnesse of Cities* (1635) 20

FROM Gabriel Plattes, *A Discovery of Infinite Treasure* (1639) 23

FROM John Graunt, *Natural and Political Observations* (1662) 25

FROM Charles de Montesquieu, *The Spirit of the Laws* (1750) 28

FROM David Hume, "Of the Populousness of Ancient Nations" (1742) 33

FROM Robert Wallace, *A Dissertation on the Numbers of Mankind, in Antient and Modern Times* (1753) 39

FROM Benjamin Franklin, "Observations Concerning the Increase of Mankind" (1755) 44

FROM Thomas Short, *A Comparative History of the Increase and Decrease of Mankind in England* (1767)   48

FROM Richard Price, *Observations on Reversionary Payments* (1772)   51

PART 2: THE MALTHUS WARS

FROM William Godwin, *An Enquiry Concerning Political Justice* (1793)   61

FROM Marquis de Condorcet, *Outlines of an Historical View of the Progress of the Human Mind* (1795)   66

FROM Thomas Robert Malthus, *An Essay on the Principle of Population* (1798)   72

FROM William Godwin, *Of Population* (1820)   82

FROM Thomas Robert Malthus, *An Essay on the Principle of Population* (1826)   89

FROM Thomas Robert Malthus, *A Summary View of the Principle of Population* (1830)   91

FROM Mary Shelley, *The Last Man* (1826)   93

PART 3: EVOLVING DEBATES

FROM Charles Darwin, "Extracts from an Unpublished Work on Species" (1839)   102

FROM Petr Kropotkin, *Mutual Aid: A Factor of Evolution* (1902)   107

FROM W. Stanley Jevons, *The Coal Question* (1865)   112

FROM Alfred Russel Wallace, "Free-Trade Principles and the Coal Question" (1873)   116

FROM John Stuart Mill, *Principles of Political Economy* (1848)   121

FROM John Ruskin, *Unto This Last: Four Essays on the First Principles of Political Economy* (1862)   124

FROM Annie Besant, *The Law of Population and Its Relation to Socialism* (1886)   128

FROM John Maynard Keynes, *The Economic Consequences of the Peace* (1919)   131

FROM Aldous Huxley, "What Is Happening to Our Population?" (1934)   134

FROM Josué de Castro, "The Cycle of the Crab" (1937)   138

PART 4: THE POPULATION BOMB

FROM William Vogt, *The Road to Survival* (1948)   147

FROM Radhakamal Mukerjee, "Population Theory and Politics" (1941)   150

FROM John Boyd Orr, *The White Man's Dilemma* (1953)   156

FROM Paul Ehrlich, *The Population Bomb* (1968)   159

FROM Garrett Hardin, "The Tragedy of the Commons" (1968)   164

FROM Committee on Agriculture, House of Representatives, *Malthus and America: A Report about Food and People* (1974)   169

FROM Barry Commoner, "A Bulletin Dialogue on *The Closing Circle*: Response" (1972)   174

FROM Mahmood Mamdani, "The Ideology of Population Control" (1976)   178

FROM Amartya Sen, "Famines as Failures of Exchange Entitlements" (1976)   181

FROM Norman Borlaug, "The Green Revolution, Peace, and Humanity" (1970)   184

FROM Elinor Ostrom, *Governing the Commons* (1990)   189

FROM Julian Simon, "Resources, Population, Environment: An Oversupply of False Bad News" (1980)   193

PART 5: THE MALTHUS WARS TODAY

FROM Jessica Tuchman Mathews, "Redefining Security" (1989)   203

FROM Robert D. Kaplan, "The Coming Anarchy" (1994)   206

FROM Jared Diamond, *Collapse: How Societies Choose to Fail or Succeed* (2005)   209

FROM Jack A. Goldstone, "The New Population Bomb: The Four Megatrends That Will Change the World" (2010)   213

FROM John Beddington, "Professor Sir John Beddington's Speech at SDUK 09" (2009)   217

FROM Joel E. Cohen, "Population and Climate Change" (2010)   222

FROM Brian O'Neill et al., "Global Demographic Trends and Future Carbon Emissions" (2010)   225

FROM Paul J. Crutzen, "Geology of Mankind" (2002)   228

FROM Johan Rockström et al., "Planetary Boundaries: Exploring the Safe Operating Space for Humanity" (2009)   230

FROM Committee on Women, Population, and the Environment, "Women, Population, and the Environment: Call for a New Approach" (1993)   233

FROM Betsy Hartmann, "Population, Environment and Security: A New Trinity" (1998)   236

FROM Winona LaDuke, *All Our Relations* (1999)   241

FROM Jade Sasser, "From Darkness into Light: Race, Population, and Environmental Advocacy" (2014)   245

Index   249

FOREWORD

The Many Moments of Malthusianism

PAUL S. SUTTER

Population is the third rail of modern environmental politics. Over the past half century, even as population growth has indirectly powered the acceleration of human impacts on the global environment, most environmental activists have not wanted to touch the issue. And for good reason. Modern environmental politics in the Western world emerged during the quarter century after World War II, a period that the historian Tom Robertson called "the Malthusian moment," when population growth and environmental concerns were inextricably linked. But the blowback was swift and damaging. Population doomsayers such as Paul and Anne Ehrlich, whose *The Population Bomb* appeared in 1968, were criticized not only for the inaccuracy of their predictions of impending global famine but also because their theorizing tended to target the developing world as "the problem." Even as the developed world consumed far more resources, and thus had a more substantial environmental footprint, the slums of Calcutta exercised a stronger influence on the dystopian imaginations of Western environmentalists than did the suburbs of New Jersey or California. Moreover, draconian proposals to solve the population problem quickly raised human rights issues, and, within the United States at least, the centrality of population concerns to environmental politics led some to advocate for strict immigration restriction, part of an unsavory lifeboat politics that divided the environmental community.

Perhaps most importantly, developing nations pushed back in the international arena, arguing that they had the right to develop and that, in doing so, they would eventually solve the population problem by raising standards of living, which would in turn lower birth rates. In this way, the Malthusian moment gave way to the "sustainability moment," a period during which concerns about population growth were subsumed within a more equitable, if also sometimes oxymoronic, discourse on sustainable development.

The decline of a singular focus on the population-resource nexus in modern environmental politics was a necessary development because of the fraught relationship between human population sizes, rates of resource use, and their subsequent environmental impacts. It was also necessary given the dangerously reductive lines of reasoning that sometimes marked the Malthusian moment. Indeed, one of the great lessons of this period was the imperative to sniff out pernicious ideas about the *qualities* of populations in a discourse otherwise focused on quantitative concerns. But our collective inability or unwillingness to talk about population growth since the 1970s has also been a problem. When I was born in 1965, there were approximately 3.3 billion humans on earth. Fifty-six years later, as I write, the current world population is approximately 7.8 billion. That's 4.5 billion people added to the planet's population during my brief existence, a staggering development around which I find it difficult to wrap my environmental historian's mind. To a certain extent, the growing scholarly and popular focus on concepts such as the Anthropocene and the Great Acceleration have returned population growth to the conversation as a gateway metric for understanding the material consequences of an increasingly human age, but our efforts to fully historicize this period of unprecedented population growth are lagging.

Into this complex moment arrives Robert Mayhew's *Debating Malthus*, a pathbreaking primary source collection on the environmental history of population thinking, one that aims to clear, regrade, and blaze the overgrown path of Malthusian history. Mayhew is an ideal guide, for he is one of our generation's leading scholars of Malthusianism and the author of the acclaimed book *Malthus: The Life and Legacies of an Untimely Prophet* (2014). Mayhew's purpose in this volume is not to tackle the problem of the population-resource nexus per se; rather, it is to help us engage with and understand the history of Malthusianism and its relationship to environmental thinking during the early modern and modern eras. Such an understanding, he hopes, will encourage new conversations and debates about population and its environmental dimensions.

The pith of the Malthusian idea was expressed in two brief sentences in Thomas Malthus's *Essay on the Principle of Population*, first published in 1798: "Population, when unchecked, increases in a geometrical ratio. Subsistence increases only in an arithmetical ratio." There lies the rub—that population apparently increases faster than the resources needed to support it, raising questions about the capacity of the environment to support growing human numbers. This simple formulation has exercised an outsized, overly static, and often problematic influence during the last several centuries, in part because we have not understood the histories—and historicity—of the concepts that have both informed and come to colonize Malthusianism. Population, resources, environment—these are not simply objective and unchanging things that stand in self-evident relationship to one another. Rather, they are complex ideas with intersecting histories that have shaped a rich series of debates. *Debating Malthus*, then, is less a material history of an objective problem than it is an intellectual history, through deftly curated primary sources, of the concepts that have, over time, shaped and reshaped our understanding of the Malthusian problem.

Debating Malthus traces what we might see as five Malthusian moments. Part 1 demonstrates that Malthus himself did not invent the discourse. During the early modern period, population growth became attached to statecraft mostly as a positive development, with observers beginning to wonder what the natural limitations to such salutary growth might be. In part 2, Mayhew shows how Malthus, though not the first person to link population growth to nature's limitations, was most important for intervening in an Enlightenment conversation about the relationship between populations and progress. Those debates demonstrate that Malthusianism emerged in a particular historical context as an alloy that later debates would heat and reshape. Part 3 examines Malthusianism during the century after Malthus's death, with an emphasis on the powerful role that Darwinian evolution played in renovating Malthusian thinking and applying it even more broadly to understandings of the natural world. This part also shows how Darwinian thinking bled dangerously into social Darwinism and then eugenics, even as it also informed modern notions of collectivism, reproductive justice, empire, and the implications of our growing reliance on fossil fuels. Population, resources, and the environment were all becoming more capacious concepts. The subject of part 4 is the postwar Malthusian moment, a period during which debates became truly international, more dominated by Americans than Europeans, and increasingly engaged by intellectuals from the so-called Third World. This period also saw Malthusian concerns become more strongly linked to their ecological consequences, what Mayhew calls "Green Malthusianism," as well as to Cold War geopolitics and the era's catastrophic fears. No concept better captured this new Malthusian configuration than the "population bomb." Finally, part 5 is a denouement of sorts, one that examines the modulating of Malthusianism in a post–Cold War world, when population bombs were less a concern than climate disasters, fears of ecological collapse, and the security threats posed by bulging global demographics. This most recent period also has seen a new feminist engagement with Malthusian formulations and fears and postcolonial and multispecies critiques of the entire discourse.

Together, these parts and the well-chosen documents that constitute them provide convincing evidence that Malthusian thinking has always been more complex, contextual, changing, and contested than we have assumed. The powerful lesson that emerges, of course, is that our current thinking about population, resources, and the environment must also be powerfully shaped by our own historical context. The gift of *Debating Malthus* is the opportunity it provides to historically situate our contemporary conversations about population, resources, and the environment. The sources suggest that the postwar Malthusian moment was but one of many, a moment in which an emerging concept of "the environment" and an environmental movement had as much to do with reshaping population thinking as vice versa.

That Malthusianism has long been a protean and contested intellectual field is poignantly demonstrated by the shifting sands of the discourse in our present moment. If recent media coverage is any indication, the world's new population "problem" may well be declining birth rates and what they portend for our social and economic future. As I write, the 2020 Census has just shown the slowest rates of US population growth in decades, China has recently allowed couples to have three children because of its own stalling demographic growth, and large parts of Europe and Asia are facing futures of sustained population declines and the graying of their populations that threaten their social and economic futures. By mid-century, many demographers predict, global population will likely enter a period of steady decline, or perhaps even an exponential spiral downward. While such developments might well be cause for Malthusian celebration, this is not the first time that such "reverse Malthusianism" has entered the conversation, and flipping the terms of the debate does not guarantee that we escape the simplifying logics chronicled in this book. Indeed, it's not yet clear what sustained population decline might mean for resource consumption, economic equity, or environmental protection. What is clear is that we need a new generation of citizens who are conversant in the long and complex history of thinking about population and the environment if we are to thoughtfully, justly, and effectively shape the future material relationships between people, the resources they need, and the environments they value. *Debating Malthus* is an essential resource for that next generation, a conversation starter par excellence.

ACKNOWLEDGMENTS

The idea for this volume emerged in the process of writing my previous monograph, *Malthus: The Life and Legacies of an Untimely Prophet* (2014). In particular, when looking to run an advanced undergraduate course on population and environmental thinking, it became clear there was no sourcebook suitable for that audience. I would like to thank Paul S. Sutter as the series editor of Weyerhaeuser Environmental Books for his enthusiastic support of this project. That enthusiasm was shared at the University of Washington Press by Regan Huff, the senior acquisitions editor who commissioned this project, and by Andrew Berzanskis, the senior acquisitions editor who has seen this project to completion. I would particularly like to thank Paul and Andrew for their patience as family circumstances delayed the completion of this project; many less genial souls would have withdrawn when delays ebbed from months to a year and more, and I am grateful that they never looked at matters in this way. I hope the wait was worth it! Ted McCormick offered suggestions for the selections in part 1, and Alison Bashford advised on part 4, particularly with respect to the fascinating ideas of Radhakamal Mukerjee. Neither are responsible for my final choices. Two anonymous readers for the press were "critical" in exactly the way any author wants: exacting but alert to the ambitions of the project and constructive in pushing me to improve the finished manuscript. Thanks also to Federico Ferretti for his advice regarding Josué de Castro and for providing the translation of Castro's "The Cycle of the Crab" used here. I would also like to thank the cohorts of students at the University of Bristol who have undertaken a course that shares its title with this book; in trialing this material with them, I have been led to change and improve the selections offered and sharpen the points at issue. Finally, the book is dedicated to my son, Samuel: jowled things . . .

The University of Washington Press and the author acknowledge permission to reprint material under copyright. If any other copyright holders feel their claims have not been acknowledged, they should contact the publisher.

A NOTE REGARDING TEXTS AND USAGE

Texts have been lightly edited and modernized for the earlier selections in terms of grammar and punctuation to aid readability. Equally, I have wanted to retain something of the feel for the fact that these texts come from Peter Laslett's "world we have lost," enforcing textually for the reader the alterity of the past. For the more recent selections, all the original academic referencing has been removed except in those few cases where one author cross references another author also included in this volume. This was thought to aid the sense of a "dialogue" between the material in this volume. All original notes have been removed, such that all notes in this volume are editorial.

The aim of this collection of excerpts is to array some of the most influential texts that have linked population, resources, and the environment in the arguments of the past half millennium of thinking in (mainly) Anglophone thought. And yet it would be naïve to stop there in trying to characterize the goals of this volume. Any project that seeks to pick out "important" contributions must occlude others. It will also by the very fact of its construction build some form of narrative that has valences of partisanship. *Debating Malthus* focuses on the Anglophone tradition of debating population and the environment, partly because of the Anglophone readership of this book, but the procrustean nature of this decision must be acknowledged: if, for example, Malthus engaged with Condorcet in the original French and with Johann Süssmilch's pioneering work on parish registers in German, we can immediately see the limits of framing the debate as Anglophone. In short, many if not most of the commentators excerpted in this collection read in languages other than English, and therefore the geographical limits of their conversations cannot be fully reflected in the selections offered here. A second spatial occlusion beyond the linguistic is also worth noting in that there are other traditions of reflecting on population, statecraft, and the physical environment in other parts of the globe that are not included here. The only justification for neglecting these traditions in this volume must be that the selections offered here are already so radically abbreviated that to try to incorporate other traditions would mean each is so sparingly represented as to amount to a meaningless caricature. And yet, of course, intellectual traditions are not hermetically sealed units, for that would make them even less interactive than tectonic plates. The gains in terms of depth of coverage allowed by the Anglophone focus must be weighed against the acknowledged losses that result from neglecting the considerable cross-fertilization of ideas and the interactional nature of demographic thought, things inevitably lost or at least underplayed by the logic of selection developed here.

And yet the presuppositions that drive *Debating Malthus* in terms of its logics of inclusion and exclusion need not be purely self-denying ordinances to its readership. On the contrary, resources for reading "against the grain" can be found in several ways. The self-awareness of the limits to canonicity that this volume embodies and that the previous paragraph laid bare immediately invite the reader to look for other routeways. First, for all the smoothing that the narrative introductions to each of the five parts generate, the selected readings and the mention in the introductions of other authors not included in this book give the reader starting points for telling different stories, for plotting different paths. Second, the excerpted texts can be read in ways not imagined by the editor who selected them and for patterns across the parts or within them that tell different stories. Finally, different readerships will make different interactional stories in the collision between the readings offered in this volume and their knowledge bases, stories that will extend beyond and challenge those that are offered by the canon of selections offered here and the narrative framework into which they are incorporated by the editor. These stories can effectively challenge and complicate the temporal, linguistic, and spatial decisions *Debating Malthus* embodies.

DEBATING MALTHUS

INTRODUCTION

On an Overgrown Path—Linking Population and Environmental History

The overarching contention of *Debating Malthus* is that thinking about population has been an important part of and driver for the environmental ideas over the past half millennium in Anglophone and European thought. As such, any attempt to develop environmental histories without an awareness of population debates is missing an important element of its story. In more detail, and as this collection of excerpts shows, the concept of "population" has developed in lockstep with notions of food and resource availability, of sustainability, and of ecology and ecosystems. An enduring and essential strand of the attempt to reason about the relationship between human societies and their physical settings has been mediated via a concern with population, in terms of its total size, its rate of growth, and its structure. The readings offered in *Debating Malthus* open a vista onto the fact that our modern concept of "the environment" would not have formed as it has without the contested notions of population as an essential contributor and interlocutor. The concepts of "population," "resource," and "environment" have been developed in interdependency rather than as separate ideas that come together but infrequently or fortuitously.

To make good this overarching contention as to the significance of population to environmental history, we can break down the narrative *Debating Malthus* offers into three component parts: population, resources, and the environment. First, over the five hundred years covered in this volume, *population* itself evolves considerably as a concept. That history is of great importance for environmental and intellectual historians. At the outset, population is by and large an aggregate imagined as something to be governed by the sovereign, a conception that ultimately has ancient and biblical roots. The quantification of population is gestured toward in the political arithmetic of the seventeenth century, but it is only in the age of the census (the first US census was in 1790, and the UK followed suit in 1801, although it was by no means the first European enumeration), which is also the age of Thomas Robert Malthus, that the descriptive notion of an aggregate can be supplemented by numerical reasoning about that aggregate. Census data allowed for the development of concepts that were crucial to how population thinking has been incorporated into environment debates over the past two centuries. Concerns about population density and rates of population growth, for example, could have little empirical traction before accurate demographic enumeration. Malthus, writing on the cusp of this development, made claims about geometrical population growth rates but had inadequate evidence. As later documents in this volume show, conceptions of population have grown more sophisticated with the passage of time. Thus, postwar discussions started to consider not just a population size and rate of change but also per capita consumption, developing notions of a population's "resource footprint" or the "ghost acres" required to feed it. Latterly, the ways in which the age structure, household size, and urbanization of a population determine its environmental impact have also been investigated, as have the inflections caused by looking at a population's stratification by gender, race, and the like. As such, population is not a self-evident "thing" but a concept with a complex history that has twinned it with resources and the natural environment in evolving ways over the years.

Second, which type of *resource* it is feared population may stress, destroy, exhaust, or overtop has changed over time. In other words, how population may imperil sustainability has been historically mutable. As such, the notion of a key or vulnerable resource on which humans are reliant has its own history that needs to be traced. In the early modern period, territory was often seen as the key resource with which to correlate population. In the age of Malthus, the focus was on food. Malthus accepted there were vast territories on the globe unencumbered by people, but he did not see this as a solution to the population "problem," unlike his opponents the Marquis de Condorcet and William Godwin. It was the superior growth rate of population relative to food that for Malthus set the terms of a resource scarcity problem, not the availability or otherwise of territory. Of course, food scarcity and security remained central to population-resource discussions right down to the postwar era, but it was joined by other resource concerns. Thus, as an agrarian, organic economy was replaced by an industrial, fossil fuel regime in the nineteenth century, scholars such as William Jevons started to see population as overtopping coal not corn. Coal had, via mechanization and transport, allowed vast underutilized lands to be opened up in the ways Godwin had imagined, and this had scotched Malthus's food scarcity concerns via de facto territorial abundance at least temporarily. But coal had also allowed a larger population to grow that would exhaust finite fossil fuel resources and then be left in an even more parlous state of collapse than Malthus had feared by virtue of its reliance on a non-renewable resource. This fear would be replayed by John Maynard Keynes to explain the outbreak of World War I and again in the 1970s with a switch in the latter case of the "carbon anxiety" from coal to oil with anxieties that "peak oil" had been reached in the OPEC oil crisis.

In between the coal and oil fears, there had grown a separate set of concerns that the limited resource that population growth would overtop was the natural environment itself. This argument had three stages. First, in the mid- and late nineteenth century, a "romantic," "conservationist," or "aesthetic" version of the argument was forged: population growth meant every available acre was to be cultivated, leaving no wilderness spaces that were spiritually essential for the well-being of humanity, an argument ventured and shared by thinkers as diverse as William Wordsworth, John Stuart Mill, Alfred Russel Wallace, and Theodore Roosevelt. The second stage of this argument emerging in the postwar era was the "ecosystem" or "ecological" version. Scholars such as William Vogt, Paul Ehrlich, and Garrett Hardin claimed that population growth and/or the explosion of per capita consumption would overtop the amount of services that the global ecosystem could provide and the amount of humanly produced waste it could absorb. This second stage of framing ecosystems/a global ecosystem as a limited resource has itself mutated in recent decades to a concern with the carrying capacity of the globe's atmosphere. The third stage, then, is the suggestion that population may overtop the atmosphere as a renewable but limited resource that creates a habitable home for humanity.

Finally, attending to population discourse allows us to trace genealogies of *the environment* as a concept. At the start of the period covered by the excerpts in this book, the notion of a single, surrounding, and sustaining physical milieu on which humans were reliant was conveyed by a constellation of terms and concepts of which the most protean—"nature"—was perhaps the most common. This is certainly the term most commonly used by Malthus, for example, but it flexed between meanings of natural law, natural history, and human nature such that its precise connotations in any given context were and are always slippery, as Robert Boyle noted presciently in the late seventeenth century. Beyond "nature," a host of other terms were applied, notably "world," "earth," and "globe," these being terms that were at least as much cosmological and conceptual as they were scalar and geographical in the early modern period. Likewise, "climate" was more than atmospheric and "terrain" more than geomorphological in this era, each reaching out to a more totalizing concept such as that we now understand by the term "environment." This set of terms was joined in Malthus's work by the notion of a *limited* environment that could be depleted by population's usage of it and later particularly by the emergent nineteenth-century conception of the natural world as something that needed preserving or conserving from the tentacles of industrial growth and mass population's incursions, a concept of which Malthus only a half century previously had shown no cognizance whatsoever. Finally, it is in the postwar period another half century later that the term "environment" starts to be deployed, together with "ecosystem" and "ecology," in ways broadly resonant with modern usages.

Returning to the central claim of *Debating Malthus*—that population is a conceptual crucible in which modern notions of "resources" and "environment" were created, and they reciprocally created our notion of "population"—this would have been seen as a self-evident truth in the immediate postwar decades. If modern environmentalism and its object of concern—"the environment"—were fashioned as conceptual objects in the postwar era, population was one of the more important arenas in which they were forged. And yet in the intervening decades between that moment and the present day, population has dropped out of environmental analysis and been comparatively marginalized by environmental historians. Why has this been the case? Why have the paths linking population, resources, and the environment, once so well trod, become overgrown? To answer these questions, we need to look at the so-called Malthusian moment of the 1950s to the 1970s when population's role in environmental thinking reached its apogee. The Malthusian moment saw the chief protagonists, such as Ehrlich and Hardin, of an apocalyptic vision of population destroying our ability to survive on earth sell millions of books and regularly appear on prime-time television. Their doom-mongering also translated into science fiction scenarios such as *Blade Runner*.

While not synonymous, at this time population and environment were inseparable bedfellows.

Beyond the visible doom-mongering, there was also a more insidious "dark side" to environmental Malthusianism that would lead to the eclipse of the whole discursive formation, a dystopian authoritarianism that would discredit the nexus of population and the environment. We can get a flavor of the problem by thinking through some of the ideas Ehrlich and Hardin promulgated. Seeing the central problematic facing modern societies as breeding beyond the carrying capacity of the globe's ecosystem, they were happy to advocate draconian solutions to avoid mass starvation. On the domestic scene, Ehrlich suggested it might be necessary to introduce sterilants into the public water supply to reduce the birth rate. Hardin suggested that individuals had to accept full economic responsibility for their procreative decisions, and if that led to squalor and even death among the poorer sectors of society, so be it. In the American context, such messaging had an unavoidably racial undertone, disproportionately affecting as it would the poorer African American and Latin American communities as well as recent immigrants. The policy prescriptions of ecological Malthusianism's fusion of population and the environment were no more palatable on the global scale. Hardin in particular advocated a "lifeboat ethics": he argued that the population growth rates of some nations in the Global South were so high that they could not be saved from ecological destruction and should therefore be left to go to the wall. If the West tried to save all nations, they would be dragged into disaster themselves, like a lifeboat that tries to rescue too many capsized passengers at sea. Relatedly, US policy circles saw the notion of "food triage" gain traction: as in a hospital emergency, food and other aid should only be released where there was a likely return on investment, where the country might recover with assistance.

Hardin also argued famously that "the freedom to breed is intolerable," such that societies beyond the pale of food triage should develop compulsory sterilization programs to bring their populations into adjustment with resources. This chimed with mass compulsory sterilization programs of which India's was only the most famous. The United States itself had for decades run such a program for the supposedly "mentally defective," a program targeting Black communities to a vastly disproportionate extent. Such policy prescriptions also had unavoidably gendered implications: cutting against the birth of modern feminism, ecological Malthusianism objectified women's procreative bodies as objects to be controlled from above by a governmental logic that denied their agency. Hardin's work in particular was a peculiar fusion of an ecological authoritarianism with a resurgent free market economics, but in that fusion was an inescapably eugenic program in which a white male governing class would allow other races and women to fail if they did not obey a purportedly iron law of Darwinian demography. This was rendered doubly uncomfortable by the fact that the constellation of population, the environment, and eugenics developed in the 1960s was by no means treading new ground. On the contrary, and as the long history of the United States' sterilization program implied, from its first forging, eugenics had tied population and the environment via the mediating force of a Darwinian/Malthusian argument.

Eugenics—the alleged science of "good breeding"—was pioneered in the United Kingdom by Charles Darwin's cousin Francis Galton in the 1870s and continued at University College, London by Karl Pearson. Both advocated selective breeding of people, which inevitably also meant that the "less fit" should be discouraged, gently or forcibly, from having children. This would improve the "stock" of a nation's population while also preventing runaway population growth. In the United States, very similar ideas emerged either side of 1900: the conservation movement of Roosevelt and the biology of Raymond Pearl and Edward East each demanded that populations be controlled in size and improved in quality to allow for the preservation of America's natural environment as a source of spiritual improvement and an icon of national identity. This fusion of population control, race selection, and conservation clearly continued to inform the writings of the generation of environmentalists prior to Hardin and Ehrlich's Malthusian moment, as embodied in the work of writers such as Fairfield Osborn and Aldo Leopold.

Reverting to the Malthusian environmental moment, it was in response to the politics of this platform that the twinning of population and the environment came to be unpicked, a path less traveled. Demography would take on a professional tone that shunned celebrity, while environmentalism would take less draconian routes into the present day, rebuilding credibility by rolling back from authoritarian excess. This was a response to four sets of critique of ecological Malthusianism that emerged in the 1960s and eventually managed to subvert its intellectual and political credibility. First, a feminist critique of the authoritarian logic of controlling women's bodies as if their only function were reproductive emerged. Acknowledging the empowerment of women meant moving away from a (male) control of the female body and its reproduction to an approach that accepted female agency, this in both developed and developing world contexts. Second, scholars and intellectuals from the Global South argued in parallel with feminism for the agency of their nations as they determined their future trajectories, political, demographic, and environmental; the critique of the ideology of population control as quasi-colonial gained traction in this era. Both of these challenges were recognized by the influential United Nations International Conference on Population and Development in their decadal meetings of 1984 and 1994. These meetings recognized population as a "neutral" factor in development rather than an apocalyptic deal breaker for social and political development, thereby unpicking ecological Malthusianism. The 1994 meeting was the last one the United Nations held, and therefore its policy toward population, development, and ecology is implicitly still that which was agreed to then. Third, and very much tied to the critique emanating from the Global South, the eugenic undertones of ecological Malthusianism came to be unpalatable as they ran directly counter to the civil rights movement in the United States and broader arguments in liberal polities for an alertness to race relations and diversity. The United States' compulsory sterilization programs ended in the 1970s, although it would be far longer before China and India followed a similar direction. Finally, and from a very different intellectual stable, the resurgent free market economics and libertarian politics of the neoconservative movement on both sides of the Atlantic objected to ecological Malthusian's advocacy of large-scale state intervention in the lives of individuals and the flows of the market. The argument of scholars such as Julian Simon was that markets embodied the collective ambitions and intelligence of individuals such that price signals would encourage or discourage fertility and guide resource use where ecosystems or their components butted up against scarcity issues.

The four trends we have just analyzed as explaining the waning traction of environmental Malthusianism also impacted on the practice of environmental history. The immediate postwar generation of pioneering environmental historians saw population as central to their inquiries. A year before Ehrlich's bestselling tract of environmental Malthusianism, *The Population Bomb*, for example, the geographer Clarence Glacken published a pioneering history of environmental ideas, *Traces on the Rhodian Shore* (1967). Glacken addressed, as his subtitle has it, "nature and culture in Western thought from ancient times to the end of the eighteenth century" and found considerable space for discussing ideas about population and their impact on environmental thought. This was particularly apparent toward the close of the book where Glacken offered a full chapter canvassing the debates about whether population had increased or declined since antiquity that had been set in motion by Montesquieu and then carried forward by the likes of David Hume and Robert Wallace and are addressed in part 1 of this volume. Glacken went on, as the capstone of his magnum opus, to the debates between Godwin, Condorcet, and Wallace that form part 2 of *Debating Malthus*. In short, in each era Glacken covered from antiquity to the eighteenth century, the interweaving of demographic and environmental thought was a key thread. The following generation of environmental historians, responding to the same currents of ideas that were criticizing ecological Malthusianism, took their inquiries in different directions that effectively marginalized population as a topic. Environmental history moved toward social and cultural contextualization of environmental practice, perturbed by the logics of coercion that Hardin and colleagues embodied. As Paul Sutter explained, "American environmental historians retreated from engagement with intellectual history in favor of a 'cultural turn.' [. . .] The second generation of American environmental historians continued to study environmental ideas, of course, but with [. . .] more interest in how American ideas of nature were socially and culturally constructed. As environmental historians became more critical of environmentalist ideas—finding in them signs of class position, racial formation, consumer status, and uncritical borrowings from science—we tended to become suspicious of the realm of ideas in general."[1]

Putting these threads together, where in the 1960s environmentalism and population went hand in hand politically and intellectually, a twinning amply reflected in the writing of environmental history, by the 1980s, a widely shared critique of that twinning emerged from predominantly intellectually radical sources (but also had a libertarian or free market echo) and uncoupled environmentalism from population. From then to the present day, environmentalism, environmental history, and demographic analysis have followed separate paths.

Why, then, is now the time to reassess the pathways that connect these areas? First, environmental history has seen a resurgence of interest in intellectual history in recent years. The decoupling of environmental history from population needs to be reversed if it is to develop comprehensive and satisfactory narratives. One aim of *Debating Malthus* is to offer a partial record and a set of starting points for the reintegration of population into environmental history. Broadly, recent work in environmental history argues for the postwar forging of our modern conception of the environment, and in this process thinking about population and its interaction with ecosystems was a key component. A complete understanding of the modern construction of the environment as an object of study and policy cannot be attained without population's role being recognized in the Malthusian moment. Recent work also recognizes that longer genealogies of environmental awareness, concern, and policy can be traced. At one level, such genealogies can stretch back, as did Glacken's work, to antiquity, but equally Paul Warde's important contribution, *The Invention of Sustainability* (2018), has suggested a starting point around 1500. *Debating Malthus* broadly agrees with Warde's sense that the Age of Discovery, the birth of global European empires, and the weaving of global loops of commerce create a recognizably modern context for thinking about the environment and its interaction with human societies. Whether one takes the *longue durée* stretching back to antiquity or Warde's modernity as one's timescale, population cannot be ignored as a contributor and catalyst to environmental ideas, something this collection shows amply for the past half millennium. Overall, then, as environmental history reengages with intellectual history on a number of temporal scales, so it needs to tread the path it shares with population debates once more to build credible synoptic narratives.

Second, we are now over half a century after the Malthusian moment of peak concern about the nexus of population and the environment. We are starting to see the production of excellent scholarly work by environmental historians and students of politics and international relations assessing that moment. In other words, we now have sufficient critical distance from the Malthusian moment to reassess its arguments, their "dark side," and the critique to which they were subjected in a more dispassionate fashion as a passage in the history of ideas, environmental, political, and demographic. *Debating Malthus* offers readers primary texts that allow them to hear those voices in their original idioms, to place them in the longer trajectory of ideas about the population-environment nexus, and to complement the excellent scholarly environmental histories of that time that are beginning to emerge (see the further reading list at the end of this introduction).

Finally, and perhaps cutting against the previous point, we still live surrounded by debates about the population-environment nexus. As the final part of this volume shows, there are both popular and scholarly projects seeking to address the ways in which population and the environment interact. Can societies collapse in Malthusian fashion when population overshoots resources? Does such an approach explain historical events from the depopulation of Easter Island to the Rwandan Genocide? To what extent does population growth, rising affluence, and urbanization help us to model global carbon footprints and climate change? How does changing household size and structure interact with these variables? Do these very questions raise the spectre of occlusions by race, gender, and class of the sort that Ehrlich and Hardin promulgated half a century ago, and how do we combat this without descending into climate change denialism? In a context where public debate can still frame the COVID-19 pandemic as a potentially Malthusian check to excess population, sent by nature through the circuits of global capitalism as a force realigning us with nature/resources/the environment, it behooves us to learn the patterns of debate, both recent and longer term, through which population, resources, and the environment have been conjoined. To be able to adjudicate such claims, a critical citizenry needs to understand their historical underpinnings, their resonances with past debates, and the pathways through which such claims have been built and refuted. Population is not a "master key" as it might have been in the Malthusian moment half a century ago but one point in an interwoven debate that has forged past and present conceptual apparatuses about what the environment is, what threatens it, how it reciprocally might imperil or enable our societies, and why this matters. By retreading the overgrown paths linking population, resources, and the environment, *Debating Malthus* seeks to encourage those debates, both historical and contemporary. Whatever its political valences and past awkwardness, population cannot be left out of our histories of and debates about the environment.

NOTE

1 Paul S. Sutter, "Putting the Intellectual Back in Environmental History," *Modern Intellectual History* 18, no. 2 (2020): 596.

FURTHER READINGS

Bashford, Alison. *Global Population: History, Geopolitics, and Life on Earth*. New York: Columbia University Press, 2014.

Connelly, Matthew. *Fatal Misconception: The Struggle to Control World Population*. Cambridge, MA: Harvard University Press, 2008.

Glacken, Clarence J. *Traces on the Rhodian Shore: Nature and Culture in Western Thought from Ancient Times to the End of the Eighteenth Century*. Berkeley: University of California Press, 1967.

Hoff, Derek S. *The State and the Stork: The Population Debate and Policy Making in US History*. Chicago: University of Chicago Press, 2012.

Hopwood, Nick, Rebecca Flemming, and Lauren Kassell, eds. *Reproduction: Antiquity to the Present Day*. Cambridge: Cambridge University Press, 2018.

Mayhew, Robert J. *Malthus: The Life and Legacies of an Untimely Prophet*. Cambridge, MA: Harvard University Press, 2014.

McCann, Carole R. *Figuring the Population Bomb: Gender and Demography in the Mid-Twentieth Century*. Seattle: University of Washington Press, 2016.

Robertson, Thomas. *The Malthusian Moment: Global Population Growth and the Birth of American Environmentalism*. New Brunswick, NJ: Rutgers University Press, 2012.

Sabin, Paul. *The Bet: Paul Ehrlich, Julian Simon, and Our Gamble over Earth's Future*. New Haven, CT: Yale University Press, 2013.

Sutter, Paul S. "Putting the Intellectual Back in Environmental History." *Modern Intellectual History* 18, no. 2 (2020): 596–605. https://doi.org/10.1017/S1479244320000050.

Warde, Paul. *The Invention of Sustainability: Nature and Destiny c. 1500–1870*. Cambridge: Cambridge University Press, 2018.

Warde, Paul, Libby Robin, and Sverker Sörlin. *The Environment: A History of the Idea*. Baltimore: Johns Hopkins University Press, 2018.

PRIMARY SOURCE COLLECTIONS

Glass, D. V. *Numbering the People: The Eighteenth-Century Controversy and the Development of Census and Vital Statistics in Britain*. Farnborough, UK: D. C. Heath, 1973.

Mazur, Laurie Ann, ed. *Beyond the Numbers: A Reader on Population, Consumption, and the Environment*. Washington, DC: Island Press, 1994.

Mazur, Laurie Ann, ed. *A Pivotal Moment: Population, Justice, and the Environmental Challenge*. Washington, DC: Island Press, 2009.

Population Knowledge Network, ed. *Twentieth Century Population Thinking: A Critical Reader of Primary Sources*. London: Routledge, 2015.

Robin, Libby, Sverker Sörlin, and Paul Warde, eds. *The Future of Nature: Documents of Global Change*. New Haven, CT: Yale University Press, 2013.

Tobin, Kathleen A., ed. *Politics and Population Control: A Documentary History*. Westport, CT: Greenwood, 2004.

1

BEFORE MALTHUS

THE DESIRE TO TRACE THE INTERSECTIONS BETWEEN POPULATION, resource use, and environmental change is by no means the product of the age of Malthus. European attempts to reflect on these interactions go back to antiquity, encoded in political, theological, and moral treatises. For example, Plato's discussion of deforestation in Attica (*Critias* 111a–d) implicitly ties these topics together in its reflection on the rafters of large buildings; people have felled trees as a resource for their expanding societies, and this has led to deforestation and soil erosion. Similarly, medieval political thought was preoccupied with demographic issues around the multitude, the peopling of the world after the Flood, and the ways in which this had etched the landscapes of Europe and the Near East.

This part traces elements of the linkage of population, resources, and the environment in the early modern era. Selections move from the late medieval genre of advice literature for princes through the "reason of state" treatises of the seventeenth century to emergent attempts to offer more sophisticated numerical information for statecraft in the form of "political arithmetic" in the seventeenth century. More diverse conceptual and numerical debates about population and resources emerge during the eighteenth-century Enlightenment and presage the work of Malthus and his critics at the end of the eighteenth century.

In *Certayne Causes Gathered Together, Wherin Is Shewed the Decaye of England*, an anonymous text addressed to Henry VIII but only published in later 1552, the author draws his monarch's attention to the depopulation allegedly gripping England as people are evicted from their houses to allow lands to be engrossed for sheep farming. This may seem quaint in its repetitive and respectful address to His Majesty. It may also seem less than original, as Thomas More in *Utopia* (1516) some half century earlier had made the same point: "your sheep [...] that commonly are so meek and so little, now, as I hear, they have become so greedy and fierce that they devour men themselves. They devastate and depopulate fields, houses and towns." *Certayne Causes*, however, is a landmark text as it points to four persistent elements in discussions about population and the environment that would ramify down the quarter millennium of argument canvassed in this section.

First is the assumption that a large population is both desirable and evidence of good governance. *Certayne Causes* assumes that depopulation is a problem the monarch will wish to address. Secondly, a strong state is one that is both populous and agrarian. Living in an "organic economy" almost entirely predicated on the exploitation of the land to feed, clothe, and power society, the socioeconomic arrangements for working the land were central to population discussion. For the early modern age, the population-resource-environment nexus worked around debates about pasture, husbandry, agricultural innovation, and the like. As Gabriel Plattes memorably put it, "husbandry is the very nerve and sinew" that holds a people together. In looking to the land to diagnose population dynamics and dilemmas, all these writers conjoined population and the environment, however unfamiliar their modes of linkage may look today.

The third point to note is that most discussions of population started from a question that sounds Malthusian to a later era: If the power of human multiplication is so vast, what restrains human populations at a lower level? Thus, Giovanni Botero asked what prevented ancient Rome from continuing to expand in size and argues that if this question can be resolved for a city, "thereby it will be resolved for the world." In a very different context a century and a half later, David Hume and Benjamin Franklin encoded the same question: Why does the prolific power of the natural world so far exceed the growth it can realize? The documents canvassed here develop three main answers: naturalistic-cum-environmental, political-cum-moral, and what we can anachronistically call a "limits to growth" model. The naturalistic argument suggests that many physical environments are deleterious to human health and longevity, and this means that the environment effectively checks population growth. This idea is an ancient one, going back to the Hippocratic text *On Airs, Waters, and Places*. These ideas are canvassed particularly clearly in the writings of Robert Wallace and Thomas Short, with Short in particular wanting to correlate death rates with the physical environments in which they occurred. And yet even for scholars working in the Hippocratic tradition, this was not an adequate analysis on its own. As Short noted, "the healthiest situation is insufficient of itself, without establishing and maintaining a good policy." Resultantly, early modern writers argued that political and moral factors were the most important checks to population growth. Key here was the impact of politics on the land: if *Certayne Causes* discussed the engrossing of land, this remained a focus of demographic attention for Richard Price 250 years later. As Price put it, "a general account of the causes which obstruct population [. . .] insists particularly on luxury and the engrossing of farms." Price's other key explanatory variable, luxury, was also important, suggesting that moral decay from hardy values of work to enervated consumption could also explain population decline, a tradition also drawn on in the analyses of Charles de Montesquieu and Wallace. Finally, scholars also reflected on the extent to which population growth could be limited by the logistical problems of sustaining it; in modern parlance, were there negative feedback loops that checked population growth? This was central to Botero's explanation of why the population of ancient Rome reached a ceiling and to Hume's analysis of limits to growth, ancient and modern, in Rome and London.

The fourth point to note is the importance of quantification to the population-resource-environment debates of the early modern period and the coupled awareness of how inadequate the available numerical data was. *Certayne Causes* tries to estimate the number of ploughs lost in the English countryside due to the engrossing of lands for sheep farming and then uses a proxy of how many individuals each plough could sustain to reach its estimate that England in Henry VIII's time had lost capacity sufficient to feed three hundred thousand individuals. While political arithmetic as pioneered by the likes of John Graunt improved the quantitative sophistication of debates about the linkage of population and the environment, a century later Benjamin Franklin's celebrated analysis of why colonial populations could grow so quickly was still having to make heroic assumptions about how to translate mortality data into an estimate of total population. Hume encapsulated the problem: "we know not exactly the numbers of any European kingdom or even city" such that debate was bound to remain impressionistic, mixing causes and facts.

The ways in which these elements came together to frame demographic discussion about population and its environmental grounding are most apparent in the Enlightenment debate about whether global population had expanded or contracted after the era of the Roman Empire. The debate started with Montesquieu's *Persian Letters* (1721). Montesquieu saw a direct link between population size and the fertility of the soil: "Why is it that the world is so thinly populated in comparison with former times? How is it that nature has managed to lose the prodigious fertility that she had originally?" He claims that "there is scarcely a fiftieth of the number of men on earth that there was in Caesar's time." In fact, Montesquieu had made no calculations whatsoever. The capricious nature of Montesquieu's numbers is made plain by their dramatic adjustment in posthumous editions after 1758 to suggest global population was one tenth, not one fiftieth, of its ancient tally. And yet Montesquieu's claims set in motion a set of debates about population and resource dynamics that continued for the next half century. Wallace defended and elaborated Montesquieu's depopulationist account on moral grounds, albeit touching on environmental arguments. More thorough was Hume's rebuttal of Montesquieu, which used detailed textual investigation to suggest Europe was more populous in the eighteenth century than at its zenith in the Roman era. Of particular interest was the weight Hume attached to climatic evidence of northern Europe being warmer in his era than Caesar's. For Hume, population increase would lead to deforestation, and this could explain the increased temperatures of his times. As we have already noted, the Hippocratic tradition of environmental determinism showed how the environment impacted on population size and life expectancy; Hume here looked at the reverse causation by which demographic change could alter the environment.

Montesquieu was also central to another set of debates in Enlightenment Europe that framed the population-resource-environment nexus. He argued, notably in his celebrated *The Spirit of the Laws* (1748), that societies advanced through successive stages in which their dynamics and statecraft would be distinctively different. Simply put, as society advanced, it would use the land more intensively, and this would allow it to sustain a larger population. There were precursors to such argument, as in Plattes's suggestion in 1639 that each time population reached a limit to growth, it would innovate on the land and thereby transcend that limit. But Montesquieu's stadial theory became hugely influential. A key question was whether each stage of social change was "progressive," and many came to suggest that while a settled agricultural society was an advance over its predecessors in terms of the numbers of happy lives it could sustain, the evolution from this into a mercantile and commercial society posed great threats. This was the line adopted by Price, and it also informed Franklin's analysis of colonial North America. For both, demographic data proved the point: America's rapid rate of population growth was evidence of a virtuous and happy society, whereas the urbanized societies of Europe exhibited slower population growth as people left the land for the mortality (and morality) sinkholes that were early modern cities.

In sum, the quarter millennium prior to Malthus's *Essay* saw the development of complex ideas about the interlinkage of population, resources, and the environment on which Malthus and his interlocutors would draw. Seeing a large, contented, and well-supplied population as both key to and evidence of good statecraft, scholars sought to analyze how the natural power of human multiplication was controlled. Focus attended to natural/environmental limits to population growth but always tied these with analysis of political and socioeconomic factors that tended to be deemed more significant. There was also awareness that technologies of resource production, transport, and depletion could limit the population growth, this being counterpointed by discussions of ways in which technological innovation and societal development could remove those barriers and transform their parameters. As such, a subtle set of debates had developed, despite the lack of accurate demographic data.

DOCUMENT 1.1

FROM ANON., *CERTAYNE CAUSES GATHERED TOGETHER, WHERIN IS SHEWED THE DECAYE OF ENGLAND* (1552)

WE SAY AS REASON DOES LEAD US, THAT SHEEP AND SHEEPMASTERS do cause scarcity of corne [. . .] The first loss as we do think, there is not so many ploughs used, occupied and maintained within Oxfordshire as was in King Henry VII's time, and since his first coming there lacketh 40 ploughs. Every plough was able to keep 6 persons down living [. . .] in his house, the which draweth to twelve score persons in Oxfordshire. And where the said twelve score persons were wont to have meat, drink, raiment and wages, paying scot and lot[1] to God and to our king, now there is nothing kept there but only sheep. Now these twelve score persons had need to have a living, whither shall they go: into Northamptonshire? And there is also the living of twelve score people lost, whither then shall they go? Forth from shire to shire and to be scattered thus abroad within the king's majesty's realm, where it shall please almighty God, and for lack of masters by compulsion driven some of them to beg and some to steal.

The second loss as we do think, that there is never a plough of the 40 ploughs, but he is able to till and plough to certify six persons and every plough to sell 30 quarters of grain by the year, or else he can fully pay six, seven or eight pounds by the year. 40 ploughs, 30 quarters every plough, draweth to two hundred quarters in Buckinghamshire, two hundred quarters in Oxfordshire, and two hundred quarters in Northamptonshire and so forth from shire to shire in certain shires within the king's majesty's realm of England. What shall the twelve two hundred quarters of corn do in Oxfordshire? We do think it will maintain the king's markets, and sustain the king's subjects and likewise in Buckinghamshire, and also in Northamptonshire, and so from shire to shire in certain shires within the king's majesty's realm. Furthermore it is to be considered what this twelve hundred quarters of corn is able to do within Oxfordshire. It is able to certify and suffice 15 score people by the year bread and drink, and allow every person 2 quarters of meat, and two quarters of malt by the year, whereas in the first the whole living of twelve score persons meat and drink and raiment [. . .] And the second lose bread and drink for 15 score persons by the year, which the whole number draweth to 5 hundred and 40 persons in Oxfordshire, so in Buckinghamshire, and so likewise in Northamptonshire and so forth from shire to shire within the king's realm.

And if it be as we do think and there be 4 score ploughs in every one of these shires less than there was, there is there the living lost of a thousand and 4 score persons in every one of these foresaid shires [. . .]

[. . .] we desire of God and the king's majesty, if it shall please his highness to be so good and gracious unto his poor subjects, that there might be in every shire and hundred as many ploughs used, occupied and maintained, as many households kept as was by king Henry VII's time [. . .] as we do think we should have corn enough, cattle enough and sheep enough, then will sheep and wool be in more men's hands. We shall have also white meat enough and all things necessary. And thus Jesus preserve our dread sovereign lord and king.

[. . .]

Furthermore as we do think, this realm does decay by these means, it is to understand and know that there is in England towns and villages to the number of fifty thousand and upward, and for every town and village, take them one with another throughout all, there is one plough decayed since the first year of the reign of King Henry VII. And in some towns and villages all the whole town [is] decayed since that time, and if there by for every town and village one plough decayed, since the first year of the reign of King Henry VII, then there is decayed one thousand ploughs and upward. The which one thousand ploughs, every plough were able to maintain 6 persons. That is to say: the man, the wife and four other in his house less or more. One thousand ploughs, six persons to every plough, draweth to the number of three hundred thousand that were wont to have meat, drink and raiment [. . .] and thus the realm does decay.

NOTE

1 "Scot and lot" is a term for local levies or taxes.

DOCUMENT 1.2

FROM GIOVANNI BOTERO, *THE CAUSE OF THE GREATNESSE OF CITIES* (1588; TRANS., LONDON, 1635)

IT IS ASSUREDLY A MATTER WORTHY [OF] CONSIDERATION, FROM whence it comes, that cities arrived to a certain height of magnitude and power, can pass no further, but either firmly abide therein, or else fall back again. Let us take Rome for an example. This, in the beginning, was founded by Romulus; as Dionysius Halicarnassus[1] writes, it contained three thousand three hundred men fit to bear arms. Romulus reigned seven and thirty years, in which space the city multiplied to forty seven thousand fighting men. Under Servius Tullius, after the death of Romulus, about some hundred and fifty years, were reckoned up in Rome four score thousand, fit for warlike employment. Finally, the number, by little and little, amounted to the sum of four hundred and fifty thousand men. Then do I demand, whence is it, that the people of Rome, from three thousand three hundred men of war, arrived at four hundred and fifty thousand; and from four hundred and fifty thousand, passed no further? Likewise, four hundred years ago, Milan and Venice afforded as many men as now they do: whereby it appears the increase goes no further. Some answer that plague, war, dearth and other like occasions, are the cause. But that does not satisfy: for plagues and infections have always been; wars were much more bloody in former ages, than in our days. [. . .]

Some affirm, it is because God, the moderator of all things, so disposes [matters]. No man doubts thereof: yet because the infinite wisdom of God in the administration and government of Nature uses second[ary] causes, I ask with what means the eternal providence makes the small number multiply, and gives limits and bounds to the greater? For answer of which question propounded, I may say that the same demand may be made of all human kind: because it being (three thousand years ago) multiplied from one man and woman so much, that all the provinces of the firm land and islands of the sea were filled, how is it come to pass that from those three thousand years hitherward, this augmentation has taken no further progression? But let us resolve this doubt in cities, for thereby it will be resolved for the world. We say, then, that the increase of cities proceeds, partly from the virtue generative of men, partly from the nutritive force of those cities. The generative, without doubt, which is always the same, at least from three thousand years hitherward. For as apt are men in these days for generation as they were in the times of David or Moses. Whereupon if there were no other impediment, the propagation endlessly would multiply and the increase of cities be without limit. But if it proceeds no further, it behoves us to say, it is wrought by the defect of nutriment and sustenance. Now, food is imported either from the territory of our city or from other countries, so that if a city would increase, it behoves victuals be thither brought from far. To cause that victual be brought from far, it is necessary the virtue attractive be so great that it surmount and overcome roughness of places, height of hills, depth of valleys, swiftness of rivers, perils of sea, treacheries of pirates, instability of winds, greatness of expense, badness of ways and passages [. . .] length of time which is required for conduct; the dearth and scantiness in places, from whence merchandise is to be conveyed; natural hate of nations, contrariety of sects and such like, which take increase, according as the people and the affairs of the cities multiply, become finally such, and so great, that they exceed all diligence and human industry. [. . .]

There may also be added to the former, that great cities are much more subject to dearth than little because they need a greater quantity of victuals. They are also subject to the plague, for the infection more easily fastens there, and with greater mortality; finally, they are subject to all the difficulties repeated by us, because they stand in need of more. So, although men were as apt for generation in the height of Rome's greatness as in the beginning thereof, yet the multitudes of people augmented not by proportion, for the virtue nutritive of the city had no force to pass any further, because the inhabitants, in process of time not having greater commodity of victuals either never married, or, if they married, their children through misery or necessity came to nothing, but forsaking their country, endeavoured to better their fortune by transmutation of place. Which mischief, the Romans [being] desirous to prevent, made choice of many poor citizens and sent them into the colonies where, like trees transplanted, they might better their estates, live more commodiously, and so might multiply. For the same reason, mankind being increased to a certain multitude, has not proceeded any further (and for three thousand years since, and more, the world was as fully replete with men, as now at this present). For the fruits of the earth, and abundance of victual, comports not with greater number of people. Men began to be propagated in Mesopotamia, and augmenting by little and little, they expatiated here and there, and having replenished the continent, they passed to the islands of the sea, and from our parts, by little and little arrived at those Countries, which we entitle the New World. Besides there is not anything for which men fight more furiously than for territory, food and convenience of habitation.

NOTE

1 Dionysius of Halicarnassus was a first-century BCE Greek historian.

DOCUMENT 1.3

FROM GABRIEL PLATTES, *A DISCOVERY OF INFINITE TREASURE* (1639)

[T]HREE SEVERAL TIMES THE PEOPLE GROWING TOO NUMEROUS FOR their maintenance, God has given understanding to men to improve the earth in such a wonderful manner, that it was able to maintain double the number, and so he that made mouths, sent meat by teaching them understanding how to get it. For when there were but few, they were maintained by fish, fowl, venison, and fruits freely provided by Nature. But when they grew too numerous for that food, they found out the spade and used industry to augment their food by their endeavours. Then they growing too numerous again, were compelled to use the plough, the chiefest of all engines, and happily found out. Whereby all commonwealths have ever since been maintained, and at length this invention would not serve the turn either without new skill in the using of it. For at first they used to till the land until the fatness thereof was spent, and so to let it lie a long time to gather fatness again of itself and in the meantime to till fresh land. But when they grew too numerous for the food gotten that way, they were compelled to find out the fallowing and manuring of the land, by which invention the land recovered more fatness in one year, than before in many years. And so a country would maintain double the number of people more than before. Now the people are grown numerous again, requiring new improvements which are discovered in this little book, and shall be shown by irrefragable demonstration and infallible experience. Also it shall be made manifest that by the common course of husbandry used at this day, the barrenness does by little and little increase, and the fertility decrease every year more and more, which in regard that the people do increase wonderfully, must needs at length produce a horrible mischief, and cause the commonwealth to be oppressed with poverty and beggary.

When as by these new inventions and improvements being industriously practised, their wealth shall not be diminished, but contrary ways wonderfully increased, though people shall grow wonderfully numerous.

And this business is not to be slightly thought upon, for so much as husbandry is the very nerve and sinew which holds together all the joints of a monarchy.

Neither is invention to be lightly regarded, for all workmanship without invention resolves itself into the workman's belly, as may be manifestly seen. For before the plough was invented, and before horses, oxen and cattle were taught to do the works which men did before, all their labour came to nothing, but only to fill the belly. But since that time, by the benefit of these and other inventions, we see what castles have been built in time of wars, and what churches in time of peace, what famous towns, cities and schools, and other things conducive for the common good. Also by this means men were spared from servile labours, that they might attain to knowledge to be statesmen, clergymen, lawyers, physicians, merchants, tradesmen, etc without which no commonwealth can subsist.

And for so much as the new world called America does for the present give aid and succour for the maintenance of the surplus of people increased in those countries, yet in regard that the finding of new worlds is not likely to be a perpetual trade, it seems to agree with providence, to begin to improve the lands formerly peopled, in such manner that by their industry there may be raised maintenance for double the number.

DOCUMENT 1.4

FROM JOHN GRAUNT, *NATURAL AND POLITICAL OBSERVATIONS* (1662)

IT MAY BE NOW ASKED, TO WHAT PURPOSE TENDS ALL THIS LABORIOUS buzzling, and groping? To know,

1. The number of the People?

2. How many *Males*, and *Females*?

3. How many Married, and Single?

4. How many *Teeming*[1] Women?

5. How many of every *Septenary*,[2] or *Decade* of years in *age*?

6. How many Fighting Men?

7. How much *London* is, and by what steps it hath increased?

8. In what time the Housing is replenished after a *Plague*?

9. What proportion die of each general and particular *Casualties*?[3]

10. What years are Fruitful, and Mortal, and in what Spaces, and Intervals, they follow each other?

11. In what proportion Men neglect the *Orders* of the Church, and *Sects* have increased?

12. The disproportion of Parishes?

13. Why the *Burials* in *London* exceed the Christenings, when the contrary is visible in the Country?

[. . .] I answer [. . .] by complaining, that whereas the Art of Governing, and the true *Politics*, is how to preserve the Subject in *Peace*, and *Plenty*, that men study only that part of it, which teaches how to supplant, and over-reach one another, and how, not by fair out-running, but by tripping up each other's heels, to win the Prize.

Now, the Foundation, or Elements of this honest harmless *Policy* is to understand the Land, and the hands of the Territory to be governed, according to all their intrinsic and accidental differences. As for example, it were good to know the *Geometrical* Content, Figure, and Situation of all the Lands of a *Kingdom*, especially according to its most natural, permanent, and conspicuous Bounds. It were good to know how much hay an acre of every sort of meadow will bear? How many cattle the same weight of each sort of hay will feed and fatten? What quantity of grain, and other commodities the same acre will bear in one, three or seven years *communibus annis*?[4] Unto what use each soil is most proper? All which particulars I call the intrinsic value: for there is also another value merely accidental, or extrinsic, consisting of the Causes, why a parcel of land, lying near a good market, may be worth double to another parcel, though but of the same intrinsic goodness; which answers the queries, why lands in the *North* of *England* are worth but sixteen years purchase, and those of the *West* above eight and twenty. It is no less necessary to know how many People there be of each Sex, State, Age, Religion, Trade, Rank or Degree, etc by the knowledge whereof trade, and government may be made more certain and regular. For if men know the people, as aforesaid, they might know the consumption they would make, so as trade might not be hoped for where it is impossible. As for instance, I have heard much complaint, that trade is not set up in some of the *South-Western* and *North-Western* parts of Ireland, there being so many excellent harbours for that purpose, whereas in several of those places I have also heard, that there are few other inhabitants, but such as live *ex sponte creatis*,[5] and are unfit subjects of trade, as neither employing others, nor working themselves.

[. . .]

I conclude, that a clear knowledge of all these particulars, and many more, whereat I have shot but at rovers, is necessary in order to good, certain and easy government, and even to balance parties and factions both in *Church* and *State*.

NOTES

1. "Teeming" here means fertile.
2. A septenary is a period of seven years. It was at least as common to divide the human life span into septenaries as into decades, that is, periods of ten years.
3. "Casualties," or chances, here means causes.
4. *Communibus annis*: in an average year.
5. *Ex sponte creatis*: from the fruits of nature, that is, from naturally occurring produce rather than agriculture.

DOCUMENT 1.5

FROM CHARLES DE MONTESQUIEU, *THE SPIRIT OF THE LAWS* (1748; THOMAS NUGENT TRANS., 1750)

BOOK XXIII: "OF LAWS IN THE RELATION THEY BEAR TO THE NUMBER OF INHABITANTS"

Chapter XIV: Of the Productions of the Earth Which Require a Greater of a Less Number of Men

Pasture-lands are but little peopled, because they find employment only for a few. Corn-lands employ a great many men, and vineyards infinitely more.

It has been a frequent complaint in England, that the increase of pasture-land diminished the inhabitants;[1] and it has been observed in France, that the prodigious number of vineyards is one of the great causes of the multitude of people.

Those countries where coal-pits furnish a proper substance for fuel, have this advantage over others, that not having the same occasion for forests, the lands may be cultivated.

In countries productive of rice, they are at great pains in watering the land; a great number of men must therefore be employed. Besides, there is less land required to furnish subsistence for a family, than in those which produce other kinds of grain. In fine,² the land which is elsewhere employed in raising cattle, serves immediately for the subsistence of man; the labour, which in other places is performed by cattle, is there performed by men; so that the culture of the soil, becomes to man an immense manufacture.

Chapter XV: Of the Number of Inhabitants with Relation to the Arts

When there is an agrarian law, and the lands are equally divided, the country may be extremely well peopled, though there are but few arts; because every citizen receives from the cultivation of his land whatever is necessary for his subsistence, and all the citizens together consume all the fruits of the earth. Thus it was in some republics.

In our present situation, in which lands are so unequally distributed, they produce much more than those who cultivate them can consume; if the arts therefore should be neglected, and nothing minded but agriculture, the country could not be peopled. Those who cultivate, having corn to spare, nothing would engage them to work the following year; the fruits of the earth would not be consumed by the indolent; for these would having nothing with which they could purchase them. It is necessary then that the arts should be established, in order that the produce of the land may be consumed by the labourer and the artificer. In a word, it is now proper that many should cultivate much more than is necessary for their own use. For this purpose, they must have a desire of enjoying superfluities; and these they can receive only from the artificer.

Those machines which are designed to abridge art, are not always useful. If a piece of workmanship is of a moderate price, such as is equally agreeable to the maker and the buyer, those machines which would render the manufacture more simple, or in other words, diminish the number of workmen, would be pernicious. And if water-mills were not every where established, I should not have believed them so useful as is pretended, because they have deprived an infinite multitude of their employment, a vast number of persons of the use of water, and a great part of the land of its fertility.

Chapter XVI: The Concern of the Legislator in the Propagation of the Species

Regulations on the number of citizens depend greatly on circumstances. There are countries in which nature does all; the legislator then has nothing to do. What need is there of inducing men by laws to propagation when a fruitful climate yields a sufficient number of inhabitants? Sometimes the climate is more favourable than the soil; the people multiply, and are destroyed by famine: this is the case of China. Hence a father sells his daughters and exposes his children. [. . .]

Chapter XVII: Of Greece and the Number of Its Inhabitants:

That effect which in certain countries of the East springs from physical causes was produced in Greece by the nature of the government. The Greeks were a great nation, composed of cities, each of which had a distinct government and separate laws. They had no more the spirit of conquest and ambition than those of Switzerland, Holland, and Germany have at this day. In every republic the legislator had in view the happiness of the citizens at home, and their power abroad, lest it should prove inferior to that of the neighbouring cities. Thus, with the enjoyment of a small territory and great happiness, it was easy for the number of the citizens to increase to such a degree as to become burdensome. This obliged them incessantly to send out colonies, and, as the Swiss do now, to let their men out to war. Nothing was neglected that could hinder the too great multiplication of children. [. . .]

Chapter XXIV: The Changes Which Happened in Europe with Regard to the Number of Inhabitants

In the state Europe was in [after the fall of the Roman Empire] one would not imagine it possible for it to be retrieved, especially when under Charlemagne it formed only one vast empire. But by the nature of government at that time it became divided into an infinite number of petty sovereignties, and as the lord or sovereign, who resided in his village or city, was neither great, rich, powerful, nor even safe but by the number of his subjects, every one employed himself with a singular attention to make his little country flourish. This succeeded in such a manner that notwithstanding the irregularities of government, the want of that knowledge which has since been acquired in commerce, and the numerous wars and disorders incessantly arising, most countries of Europe were better peopled in those days than they are even at present. I have not time to treat fully of this subject, but I shall cite the prodigious armies engaged in the Crusades, composed of men of all countries. Puffendorf[3] says that in the reign of Charles IX there were in France twenty millions of men. It is the perpetual reunion of many little states that has produced this diminution. Formerly, every village of France was a capital; there is at present only one large one. Every part of the state was a centre of power; at present all has a relation to one centre, and this centre is in some measure the state itself.

Chapter XXV: The Same Subject Continued:

Europe, it is true, has for these two ages past greatly increased its navigation; this has both procured and deprived it of inhabitants. Holland sends every year a great number of mariners to the Indies, of whom not above two-thirds return; the rest either perish or settle in the Indies. The same thing must happen to every other nation concerned in that trade. We must not judge of Europe as of a particular state engaged alone in an extensive navigation. This state would increase in people, because all the neighbouring nations would endeavour to have a share in this commerce, and mariners would arrive from all parts. Europe, separated from the rest of the world by religion, by vast seas and deserts, cannot be repaired in this manner.

Chapter XXVI: Consequences

From all this we may conclude that Europe is at present in a condition to require laws to be made in favour of the propagation of the human species. The politics of the ancient Greeks incessantly complain of the inconveniences attending a republic, from the excessive number of citizens; but the politics of this age call upon us to take proper means to increase ours. [. . .]

Chapter XXVIII: By What means We may Remedy a Depopulation:

When a state is depopulated by particular accidents, by wars, pestilence, or famine, there are still resources left. The men who remain may preserve the spirit of industry; they may seek to repair their misfortunes, and calamity itself may make them become more industrious. This evil is almost incurable when the depopulation is prepared beforehand by interior vice and a bad government. When this is the case, men perish with an insensible and habitual disease; born in misery and weakness, in violence or under the influence of a wicked administration, they see themselves destroyed, and frequently without perceiving the cause of their destruction. Of this we have a melancholy proof in the countries desolated by despotic power, or by the excessive advantages of the clergy over the laity.

In vain shall we wait for the succour of children yet unborn to re-establish a state thus depopulated. There is not time for this; men in their solitude are without courage or industry. With land sufficient to nourish a nation, they have scarcely enough to nourish a family. The common people have not even a property in the miseries of the country, that is, in the fallows with which it abounds. The clergy, the prince, the cities, the great men, and some of the principal citizens insensibly become proprietors of all the land which lies uncultivated; the families who are ruined have left their fields, and the labouring man is destitute. In this situation they should take the same measures throughout the whole extent of the empire which the Romans took in a part of theirs; they should practise in their distress what these observed in the midst of plenty; that is, they should distribute land to all the families who are in want, and procure them materials for clearing and cultivating it. This distribution ought to be continued so long as there is a man to receive it, and in such a manner as not to lose a moment that can be industriously employed.

NOTES

1. See document 1.1 for an example.
2. "In fine" means in sum or in summary.
3. Puffendorf refers to seventeenth-century German jurist Samuel von Pufendorf.

DOCUMENT 1.6

FROM DAVID HUME, "OF THE POPULOUSNESS OF ANCIENT NATIONS" (1742), IN *ESSAYS & TREATISES ON SEVERAL SUBJECTS* (1760)

[I]S IT CERTAIN, THAT ANTIQUITY WAS SO MUCH MORE POPULOUS, AS is pretended? The extravagancies of VOSSIUS,[1] with regard to this subject, are well known. But an author of much greater genius and discernment[2] has ventured to affirm, that, according to the best computations which these subjects will admit of, there are not now, on the face of the earth, the fiftieth part of mankind, which existed in the time of JULIUS CÆSAR. It may easily be observed, that the comparison, in this case, must be imperfect, even though we confine ourselves to the scene of ancient history; EUROPE, and the nations round the MEDITERRANEAN. We know not exactly the numbers of any EUROPEAN kingdom, or even city, at present: How can we pretend to calculate those of ancient cities and states, where historians have left us such imperfect traces? For my part, the matter appears to me so uncertain, that, as I intend to throw together some reflections on that head, I shall intermingle the enquiry concerning *causes* with that concerning *facts*; which ought never to be admitted, where the facts can be ascertained with any tolerable assurance.

In general, we may observe, that the question, with regard to the comparative populousness of ages or kingdoms, implies important consequences, and commonly determines concerning the preference of their whole police, their manners, and the constitution of their government. For as there is in all men, both male and female, a desire and power of generation, more active than is ever universally exerted, the restraints, which they lie under, must proceed from some difficulties in their situation, which it belongs to a wise legislature carefully to observe and remove. Almost every man who thinks he can maintain a family will have one; and the human species, at this rate of propagation, would more than double every generation. How fast do mankind multiply in every colony or new settlement; where it is an easy matter to provide for a family; and where men are nowise straitened or confined, as in long established governments? History tells us frequently of plagues, which have swept away the third or fourth part of a people: Yet in a generation or two, the destruction was not perceived; and the society had again acquired their former number. The lands which were cultivated, the houses built, the commodities raised, the riches acquired, enabled the people, who escaped, immediately to marry, and to rear families, which supplied the place of those who had perished. And for a like reason, every wise, just, and mild government, by rendering the condition of its subjects easy and secure, will always abound most in people, as well as in commodities and riches. A country, indeed, whose climate and soil are fitted for vines, will naturally be more populous than one which produces corn only, and that more populous than one which is only fitted for pasturage. In general, warm climates, as the necessities of the inhabitants are there fewer, and vegetation more powerful, are likely to be most populous: But if every thing else be equal, it seems natural to expect, that, wherever there are most happiness and virtue, and the wisest institutions, there will also be most people.

[. . .]

[In antiquity] there was then much land uncultivated, and put to no manner of use; and he[3] ascribes it as a great praise to PERTINAX,[4] that he allowed every one to take such land either in ITALY or elsewhere, and cultivate it as he pleased, without paying any taxes. *Lands uncultivated, and put to no manner of use!* This is not heard of in any part of CHRISTENDOM; except in some remote parts of HUNGARY; as I have been informed. And it surely corresponds very ill with that idea of the extreme populousness of antiquity, so much insisted on.

We learn from VOPISCUS,[5] that there was even in ETRURIA much fertile land uncultivated, which the Emperor AURELIAN[6] intended to convert into vineyards, in order to furnish the ROMAN people with a gratuitous distribution of wine; a very proper expedient for depopulating still farther that capital and all the neighbouring territories.

It may not be amiss to take notice of the account which POLYBIUS[7] gives of the great herds of swine to be met with in TUSCANY and LOMBARDY, as well as in GREECE, and of the method of feeding them which was then practised. "There are great herds of swine," says he, "throughout all ITALY, particularly in former times, through ETRURIA and CISALPINE GAUL. And a herd frequently consists of a thousand or more swine. [. . .]"

May we not infer from this account, that the north of ITALY, as well as GREECE, was then much less peopled, and worse cultivated, than at present? How could these vast herds be fed in a country so full of inclosures, so improved by agriculture, so divided by farms, so planted with vines and corn intermingled together? I must confess, that POLYBIUS'S relation has more the air of that economy which is to be met with in our AMERICAN colonies, than the management of a EUROPEAN country.

We meet with a reflection in ARISTOTLE'S Ethics,[8] which seems unaccountable on any supposition, and by proving too much in favour of our present reasoning, may be thought really to prove nothing. That philosopher, treating of friendship, and observing, that this relation ought neither to be contracted to a very few, nor extended over a great multitude, illustrates his opinion by the following argument. "In like manner," says he, "as a city cannot subsist, if it either have so few inhabitants as ten, or so many as a hundred thousand; so is there a mediocrity required in the number of friends; and you destroy the essence of friendship by running into either extreme." What! impossible that a city can contain a hundred thousand inhabitants! Had ARISTOTLE never seen nor heard of a city so populous? This, I must own, passes my comprehension.

PLINY tells us that SELEUCIA, the seat of the GREEK empire in the East, was reported to contain 600,000 people. CARTHAGE is said by STRABO to have contained 700,000.[9] The inhabitants of PEKIN are not much more numerous. LONDON, PARIS, and CONSTANTINOPLE, may admit of nearly the same computation; at least, the two latter cities do not exceed it. ROME, ALEXANDRIA, ANTIOCH, we have already spoken of. From the experience of past and present ages, one might conjecture that there is a kind of impossibility, that any city could ever rise much beyond this proportion. Whether the grandeur of a city be founded on commerce or on empire, there seem to be invincible obstacles, which prevent its farther progress. The seats of vast monarchies, by introducing extravagant luxury, irregular expense, idleness, dependence, and false ideas of rank and superiority, are improper for commerce. Extensive commerce checks itself, by raising the price of all labour and commodities. When a great court engages the attendance of a numerous nobility, possessed of overgrown fortunes, the middling gentry remain in their provincial towns, where they can make a figure on a moderate income. And if the dominions of a state arrive at an enormous size, there necessarily arise many capitals, in the remoter provinces, whither all the inhabitants, except a few courtiers, repair for education, fortune, and amusement. LONDON, by uniting extensive commerce and middling empire, has, perhaps, arrived at a greatness, which no city will ever be able to exceed.

Choose DOVER or CALAIS for a center: Draw a circle of two hundred miles radius: You comprehend LONDON, PARIS, the NETHERLANDS, the UNITED PROVINCES, and some of the best cultivated parts of FRANCE and ENGLAND. It may safely, I think, be affirmed, that no spot of ground can be found, in antiquity, of equal extent, which contained near so many great and populous cities, and was so stocked with riches and inhabitants. To balance, in both periods, the states, which possessed most art, knowledge, civility, and the best police, seems the truest method of comparison.

It is an observation of L'ABBE DU BOS,[10] that ITALY is warmer at present than it was in ancient times. "The annals of ROME tell us," says he, "that in the year 480 *ab U.C.*[11] the winter was so severe that it destroyed the trees. The TYBER froze in ROME, and the ground was covered with snow for forty days. When JUVENAL[12] describes a superstitious woman, he represents her as breaking the ice of the TYBER, that she might perform her ablutions:

> Hybernum fracta glacie descendet in amnem,
> Ter matutino Tyberi mergetur.[13]

He speaks of that river's freezing as a common event. Many passages of HORACE[14] suppose the streets of ROME full of snow and ice. We should have more certainty with regard to this point, had the ancients known the use of thermometers: But their writers, without intending it, give us information, sufficient to convince us, that the winters are now much more temperate at ROME than formerly. At present the TYBER no more freezes at ROME than the NILE at CAIRO. The ROMANS esteem the winters very rigorous, if the snow lie two days, and if one sees for eight and forty hours a few icicles hang from a fountain that has a north exposure."

The observation of this ingenious critic may be extended to other EUROPEAN climates. Who could discover the mild climate of FRANCE in DIODORUS SICULUS'S[15] description of that of GAUL? "As it is a northern climate," says he, "it is infested with cold to an extreme degree. In cloudy weather, instead of rain there fall great snows; and in clear weather it there freezes so excessive hard, that the rivers acquire bridges of their own substance, over which, not only single travellers may pass, but large armies, accompanied with all their baggage and loaded waggons. And there being many rivers in GAUL, the RHONE, the RHINE, &c. almost all of them are frozen over; and it is usual, in order to prevent falling, to cover the ice with chaff and straw at the places where the road passes." *Colder than a* GALLIC *Winter*, is used by PETRONIUS[16] as a proverbial expression. ARISTOTLE says, that GAUL is so cold a climate that an ass could not live in it.

[. . .]

OVID[17] positively maintains, with all the serious affirmation of prose, that the EUXINE sea was frozen over every winter in his time; and he appeals to ROMAN governors, whom he names, for the truth of his assertion. This seldom or never happens at present in the latitude of TOMI, whither OVID was banished. All the complaints of the same poet seem to mark a rigour of the seasons, which is scarcely experienced at present in PETERSBURGH or STOCKHOLM.

TOURNEFORT,[18] a *Provençal*, who had travelled into the same country, observes, that there is not a finer climate in the world: And he asserts, that nothing but OVID'S melancholy could have given him such dismal ideas of it. But the facts, mentioned by that poet, are too circumstantial to bear any such interpretation.

[. . .]

Allowing, therefore, this remark to be just, that EUROPE is become warmer than formerly; how can we account for it? Plainly, by no other method, than by supposing, that the land is at present much better cultivated, and that the woods are cleared, which formerly threw a shade upon the earth, and kept the rays of the sun from penetrating to it. Our northern colonies in AMERICA become more temperate, in proportion as the woods are felled; but in general, every one may remark, that cold is still much more severely felt, both in North and South AMERICA, than in places under the same latitude in EUROPE.

NOTES

1. Isaac Vossius was a seventeenth-century Dutch scholar.
2. Hume here refers to a claim Montesquieu made in his *Persian Letters* (1721) but whose tenor was also endorsed in *The Spirit of the Laws* as the previous excerpt shows.
3. "He" here is Herodian, Roman historian of second and third century CE, author of *History of the Empire from the Death of Marcus*.
4. Pertinax was a second-century CE Roman soldier and politician.
5. This is probably Flavius Vopiscus, fourth-century CE historian and author of the *Historia Augusta*.
6. Aurelian is a reference to Lucius Domitius Aurelianus Augustus, Roman Emperor, 270–275 CE.
7. Polybius was a Greek historian of second century BCE, author of *The Histories*.
8. Book 9, chap. 10.
9. Pliny the Elder was author of the encyclopedic *Natural History* in the first century CE, and Strabo of Amasia was author of a seventeen-book *Geography* completed in the same century.
10. Jean-Baptiste Du Bos was an early eighteenth-century historian; this observation is probably taken from his *Histoire critique de l'établissement de la monarchie française dans les Gaules* (1734).
11. *Ab urbe condita*: from the founding of the city [of Rome]—an expression used in antiquity and by classical historians to refer to a given year in Ancient Rome.
12. Juvenal was a second-century CE Roman poet.
13. Hume essentially provides a prose translation in the previous sentence.
14. Horace was a first-century BCE Roman poet.
15. Diodorus Siculus was a first-century BCE Greek historian and author of *Bibliotheca Historica*.
16. Petronius was a Roman politician and author of a first-century CE work, the *Satyricon*.
17. Ovid was a Roman poet, 43 BCE–17/18 CE.
18. Joseph Pitton de Tournefort was a seventeenth-century French botanist and author of *Relation d'un voyage du Levant* (1717).

DOCUMENT 1.7

FROM ROBERT WALLACE, *A DISSERTATION ON THE NUMBERS OF MANKIND, IN ANTIENT AND MODERN TIMES* (1753)

[T]HERE HAS NEVER BEEN SUCH A NUMBER OF INHABITANTS ON THE earth at any one point of time, as might have been easily raised by the prolific virtue of mankind.

The causes of this paucity of inhabitants, and irregularity of increase, are manifold. Some of them may be called physical, as they depend entirely on the course of nature, and are independent of mankind. Others of them are moral, and depend on the affections, passions and institutions of men. Among the physical causes, some are more constant; as the temperature of the air, the extreme heat or cold of some climates, the barrenness of some regions of the earth, and the unfavourableness of the climate or natural product of some soils to generation. Other causes of this kind are more variable; such as, the inclemency of particular seasons, plagues, famines, earthquakes, and inundations of the sea; which sweep off great numbers of men, as well as other animals, and prevent the quicker replenishing of the earth.

That these natural causes have had a baneful influence cannot be doubted; yet it is probable that this might be prevented in some degree, perhaps even in a great measure, by the skill and industry of men, and by wholesome laws and institutions; at least, that all these natural causes taken together, excepting perhaps the incurable barrenness or unwholesomeness of some particular regions, have not so bad an effect as the moral causes, which arise from the passions and vices of men, and have a more constant and powerful influence on the world.

To this last article we may refer so many destructive wars which men have waged against one another; great poverty, corrupt institutions, either of a civil or religious kind, intemperance, debauchery, irregular amours, idleness, luxury, and whatever either prevents marriage, weakens the generating faculties of men, or renders them negligent or incapable of educating their children, and cultivating the earth to advantage. 'Tis chiefly to such destructive causes we must ascribe the small number of men. Indeed, had it not been for the errors and vices of mankind, and the defects of government and education, the earth must have been much better peopled, perhaps might have been overstocked, many ages ago: and as these causes operate more or less strongly, the earth will be better or worse peopled at different times. Hence likewise [. . .] we may suppose that the earth was much better peopled in some ancient ages, than it has been in modern times, or is at present. Nor is there any necessity to suppose, that the number of men upon the earth must have continually increased, and that, in the present age, their number is greater than at any preceding period.

Upon a more exact inquiry, perhaps, we shall find reason to conclude, that the reverse is the truth. And as the illustration of this subject is of very great importance, and is closely connected with the deepest policy and most intimate constitution of human society, an accurate examination must be useful and interesting. [. . .]

To say truth, 'tis but a very imperfect prospect we dare promise on this occasion. The subject itself is so involved in obscurity, the accounts of ancient authors are so incomplete, the matter has either not been handled at all, or handled so superficially, that much cannot be expected in a first essay; nay, after the most accurate search it will perhaps be found impossible to determine precisely at what rate mankind have either increased or decreased, in particular ages or countries; or from what causes such variations have happened. Exact registers of such things have never been kept, and indeed could never have been preserved in such an unsettled state of human affairs. [. . .]

But ere we proceed to inquire more particularly, it will be proper to lay down some general maxims taken from nature and constant observation, which may be useful to guide us in a more particular comparison.

1. A rude and barbarous people, living by hunting, fishing, or pasturage, or on the spontaneous product of the earth, without agriculture, commerce and arts, can never be so numerous as a people inhabiting the same tracts of land, who are well skilled in agriculture and civilized by commerce, since uncultivated can never maintain so many inhabitants as cultivated lands. In every country, there shall always be found a greater number of inhabitants, ceteris paribus, in proportion to the plenty of provisions it affords, as plenty will always encourage the generality of the people to marry.

Hence it is evident, that the world could not be best peopled in rude and ignorant ages, while men lived chiefly on the spontaneous fruits of the earth, and were neither instructed in agriculture, nor polished by arts or commerce, and that in whatever age we find a country grossly ignorant of agriculture, we may be assured, it must have been but thinly inhabited. From which we must conclude that, notwithstanding the numerous swarms which the northern nations sent forth into southern climes, at different times, those northern regions might have, and if barbarous and without agriculture, must have been ill peopled. For it is easy to overstock an uncultivated country, nay, such a country in the common course of things, if it does not meet with some extraordinary calamities, must necessarily be obliged, at certain times, to disburden itself of the mouths it cannot sustain.

2. As the earth could not be well peopled in rude and barbarous ages, neither are all countries, climates and soils, equally favourable to propagation. There must therefore be a great difference in respect of inhabitants, notwithstanding the best culture, discipline and constitutions.

For cold and barren heaths, rocky mountainous tracts, marshes which cannot be drained, inhospitable sands, and many other sorts of unfruitful soils, cannot produce equal quantities of food, and by consequence, *ceteris paribus*,[1] cannot be so well stored with people, as softer and more fertile climes. We may also suppose that, in certain countries, the air, or the most common food, may be more or less favourable to generation.

3. Besides the nature of the climate or soil, the number of people in every country depends greatly on its political maxims and institutions concerning the division of lands.

For if there is very nearly an equal division of the lands, and into such small shares, that they can yield little more than what is necessary to feed and clothe the labourers in a frugal and simple manner, tho' in such a situation there is little room for commerce with strangers, and none but the most simple and necessary arts can be in use, yet if the country be naturally fertile, it must of necessity be well stored with people.

Hence we may conclude, that when any ancient nation divided its lands into small shares, and when even eminent citizens had but a few acres to maintain their families, tho' such a nation had but little commerce, and had learned only a few simple and more necessary arts, it must have abounded greatly in people. This was in a particular manner the case of *Rome* for several ages. [. . .]

But if the lands be divided into very unequal shares, and, in general, may produce much more than will decently support such as cultivate them, the country may, notwithstanding, be well peopled if arts be encouraged, and the surplus above what will support the labourers of the ground be allotted for such as cultivate the arts and sciences.

Further, where the lands are very unequally divided, and are capable of maintaining many more than those who cultivate them, that country must be thinly peopled, unless elegance is studied, and proper encouragement given to the arts which conduce to it.

In every country where nothing is known but agriculture and pasturage, and a few more simple arts, such as those of building and clothing in a frugal taste, without ornament, of necessity there must be few inhabitants, unless the lands are nearly equally divided and into small portions. And in a fertile soil, the shares of land must be extremely small, if they are not able to support many more than are necessary for cultivating them. Hence in every such soil, where a great extent of property is allowed, there is room for elegance, sumptuousness and the encouragement of the arts. And in whatever country industry prevails, about what subject soever it is employed, provided the produce of it gives a price either at home or abroad, such a country may abound in people, and flourish by arts and commence: it may even flourish tho' agriculture is not encouraged to the full, and several tracts of land are much neglected. Nay such is the force of industry and commerce, that by means of them many more inhabitants may be maintained in a country, than the produce of the lands can possible support, as their food may be brought from a distance.

At the same time, if the lands of any country be neglected, the world in general must suffer for it, and the earth must contain a smaller number of inhabitants, in proportion to the numbers which might be supported by these uncultivated lands. [...]

5. As mankind can only be supported by the fruits of the earth and animal food, and it is only by agriculture, fishing and hunting, that food can be provided, to render the earth as populous as possible, these arts must be duly cherished, especially agriculture and fishing.

[...]

Having [...] formed some probable conjectures about the superior populousness of these countries in ancient times, we proceed to inquire into the causes of this phenomenon. [...]

Now, these causes are either physical or moral.

Whatever alterations may have happened in the temperature of the air, whatever decay of heat in the sun, or diminution of the salubrity and nourishing virtue of the earth, are physical causes; which may be thought to have an effect on vegetable and animal bodies, and either prevent generation, or cut off greater numbers in all the different period of life.

Causes of this nature may be supposed to operate in the same climates in different ages, and in different climates in the same age. Mankind may be greatly wasted by plagues and famines, and a fruitful land may become a desert. Yet neither do causes of this kind seem sufficient for explaining the phenomenon of so great a decay of people. Nor indeed does it appear that there has been any such alteration in the state of nature as could make any considerable difference, either over all the earth, or in particular regions: we do not therefore build on natural causes of this sort.

NOTE

1 Other things being equal.

DOCUMENT 1.8

FROM BENJAMIN FRANKLIN, "OBSERVATIONS CONCERNING THE INCREASE OF MANKIND," IN WILLIAM CLARKE, *OBSERVATIONS ON THE LATE AND PRESENT CONDITION OF THE FRENCH* (LONDON, 1755)

EUROPE IS GENERALLY FULL SETTLED WITH HUSBANDMEN, MANUFACturers, &c and therefore cannot now much increase in People. *America* is chiefly occupied by *Indians*, who subsist mostly by Hunting. But as the hunter, of all men, requires the greatest quantity of land from whence to draw his subsistence (the husbandman subsisting on much less, the gardener on still less, and the manufacturer requiring lest of all) the *Europeans* found *America* as fully settled as it well could be by hunters. Yet these having large tracts, were easily prevailed on to part with portions of territory to the new comers, who did not much interfere with the natives in hunting, and furnished them with many things they wanted.

Land being thus plenty in *America*, and so cheap as that a labouring man, that understands husbandry, can in a short time save money enough to purchase a piece of new land sufficient for a plantation, whereon he may subsist a family, such are not afraid to marry, for if they even look far enough forward to consider how their children when grown up are to be provided for, they see that more land is to be had at rates equally easy, all circumstances considered.

Hence marriages in *America* are more general, and generally more early, than in *Europe*. And if it is reckoned there, that there is but one marriage per annum among 100 persons, perhaps we may here reckon two. And if in *Europe* they have but four births to a marriage (many of their marriages being late) we may here reckon eight, of which if one half grow up, and our marriages are made, reckoning one with another at twenty years of age, our people must be doubled every twenty years.

[. . .]

Hence the prince that acquires new territory, if he finds it vacant, or removes the natives to give his own people room, the legislator that makes effectual laws for promoting of trade, increasing employment, improving land by more or better tillage, providing more food by fisheries, securing property, &c and the man that invents new trades, arts or manufactures, or new improvements in husbandry, may properly be called *fathers of their nation*, as they are the cause of the generation of multitudes by the encouragement they afford to marriage.

[. . .]

There is no short bound to the prolific nature of plants or animals, but what is made by their crowding and interfering with each other's means of subsistence. Was the face of the earth vacant of other plants, it might be gradually sowed and overspread with one kind only, as for instance, with fennel. And were it empty of other inhabitants, it might in a few ages be replenished from one nation only, as for instance, with *Englishmen*. Thus there are supposed to be now upwards of one million *English* souls *in North America* (tho' tis thought scarce 80,000 have been brought over sea) and yet perhaps there is not one the fewer in Britain, but rather many more, on account of the employment the colonies afford to manufacturers at home. This million doubling, suppose but once in 25 years, will in another century be more than the people of *England*, and the greatest number of *Englishmen* will be on this side of the water. What an accession of power to the *British* empire by sea as well as land! What an increase of trade and navigation! What numbers of ships and seamen! We have been here but little more than 100 years, and yet the force of our privateers in the late war, united, was greater, both in men and guns, than that of the whole *British* navy in Queen *Elizabeth*'s time. How important an affair then to *Britain*, is the present treaty for settling the bounds between her colonies and the *French*, and how careful should she be to secure room enough, since on the room depends so much the increase of her people?

In fine, a nation well regulated is like a polypus:[1] take away a limb, its place is soon supplied; cut it in two, and each deficient part shall speedily grow out of the part remaining. Thus if you have room and subsistence enough, as you may by dividing, make ten polypes out of one, you may of one make ten nations equally populous and powerful. Or rather, increase a nation ten fold in numbers and strength.

And since detachments of *English* from *Britain* sent to *America*, will have their places at home soon supplied and increase so largely here, why should the *Palatine Boors*[2] be suffered to swarm into our settlements, and by herding together establish their own language and manners to the exclusion of ours? Why should *Pennsylvania*, founded by the *English*, become a colony of aliens, who will shortly be so numerous as to Germanize us instead of our Anglifying them, and will never adopt our language or customs, any more than they can acquire our complexion.

Which leads me to add one remark: that the number of purely white people in the world is proportionably very small. All *Africa* is black or tawny. *Asia* chiefly tawny. *America* (exclusive of the new comers) wholly so. And in *Europe*, the *Spaniards*, *Italians*, and *French*, are generally of what we call a swarthy complexion; the more northern nations with the *English*, making the principal body of white people on the face of the earth. I could wish their numbers were increased. And while we are, as I may call it, *scouring* our planet, by clearing *America* of woods, and so making this side of our globe reflect a brighter light to the eyes of inhabitants in *Mars* and *Venus*, why should we in the sight of superior beings, darken its people? Why increase the sons of *Africa*, by planting them in America, where we have so fair an opportunity, by excluding all blacks and tawneys, of increasing the lovely white and red?

NOTES

1. "Polypus" is an archaic term for polyp.
2. This is a reference to immigrants from German territories of the Palatinate in the Holy Roman Empire.

DOCUMENT 1.9

FROM THOMAS SHORT, *A COMPARATIVE HISTORY OF THE INCREASE AND DECREASE OF MANKIND IN ENGLAND* (LONDON, 1767)

TO MAKE THE NATION MORE POPULOUS, CITIES AND TOWNS MORE healthy, and youth stronger and hardier, these three things challenge the most particular regard.

First, encourage marriage.

Secondly, suppress vice and promote virtue.

Thirdly, mend the air.

[...]

The last thing proposed was, that cities and great towns should (if possible) be provided with good air, water, wholesome habitations, clean, open, wide, and well-ventilated streets, where such things can be had. Greater sickness and mortality are often charged, more than is just, on air and water, and on smoke, dirt, closeness of the place, bad effluvia and excrements of multitudes and variety of animals &c. Tho' these things want not their bad effects, yet the vices and licentiousness of the inhabitants are often more to be blamed. The air and water of some places are not to be mended, as in low, wet, marshy grounds, having foetid, stagnant waters, and a corrupted atmosphere, loaded with contend moisture and putrid effluvia, which places, having no descent to carry off these, cannot be made healthy habitations. But some places have been very industrious and successful in this part of the policy, they have opened and cleaned their ditches and sewers, let off their sludge and nasty standing water, so that all filthiness is more easily and better carried off, their streets widened and made straight, their houses, rooms and windows built loftier, &c. But, for all these great improvements, death sometimes rides triumphant, therefore the cause must lie deeper in the prevalence of vice and immorality, which can only be pruned off by a vigilant, indefatigable, virtuous magistracy, having, and impartially executing good laws on all sorts of offenders.

[. . .]

[Drawing together material from mortality tables] It is evident [. . .] that habitations situated on a mean elevation, on hard free-standing rocks or mountains, lying near quick-purling streams. The ground about it dry, no woods or forests very near, no stagnant waters, fens or morasses, a free, open ventilation, especially in hot countries, not thrust up between steep lofty mountains, nor thrust too low among constant oozing springs, without proper descents to carry off the draining water from the hills, the increase of such places is as 20 births to 11 burials. [. . .]

The next situation, on dry, pebbly, gravelly soil, meanly situated both as to great drought and floods, having woods in view, but not too near, remote from lakes, or stagnant waters or marshes, but having brisk-running brooks, or small rivers, not far from navigable rivers in the centre of a country, the increase, in such situations, at a medium, is a third, or above.

A thick clay, on an elevated ground where no water stands, is no bad situation. Or sand and clay, or good loam, or very hard limestone under a fruitful turf, are pretty good situations. But dry, pouring sand, chalk, soft limestone &c are not the healthiest situations.

Fenny, marshy, low, wet, and long-flooded situations; spungy, oozing, soft, springy ground, always wet, near to unenclosed, dry, great woods or forests, are all unhealthy habitations, which often bury more than are born. [. . .]

But the healthiest situation is insufficient of itself, without establishing and maintaining a good policy, such as pulling down old houses, huts and kennels, and building new ones with higher rooms and larger lights; giving liberty of access to free, clean, open, fresh air; removing all nuisances; keeping clean streets, folds and yards; being provided with pure, wholesome water; taking care of their shambles, draught-houses and markets.

A third thing necessary to promote the health of a place, is an indefatigable, faithful, impartial magistracy, who exemplarily, perceptively, and executively promote virtue, morality and good order, but curb and vigorously suppress vice.

DOCUMENT 1.10

FROM RICHARD PRICE, *OBSERVATIONS ON REVERSIONARY PAYMENTS* (1772; 6TH ED., 1803)

IN GENERAL, THERE SEEMS REASON TO THINK THAT IN TOWNS (ALLOWing for particular advantages of situation, trade, police, cleanliness and openness, which some towns may have), the excess of the burials above the births, and the proportion of inhabitants dying annually, are more or less as the towns are greater or smaller. In London itself, about 160 years ago, when it was scarcely a fourth of its present bulk, the births were much nearer to the burials than they are now. But in country parishes and villages, the births almost always exceed the burials. And I believe it never happens, except in very particular situations, that more than a 40th part of the inhabitants die annually. In the four provinces of New England there is a very rapid increase of the inhabitants. But notwithstanding this, at Boston, the capital, its inhabitants would decrease, were there no supply from the country. For if the account I have seen is just, from 1731 to 1762, the burials all along exceeded the births. So remarkably do towns, in consequence of their unfavourableness to health, and the luxury which generally prevails in them, check the increase of countries.

[...]

The facts I have now taken notice of are so important that I think they deserve more attention than has been hitherto bestowed upon them. Every one knows that the strength of a state consists in the number of people. The encouragement of population, therefore, ought to be one of the first objects of policy in every state, and some of the worst enemies of population are the luxury, licentiousness, and debility produced and propagated by great towns.

I have observed that London is now increasing. But it appears that, in truth, this is an event more to be dreaded than desired. The more London increases, the more the rest of the kingdom must be deserted, the fewer hands must be left for agriculture, and, consequently, the less must be the plenty, and the higher the price of all the means of subsistence. Moderate towns being seats of refinement, emulation, and arts, may be public advantages. But great towns, long before they grow to half the bulk of London, become checks on population of too hurtful a nature, nurseries of debauchery and voluptuousness, and, in many respects, greater evils than can be compensated by any advantages.

[. . .]

[. . .] [A] general account of the causes which obstruct population [. . .] insists particularly on LUXURY and the ENGROSSING OF FARMS. [. . .] In consequence of the easy communication, lately created between the different parts of the kingdom, the London fashions and manners and pleasures, have propagated everywhere, and almost every distant town and village now vies with the capital in all kinds of expensive dissipation and amusement. This enervates and debilitates, and, together with our taxes, raises everywhere the price of the means of subsistence, checks marriage, brings on poverty, dependence and venality. With respect particularly to the custom of *engrossing farms* [. . .] a tract of land in the hands of one man, does not yield so great a return, as when employed in the hands of several, nor does it employ so many people. [. . .] The custom of engrossing farms eases landlords of the trouble attending the necessities of little tenants and the repairs of cottages. A great farmer having it more in his power to speculate and command the markets, and by drawing to himself the profits which would have supported several farmers, is capable, with less culture, of paying a higher rent. Their superiors, therefore, find their account in this evil. But it is, indeed, erecting private benefit on public calamity, and, for the sake of a temporary advantage, giving up the nation to depopulation and distress.

According to these accounts,[1] then, our people have since the year 1690, decreased near a million and a half. And the waste has fallen principally on the inhabitants of cottages, nor indeed could it fall anywhere more unhappily, for, from cottages our navies and armies are supplied, and the lower people are the chief strength and security of every state. What renders this calamity more alarming is, that the inhabitants of the cottages thrown down in the country, fly to London and other towns, there to be corrupted and perish. I know I shall be here told that the revenue thrives. But this is not a circumstance from which any encouragement can be drawn. It thrives by a cause that is likely in time to destroy both itself and the kingdom. [. . .]

[. . .]

One of the most obvious divisions of the state of mankind is into the wild and the civilized state. In the former, man is a creature rude, ignorant and savage, running about in the woods and living by hunting, or on the spontaneous productions of the earth. In this state, the means of subsistence being scarce, and a large quantity of ground necessary to support a few, there can never be any considerable increase. In the latter state, man is a creature fixed on one spot, employing himself in cultivating the ground and enjoying the advantages of science, arts, and civil government. Of this last stage, there are many different degrees or stages, from the most simple to the most refined and luxurious. The first or the simple stages of civilization are those which favour most the increase and the happiness of mankind. For in these stages, agriculture supplies plenty of the means of subsistence, the blessings of a natural and simple life are enjoyed, property is equally divided, the wants of men are few and soon satisfied, and families are easily provided for. On the contrary, in refined states of civilization property is engrossed, and the natural equality of men subverted, artificial necessities without number are created, great towns propagate contagion and licentiousness, luxury and vice prevail, and, together with them, disease, poverty, venality and oppression. And there is a limit at which, when the corruptions of civil society arrive, all liberty, virtue and happiness must be lost, and complete ruin follow. Our American colonies are at present, for the most part, in the first and happiest of the states I have described, and they afford a very striking proof of the effects of the different stages of society on population. In the inland part of North America, or the back settlements, where the most of living are most simple, and almost every one occupies land for himself, there is an increase so rapid as to have hardly any parallel. Along the sea coast, where trade has begun to introduce refinement and luxury, the inhabitants increase more slowly, and in the maritime towns (if I may judge from the bills of mortality at Boston), they do not increase at all.

But to confine my thoughts to my own country. Here, it is too evident that we are far advanced into that last and worst state of society, in which false refinement and luxury multiply wants, and debauch, enslave and depopulate.

NOTE

1 Price here refers to accounts from the English political arithmetician Charles Davenant.

2

THE MALTHUS WARS

THOMAS ROBERT MALTHUS (1766–1834) IS OFTEN DUBBED "THE founder of modern demography." Given the diversity and scope of the debates about the interrelationships between population, resources, and the environment canvassed in part 1, the adjective "modern" is clearly important as we try to make sense of the claim. It is assuredly not the case that Malthus was the first to reason seriously and extendedly either about population per se or about its relationship with food supply, resources, and the environment. Was there any difference in how population was conceptualized in the debates that began in the 1790s? Furthermore, was there a transformation in the ways in which population was linked with its biophysical bases?

We can start to answer these questions by asking why radical political tracts of the 1790s felt the need to discuss population and its setting in the physical environment. As Condorcet made clear, citing Robert Wallace as the source of the conundrum, previous tracts posed the problem of whether population might hamstring progress. As such, radical advocates of progress such as Condorcet and Godwin felt the need to forestall this argument. Combining their insights, four arguments were proposed to support the claim that the physical environment did not at present and would not in the future limit societal advance as gauged through population size and affluence. For the present, two points were made. First, large tracts of the globe were uncultivated or under-cultivated. As such, the plenitude of the physical environment could not be limiting population growth and standards of living. Secondly, problems of food availability (and it should be noted in passing that the "resource" whose limits were almost the exclusive bone of contention in this debate was food) are issues of food distribution not quantity. Corrupt governments, acting in the interests of the few, mean that stockpiling takes place, that land is used for non-productive purposes, and that therefore the price of food is artificially raised and its availability is arbitrarily restricted.

Godwin and Condorcet could see that the two arguments proffered thus far were limited. What if all the lands of the earth were to be filled and cultivated? And furthermore, if the governments of the world were to be reformed, might it not still be the case that population growth would overtop available food supply? In other words, the problem Wallace had posed and that Malthus would reinvent had yet to be scotched. Godwin and Condorcet offered two responses. The first response drew on the extensive evidence of improvements in agricultural techniques, suggesting that there was no finite quantity of food that the earth could produce. Thanks to human ingenuity and the technological advance it generated, the baseline of food production would increase over time such that an ever-greater global population could be sustained. The second response was more radical still and saw Condorcet's and Godwin's arguments reach their speculative acme. If medical advances meant people could live longer, it was possible to imagine the point at which the human life span became, if not infinite, one with no assignable limits. With the progress of reason, society will become mature as will its individual inhabitants. As such, the sexual drive will wither in Godwin's framing, and a desire to improve the quality of lives rather than their quantity will develop on Condorcet's account. The progress of reason will thus blunt the force of the argument that population growth could scupper social improvement and overtop the earth's plenitude: technological improvement will maximize our usage of the physical environment, whereas the progress of reason will ensure humans attain to a stable population at which altruism leads to the optimization of resource distribution. If modern demographic transition theory has argued that education and affluence lead to the leveling out of population growth, Condorcet and Godwin offered a similar argument in the idiom of Enlightenment speculative philosophy.

Malthus's *Essay* was a direct response to Condorcet and Godwin couched in a logic related to the limits posed by the physical environment, an entity Malthus and his interlocutors most commonly term "nature." It is important to see the limits of what Malthus is attacking in his radical opponents and the common ground they share. First, Malthus does not deny that there is still unused and under-cultivated land on the earth. But inasmuch as not all of these lands would be highly fertile and distribution creates its own frictions (as Botero had noted two centuries earlier), this does not mean that physical limits in food supply cannot exist, nor that at smaller scales we may not already be using all the good quality land, nor that such limits both absolute and distributional are exclusively the result of defective government. Second, even if not all food scarcity issues are the result of failures of governance, Malthus is not arguing that government cannot create such problems. His criticism of the Poor Laws, England's welfare system, is an example of this, with Malthus arguing that these laws make a poverty trap and thereby "create the poor which they maintain." Third, Malthus is not denying the speed and significance of agrarian and technological improvement, discussing, for example, Robert Bakewell's sheep breeding experiments. But, for Malthus, and the core of his dissention from Condorcet and Godwin, such political, distributional, and technological concerns are "mere feathers that float on the surface." The nub of Malthus's argument here is that the terms of the relationship between population and the physical environment are set by a lawlike inequality between the rate of population growth and that of food production. As such, it is nature not politics or technology that drives the problem population poses. Furthermore, for Malthus we should beware a "fantasy of reason" that is not supported by evidence. Even if the average human life span has been extended, there's no evidence it will become unlimited, and there's not a shred of evidence to support Godwin's contention that the passion between the sexes will wither with the progress of reason. As such, there is no basis on which to project a context in which the pressure of population growth on available resources will wane. At all times, in all spaces, and in all stages of social development, the imbalance between the ratios by which population and food can (allegedly—Malthus offers data for population not for food production!) grow will create a situation in which the niggardliness of nature clips the wings of socioeconomic development and personal affluence.

Returning to our initial questions, we can see the extent to which the debates of the 1790s changed the framing of the interlinkage of population, resources, and the natural environment. Above all, what was at stake politically had changed: "advice to princes" morphed into a far more direct call for political change and even revolution in Godwin and Condorcet. Malthus responded in kind, laying the problem firmly at the foot of "nature," defending the established political order. Furthermore, population and its relationship with resources became a site at which the key problematic of the Enlightenment as posed by the French Revolution could be raised: What is the empire of Reason, and are there limits to that empire? For the radical side of the argument, Reason's progress would lead to technological, medical, and agrarian advances without limit that would be matched by the progress of mind—individual and collective—toward a rationality that would prevent population growth butting up against resource limits. As such, population became a collective capable of physical and intellectual improvement, not merely an aggregate of individuals needing governance. For Malthus, such arguments were a delusion making unwarranted inferences from limited evidence and ignoring lawlike regularities connecting human societies to their biophysical foundations. These foundations made Malthus see the perpetual problem of governance as one of too many people reaching the limits to food availability, not of too few people leading to relative political weakness as had early modern political theorists.

The decades following this debate in the 1790s between radical and conservative visions of the linkage of population, food, and the environment saw arguments ramify in numerous directions, of which three should be noted here. First, Malthus's work on population continued through much-expanded editions of his *Essay* from 1803 to 1826, being joined by an extensive literature in political economy (or, as we would now term it, "economics") about population and resources. While the other great economist of the age, David Ricardo, by and large accepted Malthus's ideas in this sphere, a host of others, such as Nassau William Senior, debated and refined these ideas or sought to take them to a broader audience, as did Harriet Martineau, whose instructive fictional tales were collected as *Illustrations of Political Economy* (1832). Secondly, a generation of radical thinkers updated Condorcet and Godwin to respond to Malthus's ideas. Thus, the celebrated essayist William Hazlitt produced a four-hundred-page *Reply to the Essay on Population* (1807), combining brilliant invective with acute analysis of the social foundations of poverty and food scarcity. William Cobbett likewise spent the first decades of the nineteenth century lambasting "the monster Malthus," perhaps most notably in his extraordinary letter on the Valley of the Avon in his most popular work, *Rural Rides* (1822), in which he noted plentiful fields heaving with corn and livestock juxtaposed with a diminished and emaciated agricultural laboring class who watched their produce being carted to the "great Wen" of London. Mary Shelley's late-Romantic contribution in *The Last Man*

(1826) neatly balanced pro- and anti-Malthusian poles. Finally, prose invectives pro and contra were joined by an avalanche of numbers as censuses began to offer real numerical grist to the mill of debates about population's linkage with food resources. The first British census was taken in 1801 to join that undertaken by the fledgling United States of America eleven years earlier. Numbers could not in and of themselves adjudicate the sorts of debates the "Malthus wars" established, instead providing fodder for all parties.

The final selections hint at the extent to which the debate about the interconnection between population, resources, and the natural environment moved on in the four decades after the French Revolution. Godwin's *Of Population* (1820) shows him keen to emphasize the potential of emigration from populous nations to alleviate resource scarcity. It also shows him deploying burgeoning census data to develop an understanding of population densities and a potential global human carrying capacity. Godwin further offers quantified examples of what agricultural improvement can deliver in terms of food yields to bolster his arguments empirically. Interestingly, he also hints at the inefficiencies of the meat-based diet Britain had pioneered in terms of its resource usage before going on to claim that the so-called chemical revolution opened up the technological possibility of synthesizing nutrition from any elements on the earth's surface and thereby enabled a geometrical growth in food production to match Malthus's projected population growth. On the other side, Malthus also raises new arguments. As document 2.5 shows, he is hesitant about emigration to vacant or underutilized spaces as it demands that the rights of natives around the globe are trampled upon. This is a fairly small argument in the texture of Malthus's *Essay*, but recent scholarship has rightly focused on it as much for what it points out is missing from the debates canvassed in this section as for what it actually says. The debate about emigration as a "safety valve" for overpopulation and the exhaustion of natural resources all but entirely ignored indigeneity, that the inhabitants of the supposedly underpopulated areas of the globe might have rights to those areas and might develop complex ideas about the connections between themselves and the land. A concern with indigenous population dynamics did emerge in fragmentary form, notably in Malthus's argument that his principle of population applied to all societies across time and space. An awareness of indigenous rights and demographic thought was all but absent. Malthus here shines a slight light onto this question, but by and large both sides in the Malthus wars of this period, radicals and conservatives alike, ignored the claims and notions of indigenous peoples. This omission, so glaring to our eyes today, would continue through the debate about the interrelationships of population, resources, and the environment traced in this book until long into the postwar period, only coming to be questioned as part of the ramification of global civil rights movements (see document 5.12 for one example).

Ultimately, Godwin's and Malthus's positions remained entrenched and opposed, but the framing of population-resource questions had been transformed in their lifetimes in ways that at least partially justify the claim with which this section opened: that a "modern" framing of human population's relationship with the earth's environment was formed in this era. Key questions about resource availability were raised, as were allied concerns about its distribution. Potential biophysical limits set by the environment were discussed, as was the extent to which such limits were a moving target determined by technological change and social organization as much as being fixed by a putative entity called "nature," even if the latter remained the most common framing term for the discussion. And as Godwin and Malthus started to discuss emigration, indigenous rights, the chemical synthesis of food, and the resource footprint of a meat-based diet, so they pointed toward a world that was global, imperial, and industrial and away from the advanced, organic, and agrarian regimes in which they had been born. Even if, then, the Malthus wars can appear to be a dialogue of the deaf stretched over four decades, in the interstices and the details of their arguments, Condorcet, Godwin, and Malthus assuredly did much to set the platform for a modern framing of the relationship between population, resources, and the environment.

DOCUMENT 2.1

FROM WILLIAM GODWIN, *AN ENQUIRY CONCERNING POLITICAL JUSTICE* (1793)

AN AUTHOR WHO HAS SPECULATED WIDELY UPON SUBJECTS OF GOVernment,[1] has recommended equal, or, which was rather his idea, common property, as a complete remedy, to the usurpation and distress which are at present the most powerful enemies of human kind, to the vices which infect education in some instances, and the neglect it encounters in more, to all the turbulence of passion, and all the injustice of selfishness. But, after having exhibited this picture, not less true than delightful, he finds an argument that demolishes the whole, and restores him to indifference and despair, in the excessive population that would ensue.

One of the most obvious answers to this objection is, that to reason thus is to foresee difficulties at a great distance. Three fourths of the habitable globe is now uncultivated. The parts already cultivated are capable of immeasurable improvement. Myriads of centuries of still increasing population may probably pass away, and the earth still be found sufficient for the subsistence of its inhabitants. Who can say how long the earth itself will survive the casualties of the planetary system? Who can say what remedies shall suggest themselves for so distant an inconvenience, time enough for practical application, and of which we may yet at this time have not the smallest idea? It would be truly absurd for us to shrink from a scheme of essential benefit to mankind, lest they should be too happy, and by necessary consequence at some distant period too populous.

[...]

What follows must be considered in some degree as a deviation into the land of conjecture. [...] Let us here return to the sublime conjecture of Franklin,[2] that "mind will one day become omnipotent over matter." If over all other matter, why not over the matter of our own bodies? If over matter at ever so great a distance, why not over matter which, however ignorant we may be of the tie that connects it with the thinking principle, we always carry about with us, and which is in all cases the medium of communication between that principle and the external universe? In a word, why may not man be one day immortal?

The different cases in which thought modifies the external universe are obvious to all. It is modified by our voluntary thoughts or design. We desire to stretch out our hand, and it is stretched out. We perform a thousand operations of the same species every day, and their familiarity annihilates the wonder. They are not in themselves less wonderful than any of those modifications which we are least accustomed to conceive.—Mind modifies body involuntarily. [...] The effort of mind in resisting pain in the stories of Cranmer and Mucius Scævola is of the same kind.[3] It is reasonable to believe that that effort with a different direction might have cured certain diseases of the system. There is nothing indeed of which physicians themselves are more frequently aware, than of the power of the mind in assisting or retarding convalescence.

The application of these reasonings is simple and irresistible. If mind be now in a great degree the ruler of the system, why should it be incapable of extending its empire? If our involuntary thoughts can derange or restore the animal economy, why should we not in process of time, in this as in other instances, subject the thoughts which are at present involuntary to the government of design? If volition can now do something, why should it not go on to do still more and more? There is no principle of reason less liable to question than this, that, if we have in any respect a little power now, and if mind be essentially progressive, that power may, and, barring any extraordinary concussions of nature, infallibly will, extend beyond any bounds we are able to prescribe to it.

Nothing can be more irrational and presumptuous than to conclude, because a certain species of supposed power is entirely out of the line of our present observations, that it is therefore altogether beyond the limits of the human mind. We talk familiarly indeed of the limits of our faculties, but nothing is more difficult than to point them out. Mind, in a progressive view at least, is infinite. If it could have been told to the savage inhabitants of Europe in the times of Theseus and Achilles, that man was capable of predicting eclipses and weighing the air, of explaining the phenomena of nature so that no prodigies should remain, of measuring the distance and the size of the heavenly bodies, this would not have appeared to them less wonderful, than if we had told them of the possible discovery of the means of maintaining the human body in perpetual youth and vigour. But we have not only this analogy, showing that the discovery in question forms as it were a regular branch of the acquisitions that belong to an intellectual nature; but in addition to this we seem to have a glimpse of the specific manner in which the acquisition will be secured.

[...]

Medicine may reasonably be stated to consist of two branches, the animal and intellectual. The latter of these has been infinitely too much neglected. It cannot be employed to the purposes of a profession; or, where it has been incidentally so employed, it has been artificially and indirectly, not in an open and avowed manner. "Herein the patient must minister to himself."[4] How often do we find a sudden piece of good news dissipating a distemper? How common is the remark, that those accidents, which are to the indolent a source of disease, are forgotten and extirpated in the busy and active? It would no doubt be of extreme moment to us, to be thoroughly acquainted with the power of motives, habit, and what is called resolution, in this respect. I walk twenty miles in an indolent and half determined temper, and am extremely fatigued. I walk twenty miles full of ardour and with a motive that engrosses my soul, and I come in as fresh and alert as when I began my journey. We are sick and we die, generally speaking, because we consent to suffer these accidents. This consent in the present state of mankind is in some degree unavoidable. We must have stronger motives and clearer views, before we can uniformly refuse it.

[...]

To apply these remarks to the subject of population. The tendency of a cultivated and virtuous mind is to render us indifferent to the gratifications of sense. They please at present by their novelty, that is, because we know not how to estimate them. They decay in the decline of life indirectly because the system refuses them, but directly and principally because they no longer excite the ardour and passion of mind. It is well known that an inflamed imagination is capable of doubling and tripling the seminal secretions. The gratifications of sense please at present by their imposture. We soon learn to despise the mere animal function, which, apart from the delusions of intellect, would be nearly the same in all cases; and to value it, only as it happens to be relieved by personal charms or mental excellence. We absurdly imagine that no better road can be found to the sympathy and intercourse of minds. But a very slight degree of attention might convince us that this is a false road, full of danger and deception. Why should I esteem another, or by another be esteemed? For this reason only, because esteem is due, and only so far as it is due.

The men therefore who exist when the earth shall refuse itself to a more extended population, will cease to propagate, for they will no longer have any motive, either of error or duty, to induce them. In addition to this they will perhaps be immortal. The whole will be a people of men, and not of children. Generation will not succeed generation, nor truth have in a certain degree to recommence her career at the end of every thirty years. There will be no war, no crimes, no administration of justice as it is called, and no government. These latter articles are at no great distance; and it is not impossible that some of the present race of men may live to see them in part accomplished. But beside this, there will be no disease, no anguish, no melancholy and no resentment. Every man will seek with ineffable ardour the good of all. Mind will be active and eager, yet never disappointed. Men will see the progressive advancement of virtue and good, and feel that, if things occasionally happen contrary to their hopes, the miscarriage itself was a necessary part of that progress. They will know, that they are members of the chain, that each has his several utility, and they will not feel indifferent to that utility. They will be eager to enquire into the good that already exists, the means by which it was produced, and the greater good that is yet in store. They will never want motives for exertion; for that benefit which a man thoroughly understands and earnestly loves, he cannot refrain from endeavouring to promote.

NOTES

1 Godwin here refers to Robert Wallace; see document 1.7.
2 That is, Benjamin Franklin; see document 1.8.

3 Thomas Cranmer was burnt at the stake for heresy in 1556, and Gaius Mucius Scaevola, a sixth-century BCE Roman soldier, when captured allegedly put his hand willingly into a sacrificial flame.
4 William Shakespeare, *Macbeth*, 5.3.

DOCUMENT 2.2

FROM MARIE JEAN ANTOINE NICOLAS DE CARITAT, MARQUIS DE CONDORCET, *OUTLINES OF AN HISTORICAL VIEW OF THE PROGRESS OF THE HUMAN MIND* (1795)

IF MAN CAN PREDICT, ALMOST WITH CERTAINTY, THOSE APPEARANCES of which he understands the laws; if, even when the laws are unknown to him, experience or the past enables him to foresee, with considerable probability, future appearances; why should we suppose it a chimerical undertaking to delineate, with some degree of truth, the picture of the future destiny of mankind from the results of its history? The only foundation of faith in the natural sciences is the principle, that the general laws, known or unknown, which regulate the phenomena of the universe, are regular and constant; and why should this principle, applicable to the other operations of nature, be less true when applied to the development of the intellectual and moral faculties of man? In short, as opinions formed from experience, relative to the same class of objects, are the only rule by which men of soundest understanding are governed in their conduct, why should the philosopher be proscribed from supporting his conjectures upon a similar basis, provided he attribute to them no greater certainty than the number, the consistency, and the accuracy of actual observations shall authorise?

[. . .]

Will not every nation one day arrive at the state of civilization attained by those people who are most enlightened, most free, most exempt from prejudices, as the French, for instance, and the Anglo-Americans? Will not the slavery of countries subjected to kings, the barbarity of African tribes, and the ignorance of savages gradually vanish? Is there upon the face of the globe a single spot the inhabitants of which are condemned by nature never to enjoy liberty, never to exercise their reason?

[. . .]

In fine, may it not be expected that the human race will be meliorated by new discoveries in the sciences and the arts, and, as an unavoidable consequence, in the means of individual and general prosperity; by farther progress in the principles of conduct, and in moral practice; and lastly, by the real improvement of our faculties, moral, intellectual and physical, which may be the result either of the improvement of the instruments which increase the power and direct the exercise of those faculties, or of the improvement of our natural organization itself?

[. . .] we shall find the strongest reasons to believe, from past experience, from observation of the progress which the sciences and civilization have hitherto made, and from the analysis of the march of the human understanding, and the development of its faculties, that nature has fixed no limits to our hopes.

[. . .]

If we pass to the progress of the arts, those arts particularly the theory of which depends on these very same sciences, we shall find that it can have no inferior limits; that their processes are susceptible of the same improvement, the same simplifications, as the scientific methods; that instruments, machines, looms, will add every day to the capabilities and skill of man—will augment at once the excellence and precision of his works, while they will diminish the time and labour necessary for executing them; and that then will disappear the obstacles that still oppose themselves to the progress in question, accidents which will be foreseen and prevented; and lastly, the unhealthiness at present attendant upon certain operations, habits and climates.

A smaller portion of ground will then be made to produce a proportion of provisions of higher value or greater utility; a greater quantity of enjoyment will be procured at a smaller expense of consumption; the same manufactured or artificial commodity will be produced at a smaller expense of raw materials, or will be stronger and more durable; every soil will be appropriated to productions which will satisfy a greater number of wants with the least labour, and taken in the smallest quantities. Thus the means of health and frugality will be increased, together with the instruments in the arts of production, of curing commodities and manufacturing their produce, without demanding the sacrifice of one enjoyment by the consumer.

Thus, not only the same species of ground will nourish a greater number of individuals, but each individual, with a less quantity of labour, will labour more successfully, and be surrounded with greater conveniences.

It may, however, be demanded, whether, amidst this improvement in industry and happiness, where the wants and faculties of men will continually become better proportioned, each successive generation possess more various stores, and of consequence in each generation the number of individuals be greatly increased; it may, I say, be demanded, whether these principles of improvement and increase may not, by their continual operation, ultimately lead to degeneracy and destruction? Whether the number of inhabitants in the universe at length exceeding the means of existence, there will not result a continual decay of happiness and population, and a progress towards barbarism, or at least a sort of oscillation between good and evil? Will not this oscillation, in societies arrived at this epoch, be a perennial source of periodical calamity and distress? In a word, do not these considerations point out the limit at which all farther improvement will become impossible, and consequently the perfectibility of man arrive at a period which in the immensity of ages it may attain, but which it can never pass?

There is, doubtless, no individual that does not perceive how very remote from us will be this period: but must it one day arrive? It is equally impossible to pronounce on either side respecting an event, which can only be realized at an epoch when the human species will necessarily have acquired a degree of knowledge, of which our short-sighted understandings can scarcely form an idea. And who shall presume to foretell to what perfection the art of converting the elements of life into substances suited for our use, may, in a progression of ages, be brought?

But supposing the affirmative, supposing it actually to take place, there would result from it nothing alarming, either to the happiness of the human race, or its indefinite perfectibility; if we consider, that prior to this period the progress of reason will have walked hand in hand with that of the sciences; that the absurd prejudices of superstition will have ceased to infuse into morality a harshness that corrupts and degrades, instead of purifying and exalting it; that men will then know, that the duties they may be under relative to propagation will consist not in the question of giving *existence* to a greater number of beings, but *happiness*; will have for their object, the general welfare of the human species; of the society in which they live; of the family to which they are attached; and not the puerile idea of encumbering the earth with useless and wretched mortals. Accordingly, there might then be a limit to the possible mass of provision, and of consequence to the greatest possible population, without that premature destruction, so contrary to nature and to social prosperity, of a portion of the beings who may have received life, being the result of those limits.

[. . .]

All the causes which contribute to the improvement of the human species, all the means we have enumerated that insure its progress, must, from their very nature; exercise an influence always active, and acquire an extent for ever increasing. The proofs of this have been exhibited, and from their development in the work itself they will derive additional force: accordingly we may already conclude, that the perfectibility of man is indefinite. Meanwhile we have hitherto considered him as possessing only the same natural faculties, as endowed with the same organization. How much greater would be the certainty, how much wider the compass of our hopes, could we prove that these natural faculties themselves, that this very organization, are also susceptible of melioration? And this is the last question we shall examine.

The organic perfectibility or deterioration of the classes of the vegetable, or species of the animal kingdom, may be regarded as one of the general laws of nature.

This law extends itself to the human race; and it cannot be doubted that the progress of the sanative art, that the use of more wholesome food and more comfortable habitations, that a mode of life which shall develop the physical powers by exercise, without at the same time impairing them by excess; in fine, that the destruction of the two most active causes of deterioration, penury and wretchedness on the one hand, and enormous wealth on the other, must necessarily tend to prolong the common duration of man's existence, and secure him a more constant health and a more robust constitution. It is manifest that the improvement of the practice of medicine, become more efficacious in consequence of the progress of reason and the social order, must in the end put a period to transmissible or contagious disorders, as well to those general maladies resulting from climate, aliments, and the nature of certain occupations. Nor would it be difficult to prove that this hope might be extended to almost every other malady, of which it is probable we shall hereafter discover the most remote causes. Would it even be absurd to suppose this quality of melioration in the human species as susceptible of an indefinite advancement; to suppose that a period must one day arrive when death will be nothing more than the effect either of extraordinary accidents, or of the slow and gradual decay of the vital powers; and that the duration of the middle space, of the interval between the birth of man and this decay, will itself have no assignable limit? Certainly man will not become immortal; but may not the distance between the moment in which he draws his first breath, and the common term when, in the course of nature, without malady or accident, he finds it impossible any longer to exist, be necessarily protracted?

[...]

But may not our physical faculties, the force, the sagacity, the acuteness of the senses, be numbered among the qualities, the individual improvement of which it will be practicable to transmit? An attention to the different breeds of domestic animals must lead us to adopt the affirmative of this question, and a direct observation of the human species itself will be found to strengthen the opinion.

Lastly, may we not include in the same circle the intellectual and moral faculties? May not our parents, who transmit to us the advantages or defects of their conformation, and from whom we receive our features and shape, as well as our propensities to certain physical affections, transmit to us also that part of organization upon which intellect, strength of understanding, energy of soul or moral sensibility depend? Is it not probable that education, by improving these qualities, will at the same time have an influence upon, will modify and improve this organization itself? Analogy, an investigation of the human faculties, and even some facts, appear to authorise these conjectures, and thereby to enlarge the boundary of our hopes.

Such are the questions with which we shall terminate the last division of our work. And how admirably calculated is this view of the human race, emancipated from its chains, released alike from the dominion of chance, as well as from that of the enemies of its progress, and advancing with a firm and indeviate step in the paths of truth, to console the philosopher lamenting the errors, the flagrant acts of injustice, the crimes with which the earth is still polluted? It is the contemplation of this prospect that rewards him for all his efforts to assist the progress of reason and the establishment of liberty. He dares to regard these efforts as a part of the eternal chain of the destiny of mankind; and in this persuasion he finds the true delight of virtue, the pleasure of having performed a durable service, which no vicissitude will ever destroy in a fatal operation calculated to restore the reign of prejudice and slavery. This sentiment is the asylum into which he retires, and to which the memory of his persecutors cannot follow him: he unites himself in imagination with man restored to his rights, delivered from oppression, and proceeding with rapid strides in the path of happiness; he forgets his own misfortunes while his thoughts are thus employed; he lives no longer to adversity, calumny and malice, but becomes the associate of these wiser and more fortunate beings whose enviable condition he so earnestly contributed to produce.

DOCUMENT 2.3

FROM THOMAS ROBERT MALTHUS, *AN ESSAY ON THE PRINCIPLE OF POPULATION* (1798)

THE GREAT AND UNLOOKED FOR DISCOVERIES THAT HAVE TAKEN place of late years in natural philosophy, the increasing diffusion of general knowledge from the extension of the art of printing, the ardent and unshackled spirit of inquiry that prevails throughout the lettered and even unlettered world, the new and extraordinary lights that have been thrown on political subjects which dazzle and astonish the understanding, and particularly that tremendous phenomenon in the political horizon, the French Revolution, which, like a blazing comet, seems destined either to inspire with fresh life and vigour, or to scorch up and destroy the shrinking inhabitants of the earth, have all concurred to lead many able men into the opinion that we were touching on a period big with the most important changes, changes that would in some measure be decisive of the future fate of mankind.

It has been said that the great question is now at issue, whether man shall henceforth start forwards with accelerated velocity towards illimitable, and hitherto unconceived improvement, or be condemned to a perpetual oscillation between happiness and misery, and after every effort remain still at an immeasurable distance from the wished-for goal.

[...]

I have read some of the speculations on the perfectibility of man and of society with great pleasure.[1] I have been warmed and delighted with the enchanting picture which they hold forth. I ardently wish for such happy improvements. But I see great, and, to my understanding, unconquerable difficulties in the way to them. These difficulties it is my present purpose to state, declaring, at the same time, that so far from exulting in them, as a cause of triumph over the friends of innovation, nothing would give me greater pleasure than to see them completely removed.

The most important argument that I shall adduce is certainly not new. The principles on which it depends have been explained in part by Hume, and more at large by Dr Adam Smith.[2] It has been advanced and applied to the present subject, though not with its proper weight, or in the most forcible point of view, by Mr Wallace,[3] and it may probably have been stated by many writers that I have never met with. I should certainly therefore not think of advancing it again, though I mean to place it in a point of view in some degree different from any that I have hitherto seen, if it had ever been fairly and satisfactorily answered.

The cause of this neglect on the part of the advocates for the perfectibility of mankind is not easily accounted for. I cannot doubt the talents of such men as Godwin and Condorcet. I am unwilling to doubt their candour. To my understanding, and probably to that of most others, the difficulty appears insurmountable. Yet these men of acknowledged ability and penetration scarcely deign to notice it, and hold on their course in such speculations with unabated ardour and undiminished confidence. [. . .]

In entering upon the argument I must premise that I put out of the question, at present, all mere conjectures, that is, all suppositions, the probable realization of which cannot be inferred upon any just philosophical grounds. A writer may tell me that he thinks man will ultimately become an ostrich. I cannot properly contradict him. But before he can expect to bring any reasonable person over to his opinion, he ought to shew that the necks of mankind have been gradually elongating, that the lips have grown harder and more prominent, that the legs and feet are daily altering their shape, and that the hair is beginning to change into stubs of feathers. And till the probability of so wonderful a conversion can be shewn, it is surely lost time and lost eloquence to expatiate on the happiness of man in such a state; to describe his powers, both of running and flying, to paint him in a condition where all narrow luxuries would be contemned, where he would be employed only in collecting the necessaries of life, and where, consequently, each man's share of labour would be light, and his portion of leisure ample.

I think I may fairly make two postulata.

First, That food is necessary to the existence of man.

Secondly, That the passion between the sexes is necessary and will remain nearly in its present state.

These two laws, ever since we have had any knowledge of mankind, appear to have been fixed laws of our nature, and, as we have not hitherto seen any alteration in them, we have no right to conclude that they will ever cease to be what they now are, without an immediate act of power in that Being who first arranged the system of the universe, and for the advantage of his creatures, still executes, according to fixed laws, all its various operations.

I do not know that any writer has supposed that on this earth man will ultimately be able to live without food. But Mr Godwin has conjectured that the passion between the sexes may in time be extinguished. As, however, he calls this part of his work a deviation into the land of conjecture, I will not dwell longer upon it at present than to say that the best arguments for the perfectibility of man are drawn from a contemplation of the great progress that he has already made from the savage state and the difficulty of saying where he is to stop. But towards the extinction of the passion between the sexes, no progress whatever has hitherto been made. It appears to exist in as much force at present as it did two thousand or four thousand years ago. There are individual exceptions now as there always have been. But, as these exceptions do not appear to increase in number, it would surely be a very unphilosophical mode of arguing to infer, merely from the existence of an exception, that the exception would, in time, become the rule, and the rule the exception.

Assuming then my postulata as granted, I say, that the power of population is indefinitely greater than the power in the earth to produce subsistence for man.

Population, when unchecked, increases in a geometrical ratio. Subsistence increases only in an arithmetical ratio. A slight acquaintance with numbers will shew the immensity of the first power in comparison of the second.

By that law of our nature which makes food necessary to the life of man, the effects of these two unequal powers must be kept equal.

This implies a strong and constantly operating check on population from the difficulty of subsistence. This difficulty must fall somewhere and must necessarily be severely felt by a large portion of mankind.

Through the animal and vegetable kingdoms, nature has scattered the seeds of life abroad with the most profuse and liberal hand. She has been comparatively sparing in the room and the nourishment necessary to rear them. The germs of existence contained in this spot of earth, with ample food, and ample room to expand in, would fill millions of worlds in the course of a few thousand years. Necessity, that imperious all pervading law of nature, restrains them within the prescribed bounds. The race of plants and the race of animals shrink under this great restrictive law. And the race of man cannot, by any efforts of reason, escape from it. Among plants and animals its effects are waste of seed, sickness, and premature death. Among mankind, misery and vice. The former, misery, is an absolutely necessary consequence of it. Vice is a highly probable consequence, and we therefore see it abundantly prevail, but it ought not, perhaps, to be called an absolutely necessary consequence. The ordeal of virtue is to resist all temptation to evil.

This natural inequality of the two powers of population and of production in the earth, and that great law of our nature which must constantly keep their effects equal, form the great difficulty that to me appears insurmountable in the way to the perfectibility of society. All other arguments are of slight and subordinate consideration in comparison of this. I see no way by which man can escape from the weight of this law which pervades all animated nature. No fancied equality, no agrarian regulations in their utmost extent, could remove the pressure of it even for a single century. And it appears, therefore, to be decisive against the possible existence of a society, all the members of which should live in ease, happiness, and comparative leisure; and feel no anxiety about providing the means of subsistence for themselves and families.

[. . .]

I said that population, when unchecked, increased in a geometrical ratio, and subsistence for man in an arithmetical ratio.

Let us examine whether this position be just.

[. . .]

In a state [. . .] of great equality and virtue, where pure and simple manners prevailed, and where the means of subsistence were so abundant that no part of the society could have any fears about providing amply for a family, the power of population being left to exert itself unchecked, the increase of the human species would evidently be much greater than any increase that has been hitherto known.

In the United States of America, where the means of subsistence have been more ample, the manners of the people more pure, and consequently the checks to early marriages fewer, than in any of the modern states of Europe, the population has been found to double itself in twenty-five years.[4]

This ratio of increase, though short of the utmost power of population, yet as the result of actual experience, we will take as our rule, and say, that population, when unchecked, goes on doubling itself every twenty-five years or increases in a geometrical ratio.

Let us now take any spot of earth, this Island for instance, and see in what ratio the subsistence it affords can be supposed to increase. We will begin with it under its present state of cultivation.

If I allow that by the best possible policy, by breaking up more land and by great encouragements to agriculture, the produce of this Island may be doubled in the first twenty-five years, I think it will be allowing as much as any person can well demand.

In the next twenty-five years, it is impossible to suppose that the produce could be quadrupled. It would be contrary to all our knowledge of the qualities of land. The very utmost that we can conceive, is, that the increase in the second twenty-five years might equal the present produce. Let us then take this for our rule, though certainly far beyond the truth, and allow that, by great exertion, the whole produce of the Island might be increased every twenty-five years, by a quantity of subsistence equal to what it at present produces. The most enthusiastic speculator cannot suppose a greater increase than this. In a few centuries it would make every acre of land in the Island like a garden.

Yet this ratio of increase is evidently arithmetical.

It may be fairly said, therefore, that the means of subsistence increase in an arithmetical ratio.

Let us now bring the effects of these two ratios together.

The population of the Island is computed to be about seven millions, and we will suppose the present produce equal to the support of such a number. In the first twenty-five years the population would be fourteen millions, and the food being also doubled, the means of subsistence would be equal to this increase. In the next twenty-five years the population would be twenty-eight millions, and the means of subsistence only equal to the support of twenty-one millions. In the next period, the population would be fifty-six millions, and the means of subsistence just sufficient for half that number. And at the conclusion of the first century the population would be one hundred and twelve millions and the means of subsistence only equal to the support of thirty-five millions, which would leave a population of seventy-seven millions totally unprovided for.

[...]

But to make the argument more general [. . .] let us take the whole earth, instead of one spot, and suppose that the restraints to population were universally removed. If the subsistence for man that the earth affords was to be increased every twenty-five years by a quantity equal to what the whole world at present produces, this would allow the power of production in the earth to be absolutely unlimited, and its ratio of increase much greater than we can conceive that any possible exertions of mankind could make it.

Taking the population of the world at any number, a thousand millions, for instance, the human species would increase in the ratio of—1, 2, 4, 8, 16, 32, 64, 128, 256, 512, etc. and subsistence as—1, 2, 3, 4, 5, 6, 7, 8, 9, 10, etc. In two centuries and a quarter, the population would be to the means of subsistence as 512 to 10, in three centuries as 4096 to 13, and in two thousand years the difference would be almost incalculable, though the produce in that time would have increased to an immense extent.

[...]

[C]heck[s] remain now to be considered.

Among plants and animals the view of the subject is simple. They are all impelled by a powerful instinct to the increase of their species, and this instinct is interrupted by no reasoning or doubts about providing for their offspring. Wherever therefore there is liberty, the power of increase is exerted, and the superabundant effects are repressed afterwards by want of room and nourishment, which is common to animals and plants, and among animals by becoming the prey of others.

The effects of this check on man are more complicated.

Impelled to the increase of his species by an equally powerful instinct, reason interrupts his career and asks him whether he may not bring beings into the world for whom he cannot provide the means of subsistence. In a state of equality, this would be the simple question. In the present state of society, other considerations occur. Will he not lower his rank in life? Will he not subject himself to greater difficulties than he at present feels? Will he not be obliged to labour harder? and if he has a large family, will his utmost exertions enable him to support them? May he not see his offspring in rags and misery, and clamouring for bread that he cannot give them? And may he not be reduced to the grating necessity of forfeiting his independence, and of being obliged to the sparing hand of charity for support?

[. . .]

The way in which these effects are produced seems to be this.

We will suppose the means of subsistence in any country just equal to the easy support of its inhabitants. The constant effort towards population, which is found to act even in the most vicious societies, increases the number of people before the means of subsistence are increased. The food therefore which before supported seven millions must now be divided among seven millions and a half or eight millions. The poor consequently must live much worse, and many of them be reduced to severe distress. The number of labourers also being above the proportion of the work in the market, the price of labour must tend toward a decrease, while the price of provisions would at the same time tend to rise. The labourer therefore must work harder to earn the same as he did before. During this season of distress, the discouragements to marriage, and the difficulty of rearing a family are so great that population is at a stand. In the mean time the cheapness of labour, the plenty of labourers, and the necessity of an increased industry amongst them, encourage cultivators to employ more labour upon their land, to turn up fresh soil, and to manure and improve more completely what is already in tillage, till ultimately the means of subsistence become in the same proportion to the population as at the period from which we set out. The situation of the labourer being then again tolerably comfortable, the restraints to population are in some degree loosened, and the same retrograde and progressive movements with respect to happiness are repeated.

This sort of oscillation will not be remarked by superficial observers, and it may be difficult even for the most penetrating mind to calculate its periods. Yet that in all old states some such vibration does exist, though from various transverse causes, in a much less marked, and in a much more irregular manner than I have described it, no reflecting man who considers the subject deeply can well doubt.

Many reasons occur why this oscillation has been less obvious, and less decidedly confirmed by experience, than might naturally be expected.

One principal reason is that the histories of mankind that we possess are histories only of the higher classes. We have but few accounts that can be depended upon of the manners and customs of that part of mankind where these retrograde and progressive movements chiefly take place. [. . .]

Such a history would tend greatly to elucidate the manner in which the constant check upon population acts and would probably prove the existence of the retrograde and progressive movements that have been mentioned, though the times of their vibrations must necessarily be rendered irregular from the operation of many interrupting causes, such as the introduction or failure of certain manufactures, a greater or less prevalent spirit of agricultural enterprise, years of plenty, or years of scarcity, wars and pestilence, poor laws, the invention of processes for shortening labour without the proportional extension of the market for the commodity, and, particularly, the difference between the nominal and real price of labour, a circumstance which has perhaps more than any other contributed to conceal this oscillation from common view.

But in order more fully to ascertain the validity of these [. . .] propositions, let us examine the different states in which mankind have been known to exist.

In the rudest state of mankind, in which hunting is the principal Occupation, and the only mode of acquiring food; the means of subsistence being scattered over a large extent of territory, the comparative population must necessarily be thin. It is said, that the passion between the sexes is less ardent among the North American Indians, than among any other race of men. Yet notwithstanding this apathy, the effort towards population, even in this people, seems to be always greater than the means to support it. This appears from the comparatively rapid population that takes place whenever any of the tribes happen to settle in some fertile spot, and to draw nourishment from more fruitful sources than that of hunting; and it has been frequently remarked, that when an Indian family has taken up its abode near any European settlement, and adopted a more easy and civilized mode of life, that one woman has reared five, or six, or more children; though in the savage state, it rarely happens that above one or two in a family grow up to maturity. The same observation has been made with regard to the Hottentots near the Cape. These facts prove the superior power of population to the means of subsistence in nations of hunters; and that this power always shews itself the moment it is left to act with freedom.

[...]

[A]mong nations of shepherds, the next state of mankind [...] that these nations could not escape the general lot of misery arising from the want of subsistence, Europe, and all the fairest countries in the world, bear ample testimony. Want was the goad that drove the Scythian shepherds from their native haunts, like so many famished wolves in search of prey. Set in motion by this all powerful cause, clouds of Barbarians seemed to collect, from all points of the northern hemisphere.

[...]

In examining the next state of mankind with relation to the question before us, the state of mixed pasture and tillage, in which with some variation in the proportions, the most civilized nations must always remain; we shall be assisted in our review by what we daily see around us, by actual experience, by facts that come within the scope of every man's observation.

Notwithstanding the exaggerations of some old historians, there can remain no doubt in the mind of any thinking man, that the population of the principal countries of Europe, France, England, Germany, Russia, Poland, Sweden, and Denmark is much greater than ever it was in former times. [...]

The reason that the greater part of Europe is more populous now than it was in former times, is, that the industry of the inhabitants has made these countries produce a greater quantity of human subsistence. For, I conceive, that it may be laid down as a position not to be controverted, that, taking a sufficient extent of territory to include within it exportation and importation; and allowing some variation for the prevalence of luxury, or of frugal habits; that population constantly bears a regular proportion to the food that the earth is made to produce. In the controversy concerning the populousness of ancient and modern nations,[5] could it be clearly ascertained that the average produce of the countries in question, taken altogether, is greater now than it was in the times of Julius Cæsar, the dispute would be at once determined.

NOTES

1 That is, the writings of Godwin and Condorcet.
2 Adam Smith is a Scottish Enlightenment thinker best known for his pioneering treatise in political economy, *An Inquiry into the Nature and Causes of the Wealth of Nations* (1776).
3 Malthus here refers to Robert Wallace; see document 1.7.
4 Malthus took this argument from Benjamin Franklin (see document 1.8) via Richard Price (see document 1.10).
5 See part 1.

DOCUMENT 2.4

FROM WILLIAM GODWIN, *OF POPULATION* (1820)

THE PITH OF ALL MR. MALTHUS'S SPECULATIONS LIES IN ESTABLISHING a geometrical ratio for the power of increase in the human species, and an arithmetical ratio for the power of increase in the means of subsistence: and his capital inference is, that, at least in all old settled countries, or rather in all countries, except those where land is to be had freely, or at a very low rate, and agriculture is understood, the population is continually limited and kept down by the limits of the means of subsistence, and there is always a somewhat greater number of inhabitants, than the food of the country will fully and wholesomely nourish.

We have already enquired into the solidity of the doctrine of the Essay on Population, respecting that excessive tendency of the human species to increase. [. . .] We have seen, that it is at least problematical, whether there is a tendency in the human species to increase, and that, for any thing that appears from the enumerations and documents hitherto collected, it may be one of the first duties incumbent on the true statesman and friend of human kind, to prevent that diminution in the numbers of his fellow-men, which has been thought, by some of the profoundest enquirers, ultimately to threaten the extinction of our species.

It is proper that we should now proceed to examine the other branch of Mr. Malthus's doctrine, that which relates to the means of subsistence; concerning which he will be seen to have fallen into errors not less ill-founded and pernicious, than those which concern the possible numbers of mankind.

[. . .]

The first thing perhaps that would arrest the observation of an enlightened enquirer, who should set himself down to survey the globe we inhabit according to the latest authorities, is the scanty and sparing way in which man, of whose nature we are, and in many respects with good reason, so proud, is scattered over the face of the earth. What immense deserts, what vast tracts of yet unconquered forests, the asylum only of wild beasts, or of the most pernicious and contemptible animals, have we occasion to observe! When I travel even through many parts of England, it seems to me that I pass through a country, which has but just begun to be reclaimed from the tyranny of savage nature. I believe I may venture to affirm that there is one third of the island which does not yet feel the hands of the cultivator; not to mention the very imperfect and inadequate manner in which the other two-thirds are turned to use. Man seems formed to subdue all these, to chase the wild beasts and either to tame or destroy their species, to fell the forests, and to render the most ungrateful soil productive. If indeed we are qualified to "increase, and multiply, and replenish the earth,"[1] it might be hoped that, at a period however distant, the whole surface of all lands might be "cultivated like a garden."[2] But, for some reason or other, the very reverse of this is glaringly and deplorably the case.

[. . .]

I am desirous, on the present occasion, of shutting out everything conjectural, and which therefore by a certain class of reasoners might be called visionary. One practical way of looking at the subject is this. The habitable parts of the globe are computed to occupy a space of thirty-nine millions of square miles, and its human inhabitants to amount to six hundred millions. Of this surface China is said to constitute 1,300,000 square miles. Now, let us admit the present population of China to stand at three hundred millions of souls. How fully China is cultivated I do not know; but I have as little doubt as Mr. Malthus appears to have, that the soil of that empire might be made greatly more effective for the purposes of human subsistence, than it is at present. But let us assume, for the sake of argument, the cultivation of China for the standard of possible cultivation, and consequently its population for the standard of possible population. The earth then, if all its habitable parts could be made as fertile as China, is equal to the sustaining a population of nine thousand millions of human beings. In other words, wherever one human being is now found in existence, the earth is capable, not in theory only, and according to conceived improvements no where yet realised, but judging from approved facts, instead of that one, of subsisting fifteen.

The majority of men seem to have laboured under some deception as to the population of China. It is principally in the vast extent of an empire said to be every where so flourishing, that China is worthy of admiration. Taking from Pinkerton[3] the dimensions of China on the one hand, and of England and Wales on the other, I find that, if the latter were as well stocked with citizens as the former, it would contain 13,461,923 inhabitants, that is about three millions beyond the returns to the population-act of 1811.[4]

[. . .]

I cannot but think that the first contemplation that would have suggested itself to an enlightened philanthropist, proceeding on these premises, would have been something like the following.

Man is an admirable creature, the beauty of the world, which, if he did not exist in it, would be "a habitation of dragons, and a court for owls; the wild beast of the desert would cry to the wild beast of the islands; baboons would dance there; and its pleasant places be filled with all doleful creatures."[5] How delightful a speculation then is it, that man is endowed by all-bountiful nature with an unlimited power of multiplying his species! I would look out upon the cheerless and melancholy world which has just been described, and imagine it all cultivated, all improved, all variegated with a multitude of human beings, in a state of illumination, of innocence, and of active benevolence, to which the progress of thought, and the enlargement of mind seem naturally to lead, beyond any thing that has yet any where been realised. I would count up the acres and the square miles of the surface of the earth, and consider them all as the estate in fee simple of the human intellect. I would extend my view from China and England, countries already moderately, and but moderately peopled, to the plains of North America, of South America, of Africa, of many tracts of Asia, of the north of Europe, of Spain, and various other divisions of the prolific world. I should contemplate with delight the extensive emigrations that have taken place to North America, and plan and chalk out, as far as my capacity and endowments of study would permit me, similar emigrations to other parts of the world, that should finally make the whole earth at least as populous as China is at present.

[...]

It is with some diffidence that I would enter upon the theoretical part of the question, and enquire how far the earth may be rendered more productive to the purposes of human subsistence than it is at present. This branch of the subject however would be left imperfect, if that consideration were wholly omitted.

To the improvements of man, more particularly in art, and the application of human industry, there is no end. No sooner therefore shall we have got rid of the geometrical ratio, and the still more absurd doctrine (if indeed there be any degrees between these) of "population necessarily and constantly pressing hard against the limits of subsistence, from the present moment to the time when the whole earth shall be cultivated like a garden,"[6] than our prospects will grow very cheering indeed.

[...]

Let us come down then to the regions of common sense. And, to attain a greater degree of perspicuity in our views, let us take for the object of our consideration the countries of England and Wales.

[...]

In the first place then I would observe, that, after what has been stated, it will hardly be denied, first, that the food produced in England and Wales, if equally distributed, is more than enough for the present number of the inhabitants; or, secondly, that many tracts of land in these countries might be rendered more efficient for the subsistence of man, than they actually are.

The problem now under consideration, is, how shall a given tract of country be made to subsist more men? The problem that seems for more than a century past in England practically to have occupied the attention of those in whose direction the affair was placed, has been, How shall a given tract of country be made effective only for the subsistence of a smaller number of men?

Dr. Price[7] mentions two causes, operating in this country, which are eminently calculated to produce this effect; the engrossing of farms, and the progress of luxury.

[...]

Mr. Malthus repeatedly calls our attention, and with great propriety, to the period when the whole earth, or any considerable division of it, shall be "cultivated like a garden." Till that shall be the case, it is perfectly clear that there can be no permanent deficiency in the means of subsistence, except what is produced by the restrictions imposed on us by human institutions.

I feel inclined in this place shortly to mention the agricultural improvements of Mr. Coke of Norfolk.[8] [. . .] Mr. Coke's Norfolk estate, when he came to the succession more than forty years ago, was regarded as some of the worst land in the country. A great part of it was leased out at three shillings an acre. The entire rental amounted to £2200 *per annum*. By his example and encouragement its produce is now so far raised, that it may serve as a sort of model to the whole island. The rental has increased ten-fold: the cultivators are happy: the population is tripled. They have no longer need for a poor-house, which has accordingly been pulled down. The very land, which was lately an object of so much contempt, now produces five or six quarters of wheat, and ten of barley, *per* acre.

Mr. Coke is however at this moment a sort of phenomenon in the island. The majority of our cultivators, even in the naturally fertile counties of Shropshire and Cheshire, go on in the method of their fathers, without improvement; and, at the very time that Mr. Coke was gathering the crops abovementioned, the average produce of wheat among them was not more than two quarters *per* acre. Thus we see that by a very simple process, the example of which we have under our eye, the produce of our island might be much more than doubled. The consciousness of this, one would have thought, would have prevented any sober man, in this ill-omened hour for so unhallowed a purpose, from preaching up Mr. Malthus's doctrine of depopulation.

I mention this example [. . .] because there is a numerous class of persons, well disposed to do justice to an actual experiment, at the same time that they turn a deaf ear to what comes before them in the shape of speculation. For these reasons I have recorded the proceedings of Mr. Coke, though these are doubtless extremely trivial, compared with what I conceive, and with what Mr. Malthus assumes, of the capacity of the earth for affording subsistence to mankind.

[. . .]

To the speculations already mentioned upon the means of human subsistence, is to be added the sea. The sea occupies two-thirds of the surface of the globe: it is every where full of animal life, and nearly all that life may be rendered subservient to human subsistence. This is a species of crop that we are not called upon to sow; it needs no manure; and the farmer who takes care of it, will seldom have occasion to observe the face of the heavens, and send to the parish-minister to solicit a prayer for fine weather, or a prayer for rain. There is no long watching the progress of growth, but one fine day will be sufficient for him to bring in his stores. It has been ascertained, particularly as to the salmon-fishery, that no drafts upon this stock, however immense, occasions the smallest sensible diminution of the crop for the next season. It is upon the confidence of this fact, that some of the most serious transactions are founded, in the countries to which the question relates. Thus, in some parts of Scotland, where the drain has for years been the most considerable, the rents for a right of fishing for a certain distance, have lately been raised tenfold above what they had been. Add to which, that salmon and other fish, when cured, may be kept for almost any time, and be carried any distance up the country.

Before we quit this branch of the subject, it will be worth while to look back to Mr. Middleton's estimate of the present mode of human subsistence. He states each man to consume upon an average, *per annum*, "in bread the produce of half an acre, in roots, greens and fruit the produce of one eighth of an acre, in liquids one eighth of an acre, and in animal food two acres."[9] Here we are presented in a striking view with the knowledge, of how much would be economised as to human subsistence, by the general substitution of the vegetable for the animal productions of the earth.

[. . .]

There is however one other circumstance that requires to be mentioned, before the subject can properly be considered as exhausted. Of all the sciences, natural or mechanical, which within the last half century have proceeded with such gigantic strides, chemistry is that which has advanced the most rapidly. All the substances that nature presents, all that proceeds from earth or air, is analysed by us into its original elements. Thus we have discovered, or may discover, precisely what it is that nourishes the human body. And it is surely no great stretch of the faculty of anticipation, to say, that whatever man can decompose, man will be able to compound. The food that nourishes us, is composed of certain elements; and wherever these elements can be found, human art will hereafter discover the power of reducing them into a state capable of affording corporeal sustenance. No good reason can be assigned, why that which produces animal nourishment, must have previously passed through a process of animal or vegetable life. And, if a certain infusion of attractive exterior qualities is held necessary to allure us to our food, there is no reason to suppose that the most agreeable colours and scents and flavours may not be imparted to it, at a very small expense of vegetable substance. Thus it appears that, wherever earth, and water, and the other original chemical substances may be found, there human art may hereafter produce nourishment: and thus we are presented with a real infinite series of increase of the means of subsistence, to match Mr. Malthus's geometrical ratio for the multiplication of mankind.—This may be thought too speculative; but surely it is not more so, than Mr. Malthus's period, when the globe of earth, or, as he has since told us, the solar system, and all the "other planets circling other suns," shall be overcrowded with the multitude of their human inhabitants.

NOTES

1 Genesis 9:7.
2 This quotation is from Malthus's *Essay*.
3 John Pinkerton, *Modern Geography* (1802).
4 This was the second decennial census in England and Wales.
5 Quotation is possibly a free translation of Isaiah 34:13.
6 Malthus, *Essay*.
7 Godwin here refers to Richard Price; see document 1.10, which is Godwin's immediate source here.
8 Thomas Coke was an agricultural improver.
9 Quotation is perhaps from Charles Middleton, *A Complete System of Geography* (1778).

DOCUMENT 2.5

FROM THOMAS ROBERT MALTHUS, *AN ESSAY ON THE PRINCIPLE OF POPULATION* (6TH ED., 1826)

MAN IS NECESSARILY CONFINED IN ROOM. WHEN ACRE HAS BEEN added to acre till all the fertile land is occupied, the yearly increase of food must depend upon the melioration of the land already in possession. This is a fund; which, from the nature of all soils, instead of increasing, must be gradually diminishing. [. . .]

From the accounts we have of China and Japan, it may be fairly doubted, whether the best-directed efforts of human industry could double the produce of these countries even once in any number of years. There are many parts of the globe; indeed, hitherto uncultivated, and almost unoccupied; but the right of exterminating, or driving into a corner where they must starve, even the inhabitants of these thinly-peopled regions, will be questioned in a moral view. The process of improving their minds and directing their industry would necessarily be slow; and during this time, as population would regularly keep pace with the increasing produce, it would rarely happen that a great degree of knowledge and industry would have to operate at once upon rich unappropriated soil. Even where this might take place, as it does sometimes in new colonies, a geometrical ratio increases with such extraordinary rapidity, that the advantage could not last long. If the United States of America continue increasing, which they certainly will do, though not with the same rapidity as formerly, the Indians will be driven further and further back into the country, till the whole race is ultimately exterminated, and the territory is incapable of further extension.

These observations are, in a degree, applicable to all the parts of the earth, where the soil is imperfectly cultivated. To exterminate the inhabitants of the greatest part of Asia and Africa, is a thought that could not be admitted for a moment. To civilise and direct the industry of the various tribes of Tartars and Negroes, would certainly be a work of considerable time, and of variable and uncertain success.

DOCUMENT 2.6

FROM THOMAS ROBERT MALTHUS, *A SUMMARY VIEW OF THE PRINCIPLE OF POPULATION* (1830)

IT IS UNQUESTIONABLY TRUE, THAT IN NO COUNTRY OF THE GLOBE have the government, the distribution of property, and the habits of the people, been such as to call forth, in the most effective manner, the resources of the soil. Consequently, if the most advantageous possible change in all these respects could be supposed at once to take place, it is certain that the demand for labour, and the encouragement to production, might be such, as for a short time, in some countries, and for rather a longer time in others, to lessen the operation of the checks to population which have been described. It is specifically this truth constantly obtruding itself upon our attention, which is the great source of delusion on this subject, and creates the belief that man could always produce from the soil much more than sufficient to support himself and family. In the actual state of things, this power has perhaps always been possessed. But for it we are indebted wholly to the ignorance and bad government of our ancestors. If they had properly called forth the resources of the soil, it is quite certain that we should now have but scanty means left of further increasing our food. [. . .] That difficulty in procuring the necessaries of life which is now felt in the comparatively low wages of labour almost all over the world, and is occasioned partly by the necessary state of the soil, and partly by a premature check to the demand for produce and labour, would then be felt in a greater degree, and would less admit of any relaxation in the checks to population, because it would be occasioned wholly and necessarily by the state of the soil.

[...]

It is to the laws of nature, therefore, and not to the conduct and institutions of man, that we are to attribute the necessity of a strong check on the natural increase of population.

But, though the laws of nature which determine the rate at which population would increase if unchecked, and the very different rate at which the food required to support population could continue to increase in a limited territory, are undoubtedly the causes which render necessary the existence of some great and constant check to population, yet a vast mass of responsibility remains behind on man and the institutions of society.

In the first place, they are certainly responsible for the present scanty population of the earth. There are few large countries, however advanced in improvement, the population of which might not have been doubled or tripled, and there are many which might be ten, or even a hundred times as populous, and yet all the inhabitants be as well provided for as they are now, if the institutions of society, and the moral habits of the people, had been for some hundred years the most favourable to the increase of capital, and the demand for produce and labour.

Secondly, though man has but a trifling and temporary influence in altering the proportionate amount of the checks to population, or the degree in which they press upon the actual numbers, yet he has a great and most extensive influence on their character and mode of operation.

It is not in superseding the necessity of checks to population, in the progress of mankind to the full peopling of the earth (which may with truth be said to be a physical impossibility), but in directing these checks in such a way as to be the least prejudicial to the virtue and happiness of society, that government and human institutions produce their great effect. Here we know, from constant experience, that they have great power. Yet, even here, it must be allowed, that the power of government is rather indirect than direct, as the object to be attained depends mainly upon such a conduct on the part of individuals, as can seldom be directly enforced by laws, though it may be powerfully influenced by them.

DOCUMENT 2.7

FROM MARY SHELLEY, *THE LAST MAN* (1826)

MEANWHILE ALL WENT ON WELL IN LONDON. [. . .] CANALS, AQUE-ducts, bridges, stately buildings, and various edifices for public utility, were entered upon [. . .] to render England one scene of fertility and magnificence. [. . .] The physical state of man would soon not yield to the beatitude of the angels; disease was to be banished; labour lightened of its heaviest burden. Nor did this seem extravagant. The arts of life, and the discoveries of science had augmented in a ratio which left all calculation behind; food sprung up, so to say, spontaneously—machines existed to supply with facility every want of the population.

[. . .]

In the autumn of the year 2092 [. . .] Delight awoke in every heart, delight and exultation; for there was peace through all the world [. . .] and man died not that year by the hand of man.

"Let this last but twelve months," said Adrian; "and earth will become a Paradise. The energies of man were before directed to the destruction of his species; they now aim at its liberation and preservation. Man cannot repose, and his restless aspirations will now bring forth good instead of evil. The favoured countries of the south will throw off the iron yoke of servitude; poverty will quit us, and with that, sickness. What may not the forces, never before united, of liberty and peace achieve in this dwelling of man?"

"Dreaming, for ever dreaming [. . .]" said Ryland, the old adversary. [. . .] "Be assured that earth is not, nor ever can be heaven, while the seeds of hell are natives of her soil. When the seasons have become equal, when the air breeds no disorders, when its surface is no longer liable to blights and droughts, then sickness will cease; when men's passions are dead, poverty will depart. When love is no longer akin to hate, then brotherhood will exist: we are very far from that state at present.

[. . .]

[With the onset of a pandemic] The English [. . .] came pouring back in one great revulsive stream, back on their own country; and with them crowds of Italians and Spaniards. Our little island was filled even to bursting. [. . .] It was impossible to see these crowds of wretched, perishing creatures, late nurslings of luxury, and not stretch out a hand to save them. As at the conclusion of the eighteenth century, the English unlocked their hospitable store, for the relief of those driven from their homes by political revolution;[1] so now they were not backward in affording aid to the victims of a more wide-spreading calamity. [. . .] Adrian [. . .] addressed himself to the wealthy of the land; he made proposals in parliament little adapted to please the rich; but his earnest pleadings and benevolent eloquence were irresistible. To give up their pleasure grounds to the agriculturist, to diminish sensibly the number of horses kept for the purposes of luxury throughout the country, were means obvious, but unpleasing. Yet, to the honour of the English be it recorded, that, although natural disinclination made them delay awhile, yet when the misery of their fellow-creatures became glaring, an enthusiastic generosity inspired their decrees.

[. . .]

In the autumn of this year 2096, the spirit of emigration crept in among the few survivors. [. . .] Let us go! England is in her shroud. [. . .] Let us go!—the world is our country now, and we may choose for our residence its most fertile spot. Shall we, in these desert halls, under this wintry sky, sit with closed eyes and folded hands, expecting death? Let us rather go out and meet it gallantly:—or perhaps—for all this pendulous orb, this fair gem in the sky's diadem, is surely not plague-striken—perhaps, in some secluded nook, amidst eternal spring, and waving trees, and purling streams, we may find

Life. The world is vast, and England, though her many fields and wide spread woods seem interminable, is but a small part of her. At the close of a day's march over high mountains and through snowy vallies, we may come upon health, and committing our loved ones to its charge, replant the uprooted tree of humanity, and send to late posterity the tale of the ante-pestilential race, the heroes and sages of the lost state of things.

NOTE

1 Shelley here refers to British charitable relief to emigrants from the French Revolution.

3

EVOLVING DEBATES

MALTHUS DIED IN 1834, AND HIS OLD SPARRING PARTNER, WILLIAM Godwin, two years later. An era whose intellectual debates had been defined by the polarizing cataclysm that was the French Revolution came to a close. And yet the century after Malthus's death, as canvassed in this section, saw both a strong continuation of the debate about the interrelationship between population, resources, social justice, and the environment and a notable broadening of the terms of reference for those categories.

Perhaps most importantly for the new directions that debates about population and the environment would take in the nineteenth century, five years after Malthus's death Charles Darwin sketched his theory of natural selection. This sketch, which is included here, was published only twenty years later, in 1858, together with a parallel thesis by Alfred Russel Wallace. Taken together, these statements amounted to the public promulgation of the idea of evolution. If evolution was (and is) the single most important transformation in our understanding of the functioning of the natural world generated by modern science, population analysis was both central to the genesis of this idea and reciprocally transformed by it. Looking back from a vantage point half a century later, Wallace confirmed the centrality of Malthus's *Essay* and population thinking more generally to the genesis of the idea of evolution, noting "the effect of that was analogous to that of friction upon the specially prepared match, producing that flash of insight which led us immediately to the simple but universal law of the 'survival of the fittest,' as the long sought *effective* cause of the continuous modification and adaptation of living things."[1] This is closely echoed in a comment in *On the Origin of Species* (1859) that the survival of the fittest is "the doctrine of Malthus applied with manifold force to the whole animal and vegetable kingdoms."

That a cluster of metaphors around concepts of competition, struggle, and the war of all against all came to dominate European and North American understandings of the functioning of the natural world was in no small part predicated both on Malthus's legacy and on Darwin's and Wallace's fascination with population dynamics. These metaphors were both embraced, ramifying into the study of areas not initially indicated by Darwin and Wallace, and contested vigorously as the nineteenth century progressed by those building different understandings of how populations survived and flourished and what that told us about human relations with their environment. If Darwinian ideas were effectively the transfer of concepts from the study of human populations to an inquiry into the natural world, a diffuse movement we now label as social Darwinism saw a reverse flow of ideas, using a Darwinian understanding of how the natural world functions to understand modern social and political formations. Darwin signaled this inquiry in his *Descent of Man* (1871), but it was carried forward far more forcefully by the likes of Herbert Spencer and Thomas Huxley, who depicted societies as the product of a struggle for resources. Social Darwinism's impact was broad, being deployed as an organizing device by diverse inquiries into politics, geography, anthropology, and sociology. Social Darwinism inevitably led to anxieties about fitness: Was our society strong enough to survive, or could it face extinction at the hands of a more vibrant society? Social Darwinism, then, easily morphed into a eugenic concern with the quality of the human population as a breed that was first signaled by Darwin's cousin Francis Galton and would come to impact forcibly and (all too frequently) tragically on the population policies of Europe and North America in the decades either side of 1900.

And yet the image of nature as a Darwinian-Malthusian struggle to survive both for the population as a whole and for classes, races, and individuals within it was by no means hegemonic: on the contrary, other naturalists built different ways of framing how animals including humans survived. Such work built different conceptions of the human relationship with other cultures, with other creatures, and with the environment. Most important was the Russian geographer and naturalist Petr Kropotkin. Kropotkin's image of nature was one in which species flourished by means of "mutual aid," that is, of collective and collaborative behavior rather than competition. Kropotkin's ideas were formed by detailed fieldwork on the Russian steppes, a very different set of environments from the temperate and tropical ones studied by Darwin and Wallace. A different physical environment, then, led Kropotkin to a different understanding of population dynamics, this in turn supporting an alternative set of images of how plant, animal, and human societies functioned. In short, Kropotkin naturalized socialist and cooperative ideas of mutual aid as a different master metaphor of the relationship between populations and the environment. Another linkage of socialism, "progressive" politics, and population polemics was forged by the pioneering feminist and advocate of birth control Annie Besant, who highlighted issues of striking prescience in later Victorian England, notably issues of gender equality and what would come to be known as "reproductive justice" a century later.

If Kropotkin took us to the Russian steppes and Besant traveled to the poverty-ridden dens of London's East End, William Jevons took debates about population, resources, and the environment down the mines. Malthus's political economy of population was unpicked in his own era by the emergence of coal as a source of power and heat that circumvented the limits of food production, but within a generation of his death, nineteenth-century society was galvanized by fears of a "sooty Malthusianism." This took two forms that were hugely important to developing understandings of the relationship between human societies and their environment. First, Jevons in *The Coal Question* (1865) suggested that recourse to coal was only a temporary respite from the Malthusian pressure of an expanding population on scarce resources. Indeed, the potential for a crash as society reached resource limits was all the greater since coal as a non-renewable would simply be exhausted and at a time when it had facilitated unprecedented and unsustainable population growth. Jevons, then, adjusted Malthus's concern with food as a limited resource to respond to the shift from an organic to a fossil fuel economy in ways that would find close parallels a century later in concerns about "peak oil" and its likely aftermath in terms of societal collapse. Second, such anxieties about limited resources led to far broader concerns about the impact of a free trade economy on the natural environments on which people were reliant spiritually and aesthetically as well as economically.

In counterpoint to the political panic produced by Jevons's work, Wallace provided a window onto the social and environmental costs of coal. Wallace as the co-discoverer of evolution by means of natural selection had taken this set of ideas in a different direction from Darwin, arguing that human societies were now outside the sphere of natural selective forces thanks to their advanced brain capacities. If the use of human reason could avoid Malthusian environmental limits in general, applying this to Jevons's coal question led to some very radical ideas. First, unfettered free trade was irrational as it failed to respond to environmental limits, sacrificing the happiness and viability of future generations to present profit. Second, such a focus on the present led to the despoliation of the physical environment, black countries of smoke and soot replacing England's green and pleasant land. Resource depletion and environmental despoliation, then, led to questions about the worth of free trade capitalism (as, through a different route, had Kropotkin's work) and to ideas of prioritizing quality or value of life as opposed to quantity of population and productivity. From here it was a short step to ideas of an "optimum population" size and density determined by environmental quality. Such concerns, tied with an awareness of issues of distributional justice, permeated mainstream work in economics via John Stuart Mill's comments, inspired by the Romanticism of William Wordsworth, about the need to balance growth with the preservation of the physical environment in *Principles of Political Economy* (1848). In wanting to conjoin economic growth, social justice, and environmental concern, Mill prefigured many of the tensions and trade-offs modern environmental economics addresses. In somewhat vatic mode, no one encapsulated these concerns more presciently or more forcibly than the critic John Ruskin in *Unto This Last* (1862), a work that fulminated against the "dismal science" of political economy (as Thomas Carlyle had dubbed it) and in particular against its understanding of population. For Ruskin, ignoring that "there is no wealth but life," political economy failed to observe that human life was as reliant for sustenance, properly understood, on the cornflower and the coal tit as it was on Malthus's corn and Jevons's coal.

The nexus of debates about species evolution and competition (evolution as a model by which to understand the functioning of the natural and human world), on the one hand, and about political economy and human value (population size and quality), on the other, drove interpretations of events throughout the period. History, trade, empire, war, and exchange were all modeled in terms of the interaction of population dynamics with resources and the environment. Perhaps the most eloquent statement of a Darwinian-Malthusian understanding of human events came at the end of the period in John Maynard Keynes's celebrated reading of World War I, *The Economic*

Consequences of the Peace (1919). Presciently, Keynes feared that the punitive sanctions imposed in the Treaty of Versailles would lead to a recrudescence into war, but to build his case, he outlined the causes of the war from which Europe was just emerging. He portrayed a thoroughly Malthusian context of population growth in Europe, a social Darwinian vista of spiraling economic competition, and a reworking of Jevons's coal question in the form of dwindling resource availability. Much of Keynes's argument would be unpicked by William Beveridge, but it does show the extent to which scholars looked to population and resource limits. This kind of analysis persisted in the interwar years, forming a complex amalgam of population, environment, eugenics, and aesthetics.

In sum, the century after Malthus's death saw a continued debate about the nexus of population and resources with a considerable widening of the interpretation of both concepts. Population came to be thought of not only in terms of total numbers but also in terms of demographic structure. Population was also, and more influentially, thought of in regard to quality and optimum size in terms inherited from the application of Darwinian ideas to the human realm. The understanding of resources likewise shifted and widened from Malthus's focus on food in an organic economy to a broader bundle of resources such as coal and iron and to the issues about accessing such resources in a globalizing free trade economy. For all that a Darwinian image of struggle became a master metaphor of nature, society, and their interaction for the century after its construction, dissenting voices also pointed to different, cooperative understandings of how populations worked with respect to the natural world. Such voices also highlighted the negative consequences of unalloyed growth and competition in terms of environmental despoliation and the aesthetic and spiritual damage it wrought. The environment viewed as a source of intellectual and aesthetic satisfaction, then, as well as merely in economic terms as the means of survival, came to be factored into the nexus of population and resources.

The final selection in this part poses a question: What happens if you refuse to accept the logics of Anglophone and European debates about population, resources, and the environment? Josué de Castro was a Brazilian pacifist, campaigner, and nutritionist who worked for the United Nation's Food and Agriculture Organization after World War II. If Castro came to work within the new internationalist paradigm that we will revisit in part 4, he started by penning a set of experiments in fiction, one of which from 1937, "The Cycle of the Crab," is translated here. Moving from reportage to fiction,

Castro asks us to imagine a Brazilian population that clothes, houses, and feeds itself in ways disclosed by the environments in which it is settled rather than imposing procrustean solutions of urban industrial capitalism on that environment. Writing with different generic norms from Malthus and his nineteenth-century interlocutors, Castro presages the different, indigenous logics linking population, resources, and the environment that would resurface in the later twentieth and twenty-first centuries as the intersectionalities of race, gender, and indigeneity came to be taken seriously.

NOTE

1 Wallace, cited in Andrew Berry, ed., *Infinite Tropics: An Alfred Russel Wallace Anthology* (London: Verso, 2003), 68–69.

DOCUMENT 3.1

FROM CHARLES DARWIN, "EXTRACTS FROM AN UNPUBLISHED WORK ON SPECIES" (1839), IN C. R. DARWIN AND A. R. WALLACE, "ON THE TENDENCY OF SPECIES TO FORM VARIETIES," *JOURNAL OF THE PROCEEDINGS OF THE LINNEAN SOCIETY OF LONDON* (1858)

DE CANDOLLE,[1] IN AN ELOQUENT PASSAGE, HAS DECLARED THAT ALL nature is at war, one organism with another, or with external nature. Seeing the contented face of nature, this may at first well be doubted; but reflection will inevitably prove it to be true. The war, however, is not constant, but recurrent in a slight degree at short periods, and more severely at occasional more distant periods; and hence its effects are easily overlooked. It is the doctrine of Malthus applied in most cases with tenfold force. As in every climate there are seasons, for each of its inhabitants, of greater and less abundance, so all annually breed; and the moral restraint which in some small degree checks the increase of mankind is entirely lost. Even slow-breeding mankind has doubled in twenty-five years; and if he could increase his food with greater ease, he would double in less time. But for animals without artificial means, the amount of food for each species must, *on an average*, be constant, whereas the increase of all organisms tends to be geometrical, and in a vast majority of cases at an enormous ratio. Suppose in a certain spot there are eight pairs of birds, and that *only* four pairs of them annually (including double hatches) rear only four young, and that these go on rearing their young at the same rate, then at the end of seven years (a short life, excluding violent deaths, for any bird) there will be 2048 birds, instead of the original sixteen. As this increase is quite impossible, we must conclude either that birds do not rear nearly half their young, or that the average life of a bird is, from accident, not nearly seven years. Both checks probably concur. The same kind of calculation applied to all plants and animals affords results more or less striking, but in very few instances more striking than in man.

Many practical illustrations of this rapid tendency to increase are on record, among which, during peculiar seasons, are the extraordinary numbers of certain animals; for instance, during the years 1826 to 1828, in La Plata, when from drought some millions of cattle perished, the whole country actually *swarmed* with mice. Now I think it cannot be doubted that during the breeding-season all the mice (with the exception of a few males or females in excess) ordinarily pair, and therefore that this astounding increase during three years must be attributed to a greater number than usual surviving the first year, and then breeding, and so on till the third year, when their numbers were brought down to their usual limits on the return of wet weather. Where man has introduced plants and animals into a new and favourable country, there are many accounts in how surprisingly few years the whole country has become stocked with them. This increase would necessarily stop as soon as the country was fully stocked; and yet we have every reason to believe, from what is known of wild animals, that *all* would pair in the spring. In the majority of cases it is most difficult to imagine where the checks fall—though generally, no doubt, on the seeds, eggs, and young; but when we remember how impossible, even in mankind (so much better known than any other animal), it is to infer from repeated casual observations what the average duration of life is, or to discover the different percentage of deaths to births in different countries, we ought to feel no surprise at our being unable to discover where the check falls in any animal or plant. It should always be remembered, that in most cases the checks are recurrent yearly in a small, regular degree, and in an extreme degree during unusually cold, hot, dry, or wet years, according to the constitution of the being in question. Lighten any check in the least degree, and the geometrical powers of increase in every organism will almost instantly increase the average number of the favoured species. Nature may be compared to a surface on which rest ten thousand sharp wedges touching each other and driven inwards by incessant blows. Fully to realize these views much reflection is requisite. Malthus on man should be studied; and all such cases as those of the mice in La Plata, of the cattle and horses when first turned out in South America, of the birds by our calculation, &c., should be well considered. Reflect on the enormous multiplying power *inherent and annually in action* in all animals; reflect on the countless seeds scattered by a hundred ingenious contrivances, year after year, over the whole face of the land; and yet we have every reason to suppose that the average percentage of each of the inhabitants of a country usually remains constant. Finally, let it be borne in mind that this average number of individuals (the external conditions remaining the same) in each country is kept up by recurrent struggles against other species or against external nature (as on the borders of the Arctic regions, where the cold checks life), and that ordinarily each individual of every species holds its place, either by its own struggle and capacity of acquiring nourishment in some period of its life, from the egg upwards; or by the struggle of its parents (in short-lived organisms, when the main check occurs at longer intervals) with other individuals of the *same* or *different* species.

But let the external conditions of a country alter. If in a small degree, the relative proportions of the inhabitants will in most cases simply be slightly changed; but let the number of inhabitants be small, as on an island, and free access to it from other countries be circumscribed, and let the change of conditions continue progressing (forming new stations), in such a case the original inhabitants must cease to be as perfectly adapted to the changed conditions as they were originally. It has been shown in a former part of this work, that such changes of external conditions would, from their acting on the reproductive system, probably cause the organization of those beings which were most affected to become, as under domestication, plastic. Now, can it be doubted, from the struggle each individual has to obtain subsistence, that any minute variation in structure, habits, or instincts, adapting that individual better to the new conditions, would tell upon its vigour and health? In the struggle it would have a better *chance* of surviving; and those of its offspring which inherited the variation, be it ever so slight, would also have a better *chance*. Yearly more are bred than can survive; the smallest grain in the balance, in the long run, must tell on which death shall fall, and which shall survive. Let this work of selection on the one hand, and death on the other, go on for a thousand generations, who will pretend to affirm that it would produce no effect, when we remember what, in a few years, Bakewell effected in cattle, and Western in sheep, by this identical principle of selection?

To give an imaginary example from changes in progress on an island:—let the organization of a canine animal which preyed chiefly on rabbits, but sometimes on hares, become slightly plastic; let these same changes cause the number of rabbits very slowly to decrease, and the number of hares to increase; the effect of this would be that the fox or dog would be driven to try to catch more hares: his organization, however, being slightly plastic, those individuals with the lightest forms, longest limbs, and best eyesight, let the difference be ever so small, would be slightly favoured, and would tend to live longer, and to survive during that time of the year when food was scarcest; they would also rear more young, which would tend to inherit these slight peculiarities. The less fleet ones would be rigidly destroyed. I can see no more reason to doubt that these causes in a thousand generations would produce a marked effect, and adapt the form of the fox or dog to the catching of hares instead of rabbits, than that greyhounds can be improved by selection and careful breeding. So would it be with plants under similar circumstances. If the number of individuals of a species with plumed seeds could be increased by greater powers of dissemination within its own area (that is, if the check to increase fell chiefly on the seeds), those seeds which were provided with ever so little more down, would in the long run be most disseminated; hence a greater number of seeds thus formed would germinate, and would tend to produce plants inheriting the slightly better-adapted down.

Besides this natural means of selection, by which those individuals are preserved, whether in their egg, or larval, or mature state, which are best adapted to the place they fill in nature, there is a second agency at work in most unisexual animals, tending to produce the same effect, namely, the struggle of the males for the females. These struggles are generally decided by the law of battle, but in the case of birds, apparently, by the charms of their song, by their beauty or their power of courtship, as in the dancing rock-thrush of Guiana. The most vigorous and healthy males, implying perfect adaptation, must generally gain the victory in their contests. This kind of selection, however, is less rigorous than the other; it does not require the death of the less successful, but gives to them fewer descendants. The struggle falls, moreover, at a time of year when food is generally abundant, and perhaps the effect chiefly produced would be the modification of the secondary sexual characters, which are not related to the power of obtaining food, or to defence from enemies, but to fighting with or rivalling other males. The result of this struggle amongst the males may be compared in some respects to that produced by those agriculturists who pay less attention to the careful selection of all their young animals, and more to the occasional use of a choice mate.

NOTE

1 Darwin here refers to Augustin de Candolle, a Swiss botanist.

DOCUMENT 3.2

FROM PETR KROPOTKIN, *MUTUAL AID: A FACTOR OF EVOLUTION* (1902)

THE CONCEPTION OF STRUGGLE FOR EXISTENCE AS A FACTOR OF EVOlution, introduced into science by Darwin and Wallace, has permitted us to embrace an immensely wide range of phenomena in one single generalization, which soon became the very basis of our philosophical, biological, and sociological speculations. An immense variety of facts:—adaptations of function and structure of organic beings to their surroundings; physiological and anatomical evolution; intellectual progress, and moral development itself, which we formerly used to explain by so many different causes, were embodied by Darwin in one general conception. We understood them as continued endeavours—as a struggle against adverse circumstances—for such a development of individuals, races, species and societies, as would result in the greatest possible fulness, variety, and intensity of life. It may be that at the outset Darwin himself was not fully aware of the generality of the factor which he first invoked for explaining one series only of facts relative to the accumulation of individual variations in incipient species. But he foresaw that the term which he was introducing into science would lose its philosophical and its only true meaning if it were to be used in its narrow sense only—that of a struggle between separate individuals for the sheer means of existence. And at the very beginning of his memorable work he insisted upon the term being taken in its "large and metaphorical sense including dependence of one being on another, and including (which is more important) not only the life of the individual, but success in leaving progeny."

While he himself was chiefly using the term in its narrow sense for his own special purpose, he warned his followers against committing the error (which he seems once to have committed himself) of overrating its narrow meaning. In *The Descent of Man* he gave some powerful pages to illustrate its proper, wide sense. He pointed out how, in numberless animal societies, the struggle between separate individuals for the means of existence disappears, how *struggle* is replaced by *co-operation*, and how that substitution results in the development of intellectual and moral faculties which secure to the species the best conditions for survival. He intimated that in such cases the fittest are not the physically strongest, nor the cunningest, but those who learn to combine so as mutually to support each other, strong and weak alike, for the welfare of the community. "Those communities," he wrote, "which included the greatest number of the most sympathetic members would flourish best, and rear the greatest number of offspring." The term, which originated from the narrow Malthusian conception of competition between each and all, thus lost its narrowness in the mind of one who knew Nature.

Unhappily, these remarks, which might have become the basis of most fruitful researches, were overshadowed by the masses of facts gathered for the purpose of illustrating the consequences of a real competition for life. Besides, Darwin never attempted to submit to a closer investigation the relative importance of the two aspects under which the struggle for existence appears in the animal world, and he never wrote the work he proposed to write upon the natural checks to over-multiplication, although that work would have been the crucial test for appreciating the real purport of individual struggle. Nay, on the very pages just mentioned, amidst data disproving the narrow Malthusian conception of struggle, the old Malthusian leaven reappeared—namely, in Darwin's remarks as to the alleged inconveniences of maintaining the "weak in mind and body" in our civilized societies (ch. v). As if thousands of weak-bodied and infirm poets, scientists, inventors, and reformers, together with other thousands of so-called "fools" and "weak-minded enthusiasts," were not the most precious weapons used by humanity in its struggle for existence by intellectual and moral arms, which Darwin himself emphasized in those same chapters of *Descent of Man*.

It happened with Darwin's theory as it always happens with theories having any bearing upon human relations. Instead of widening it according to his own hints, his followers narrowed it still more. And while Herbert Spencer,[1] starting on independent but closely allied lines, attempted to widen the inquiry into that great question, "Who are the fittest?" especially in the appendix to the third edition of the *Data of Ethics*, the numberless followers of Darwin reduced the notion of struggle for existence to its narrowest limits. They came to conceive the animal world as a world of perpetual struggle among half-starved individuals, thirsting for one another's blood. They made modern literature resound with the war-cry of *woe to the vanquished*,[2] as if it were the last word of modern biology. They raised the "pitiless" struggle for personal advantages to the height of a biological principle which man must submit to as well, under the menace of otherwise succumbing in a world based upon mutual extermination. Leaving aside the economists who know of natural science but a few words borrowed from second-hand vulgarizers, we must recognize that even the most authorized exponents of Darwin's views did their best to maintain those false ideas. In fact, if we take Huxley,[3] who certainly is considered as one of the ablest exponents of the theory of evolution, were we not taught by him, in a paper on the "Struggle for Existence and its Bearing upon Man," that,

> from the point of view of the moralist, the animal world is on about the same level as a gladiators' show. The creatures are fairly well treated, and set to, fight hereby the strongest, the swiftest, and the cunningest live to fight another day. The spectator has no need to turn his thumb down, as no quarter is given.

[...]

In how far this view of nature is supported by fact, will be seen from the evidence which will be here submitted to the reader as regards the animal world, and as regards primitive man. But it may be remarked at once that Huxley's view of nature had as little claim to be taken as a scientific deduction as the opposite view of Rousseau,[4] who saw in nature but love, peace, and harmony destroyed by the accession of man. In fact, the first walk in the forest, the first observation upon any animal society, or even the perusal of any serious work dealing with animal life (D'Orbigny's, Audubon's, Le Vaillant's, no matter which),[5] cannot but set the naturalist thinking about the part taken by social life in the life of animals, and prevent him from seeing in Nature nothing but a field of slaughter, just as this would prevent him from seeing in Nature nothing but harmony and peace. Rousseau had committed the error of excluding the beak-and-claw fight from his thoughts; and Huxley committed the opposite error; but neither Rousseau's optimism nor Huxley's pessimism can be accepted as an impartial interpretation of nature.

As soon as we study animals—not in laboratories and museums only, but in the forest and the prairie, in the steppe and the mountains—we at once perceive that though there is an immense amount of warfare and extermination going on amidst various species, and especially amidst various classes of animals, there is, at the same time, as much, or perhaps even more, of mutual support, mutual aid, and mutual defence amidst animals belonging to the same species or, at least, to the same society. Sociability is as much a law of nature as mutual struggle. Of course it would be extremely difficult to estimate, however roughly, the relative numerical importance of both these series of facts. But if we resort to an indirect test, and ask Nature: "Who are the fittest: those who are continually at war with each other, or those who support one another?" we at once see that those animals which acquire habits of mutual aid are undoubtedly the fittest. They have more chances to survive, and they attain, in their respective classes, the highest development of intelligence and bodily organization. If the numberless facts which can be brought forward to support this view are taken into account, we may safely say that mutual aid is as much a law of animal life as mutual struggle, but that, as a factor of evolution, it most probably has a far greater importance, inasmuch as it favours the development of such habits and characters as insure the maintenance and further development of the species, together with the greatest amount of welfare and enjoyment of life for the individual, with the least waste of energy.

[...]

The readiness of the Russian zoologists to accept [...] [this] seems quite natural, because nearly all of them have had opportunities of studying the animal world in the wide uninhabited regions of Northern Asia and East Russia; and it is impossible to study like regions without being brought to the same ideas. I recollect myself the impression produced upon me by the animal world of Siberia when I explored the Vitim regions in the company of so accomplished a zoologist as my friend Polyakoff[5] was. We both were under the fresh impression of the *Origin of Species*, but we vainly looked for the keen competition between animals of the same species which the reading of Darwin's work had prepared us to expect, even after taking into account the remarks of the third chapter. We saw plenty of adaptations for struggling, very often in common, against the adverse circumstances of climate, or against various enemies, and Polyakoff wrote many a good page upon the mutual dependency of carnivores, ruminants, and rodents in their geographical distribution; we witnessed numbers of facts of mutual support, especially during the migrations of birds and ruminants; but even in the Amur and Usuri regions, where animal life swarms in abundance, facts of real competition and struggle between higher animals of the same species came very seldom under my notice, though I eagerly searched for them.

NOTES

1. Spencer was a nineteenth-century English philosopher, social scientist, and biologist who coined the phrase "survival of the fittest."
2. This is a proverbial phrase from Roman history, meaning that those defeated in battle can expect no quarter to be offered.
3. A nineteenth-century champion of Darwin's ideas, Thomas Henry Huxley was known informally as "Darwin's Bulldog" for his combative style.
4. Eighteenth-century French philosopher Jean-Jacques Rousseau is commonly associated with the idea that a primitive and "natural" state was the purest.
5. Kropotkin here refers to Alcide d'Orbigny, nineteenth-century French naturalist; John James Audubon, French-American naturalist and ornithologist; and François Levaillant, French naturalist and ornithologist.
6. Ivan Semyonovich Polyakov was a nineteenth-century Russian zoologist and ethnographer.

DOCUMENT 3.3

FROM W. STANLEY JEVONS, *THE COAL QUESTION* (1865)

[M]EN, AS WELL AS ALL LIVING CREATURES, TEND TO INCREASE IN AN uniform geometrical ratio. And an uniform rate of growth means an uniform ratio—an uniform percentage of increase—*uniform multiplication in uniform periods*. The law is true and necessary as a mathematical law. If children do as their fathers, they must increase like them; if they do not, some change must have occurred in character or circumstances.

Such is the principle of population as established by Malthus in his celebrated essay. Of the moral and social consequences he deduced from it I need say nothing at present. They have been accepted for the most part by political economists. But the statement *that living beings of the same nature and in the same circumstances multiply in the same geometrical ratio*, is self-evident when the meaning of the words is understood.

Now what is true of the mere number of the people is true of other elements of their condition. If our parents made a definite social advance, then, unless we are unworthy of our parents, or in different circumstances, we should make a similar advance. If our parents doubled their income, or doubled the use of iron, or the agricultural produce of the country, then so ought we, unless we are either changed in character or circumstances.

But great care is here necessary. We are getting to the gist of the subject. Even if we do not change in inward character, yet our exterior circumstances are usually changing. This is what Malthus argued. He said that though our numbers *tend* to increase in uniform ratio, we cannot expect the same to take place with the supply of food. We cannot double the produce of the soil, time after time, *ad infinitum*. When we want more off a field we cannot get it by simply doubling the labourers. Any quantity of capital, and labour, and skill may fail to do it, though discoveries from time to time do allow of a considerable increase. Yet the powers and capabilities of organic and inorganic nature always present this remarkable contrast. The former are always relative to the number of existing beings, and tend unceasingly to increase. But exterior nature presents a certain absolute and inexorable limit.

Now *the whole question turns upon the application of these views to the consumption of coal*. Our subsistence no longer depends upon our produce of corn. The momentous repeal of the Corn Laws[1] throws us from corn upon coal. It marks, at any rate, the epoch when coal was finally recognised as the staple produce of the country;—it marks the ascendency of the manufacturing interest, which is only another name for the development of the use of coal.

The application, however, is a little complicated. The quantity of coal consumed is really a quantity of two dimensions, the number of the people, and the average quantity used by each. Even if each person continued to use an invariable quantity of coal per annum, yet the total produce would increase in the same ratio as the number of the people. But added to this is the fact that we do each of us in general increase our consumption of coal. In round numbers, the population has about doubled since the beginning of the century, but the consumption of coal has increased eightfold, and more. *The consumption per head of the population has therefore increased fourfold.*

[. . .]

But the new applications of coal are of an unlimited character. [. . .] And it cannot escape the attention of any observant person that our inventions and works do multiply in variety and scale of application. Each success assists the development of previous successes, and the achievement of new ones. None of our inventions can successfully stand alone—all are bound together in mutual dependence. The iron manufacture depends on the use of the steam-engine, and the steam-engine on the iron manufacture. Coal and iron are essential either in the supply of light or water, and both these are needed in the development of our factory system. The advance of the mechanical arts gives us vast steam-hammers and mechanical tools, and these again enable us to undertake works of magnitude and difficulty before deemed insuperable. "The tendency of progress," says Sir William Armstrong, "is to quicken progress, because every acquisition in science is so much vantage ground for fresh attainment. We may expect, therefore, to increase our speed as we struggle forward."[2]

For once it would seem as if in fuel, as the source of universal power, we had found an unlimited means of multiplying our command over nature. But alas no! The coal is itself limited in quantity; not absolutely, as regards us, but so that each year we gain our supplies with some increase of difficulty. There are unlimited novelties to make our own, *had we unlimited force to use them.*

[. . .]

For the present our cheap supplies of coal, and our skill in its employment, and the freedom of our commerce with other wide lands, render us independent of the limited agricultural area of these islands, and take us out of the scope of Malthus' doctrine. We are growing rich and numerous upon a source of wealth of which the fertility does not yet apparently decrease with our demands upon it. Hence the uniform and extraordinary rate of growth which this country presents. We are like settlers spreading in a rich new country of which the boundaries are yet unknown and unfelt.

But then I must point out the painful fact that such a rate of growth will before long render our consumption of coal comparable with the total supply. In the increasing depth and difficulty of coal mining we shall meet that vague, but inevitable boundary that will stop our progress. We shall begin as it were to see the further shore of our Black Indies. The wave of population will break upon that shore, and roll back upon itself. And as settlers, unable to choose in the far inland new and virgin soil of unexceeded fertility, will fall back upon that which is next best, and will advance their tillage up the mountain side, so we, unable to discover new coal-fields as shallow as before, must deepen our mines with pain and cost.

There is too this most serious difference to be noted. A farm, however far pushed, will under proper cultivation continue to yield for ever a constant crop. But in a mine there is no reproduction, and the produce once pushed to the utmost will soon begin to fail and sink towards zero.

So far then as our wealth and progress depend upon the superior command of coal we must not only stop—we must go back.

NOTES

1 This took place in 1846. The Corn Laws were tariffs designed to prevent the importation of cereals to the United Kingdom to encourage their domestic production.
2 Nineteenth-century British industrialist William Armstrong, 1st Baron Armstrong, was an early advocate of renewable energy.

DOCUMENT 3.4

FROM ALFRED RUSSEL WALLACE, "FREE-TRADE PRINCIPLES AND THE COAL QUESTION," LETTER TO THE *DAILY NEWS* (SEPTEMBER 16, 1873)

IT HAS NOW BECOME AN AXIOM WITH ALL LIBERAL THINKERS THAT complete freedom of exchange between nations and countries of the various products each has in superabundance and can best spare, for others which it requires, is for the benefit of both parties; and this principle is thought to be so universally applicable, that even when it produces positive injury to ourselves and is certain to injure our descendants, hardly any public writer who professes liberal views ventures to propose a limitation of it. It seems clear, however, that there are limitations to its wholesome application, and that there are certain commodities which we have no right to exchange away without restriction, for others of more immediate use to the individuals or communities who happen to be in possession of them. These commodities may be briefly defined as those natural products which are practically limited in quantity, and which cannot be reproduced. What is meant may perhaps be best explained by taking what may be considered a very extreme case as an illustration. Let us suppose, for instance, a country in which the springs or wells of water were strictly limited in number, but sufficiently copious to supply all the actual needs of the community who had always had the use of them, on making a nominal payment to the owners of the land on which they were situated. Acting on the principles of unrestricted free trade, and anxious to increase their wealth, one after another of the landowners sold their springs to manufacturers, who used up all the water except that required to supply the wants of their own workpeople, thus rendering the remainder of the country almost uninhabitable. A still more extreme case, but one rather more to the point, would be that of a country possessing a surface soil of very moderate depth, but of extreme fertility, and supporting a dense population on its vegetable products. The landowners might find it very profitable to them to sell this surface soil to the wealthy horticulturists of other countries; and if the principle of free trade is unlimited, they would be justified in doing so, although they would permanently impoverish the land, and render it capable of supporting a less numerous and less healthy population in long future ages.

Most persons will admit that in both these cases the exercise of the unrestricted right of free trade becomes a wrong to mankind. [. . .] I believe, however, it may be shown that, under circumstances far worse than those here supposed, the landowners in the most civilized community on the globe do act in a very analogous manner, and, moreover, are not yet condemned by public opinion for doing so. Let us first, however, deduce from such supposed cases as those above given a general principle determining what articles of merchandise are and what are not the proper subjects of free trade. A little consideration will convince us that most animal or vegetable products or manufactured articles, the reproduction and increase of which are almost unlimited in comparatively short periods, are those whose free exchange is an unmixed benefit to mankind; the reason being that such exchange enriches both parties without impoverishing either, and, by leading to improved modes of cultivation and an increased power of production, adds continually to the sustaining power of the earth, and benefits future generations as much as it does ourselves. On the other hand, all those articles of consumption which are in any way essential to the comfort and well-being of the community, and which are, either absolutely or practically, limited in quantity and incapable of being reproduced in any period of time commensurate with the length of human life, are in a totally different category. They must be considered to be held by us in trust for the community, and for succeeding generations. They should be jealously guarded from all waste or unnecessary expenditure, and it should be considered (as it will certainly come to be regarded) as a positive crime against posterity to expend them lavishly for the sole purpose of increasing our own wealth, luxury, or commercial importance. Under this head we must class all mineral products which are extensively used in domestic economy, the arts or manufactures, and which are in any way essential to the health or well-being of the community, and more especially those which from their bulk, weight, and extensive use could not be imported from distant regions without a very serious addition to their cost, such as is pre-eminently the case with coal and iron.

Now, it will be seen that we have here to deal with a case quite as extreme in reality as those supposititious cases with which we commenced this inquiry. For coal and iron are almost as much necessaries of life to the large population of this country as are abundance of water and a fertile soil; but there is this difference, that the water might be restored to its legitimate use, and the soil might be renewed by a sufficient period of vegetable growth; whereas coal burned, and iron oxidised, are absolutely lost to mankind, and we have no knowledge of any restorative processes except after the lapse of periods so vast that they cannot enter into our calculations. It may be replied, that the quantity existing on the globe is vast enough for the necessities of mankind for any periods we need calculate on; but even if this be so (of which we are by no means certain), it may none the less be shown that numerous and widespread evils result from our present mode of recklessly expending the stores in certain countries, while the same products remain totally unused in many of the countries they are exported to. [. . .]

Briefly to state these:—In the first place, we have seriously, and perhaps permanently, increased the cost of one of the chief necessaries of life in so changeable a climate as ours—fuel. This is in itself so great and positive an evil that no considerations of mere convenience to remote nations, such as the construction of railways in New Zealand or in Honduras, ought even to be mentioned as an excuse for it. Coal in winter is a question of comfort or misery, even of life or death, to millions of the people whose happiness it is our first duty to secure; and shall we coolly tell them that the Antipodes must have railroads, and that landowners, coalowners, and contractors must make fortunes, although the necessary consequence is the yearly increasing scarcity of one of their first necessaries and greatest comforts?

In the second place, by destroying for ever a considerable and ever-increasing proportion of the mineral wealth of our country, we have rendered it absolutely less habitable and less enjoyable for our descendants, and we have not done this by any fair and justifiable use for our own necessities or enjoyments, but by the abuse of increasing to the utmost of our power the quantity we send out of the country, never mind for what purpose, so that it adds to the wealth of our landowners, capitalists, and manufacturers.

In the third place, we have brought into existence a large population wholly dependent on this excessive production and export of minerals, and therefore not capable of being permanently maintained on our soil. In proportion as other nations make use of their mineral productions, and as our own minerals, from the increasing difficulty of procuring them, become necessarily more costly, so must our excessive exports diminish, and with it must diminish our power of maintaining our present abnormal population. A period of adversity will then probably set in for us, only faintly foreshadowed in intensity and duration by those arising from mere temporary fluctuations in the demand for minerals and their manufactured products.

Fourthly, we not only injure ourselves and our successors by thus striving to get rid of our mineral treasures as fast as possible, but we probably do more harm than good to the nations to whom we export them; for we prevent them from deriving the various social and intellectual benefits which would undoubtedly arise from their being compelled to utilise for their own purposes the mineral products of their own lands. The working of mines and the establishment of manufactures bring into action such a variety of the mental faculties, and so well vary and supplement the labours and the profits of agriculture or trade, that a people who wholly neglect these branches of industry can hardly be said to live a complete and healthy national life. By considering our rich stores of coal and iron as held in trust by us for the use of the present and future populations of these islands, we should probably stimulate and advance a healthy civilization in many countries which the most lavish expenditure of our own minerals, aided by our capital and engineering skill, fail to benefit.

Lastly, I would call attention to the way in which the lavish production of minerals disfigures the country, diminishes vegetable and animal life, and destroys the fertility (for perhaps hundreds of generations) of large tracts of valuable land. It would be interesting to have a survey made of the number of acres of land covered by slag-heaps and cinder-tips at our iron and copper works, and by the waste and refuse mounds at our various mines and slate quarries, together with the land destroyed or seriously injured by smoke and deleterious gases in those "black countries"[1] which it pains the lover of nature to travel through. The extent of once fertile land thus rendered more or less permanently barren would, I believe, astonish and affright us. How strikingly contrasted, both in their motive and results, are those noble works of planting or of irrigation which permanently increase both the beauty and productiveness of a country, and carry down their blessings to succeeding generations.

NOTE

1 This term refers to any area with much coal use, but Wallace may be referring specifically to the West Midlands of England, which are often known as "The Black Country."

DOCUMENT 3.5

FROM JOHN STUART MILL, *PRINCIPLES OF POLITICAL ECONOMY* (1848)

I CONFESS I AM NOT CHARMED WITH THE IDEAL OF LIFE HELD OUT BY those who think that the normal state of human beings is that of struggling to get on; that the trampling, crushing, elbowing, and treading on each other's heels, which form the existing type of social life, are the most desirable lot of human kind, or anything but the disagreeable symptoms of one of the phases of industrial progress.

[...]

I know not why it should be matter of congratulation that persons who are already richer than any one needs to be, should have doubled their means of consuming things which give little or no pleasure except as representative of wealth; or that numbers of individuals should pass over, every year, from the middle classes into a richer class, or from the class of the occupied rich to that of the unoccupied. It is only in the backward countries of the world that increased production is still an important object: in those most advanced, what is economically needed is a better distribution, of which one indispensable means is a stricter restraint on population. Levelling institutions, either of a just or of an unjust kind, cannot alone accomplish it; they may lower the heights of society, but they cannot, of themselves, permanently raise the depths.

[. . .]

There is room in the world, no doubt, and even in old countries, for a great increase of population, supposing the arts of life to go on improving, and capital to increase. But even if innocuous, I confess I see very little reason for desiring it. The density of population necessary to enable mankind to obtain, in the greatest degree, all the advantages both of cooperation and of social intercourse, has, in all the most populous countries, been attained. A population may be too crowded, though all be amply supplied with food and raiment. It is not good for man to be kept perforce at all times in the presence of his species. A world from which solitude is extirpated, is a very poor ideal. Solitude, in the sense of being often alone, is essential to any depth of meditation or of character; and solitude in the presence of natural beauty and grandeur, is the cradle of thoughts and aspirations which are not only good for the individual, but which society could ill do without. Nor is there much satisfaction in contemplating the world with nothing left to the spontaneous activity of nature; with every rood of land brought into cultivation, which is capable of growing food for human beings; every flowery waste or natural pasture ploughed up, all quadrupeds or birds which are not domesticated for man's use exterminated as his rivals for food, every hedgerow or superfluous tree rooted out, and scarcely a place left where a wild shrub or flower could grow without being eradicated as a weed in the name of improved agriculture. If the earth must lose that great portion of its pleasantness which it owes to things that the unlimited increase of wealth and population would extirpate from it, for the mere purpose of enabling it to support a larger, but not a better or a happier population, I sincerely hope, for the sake of posterity, that they will be content to be stationary, long before necessity compels them to it.

It is scarcely necessary to remark that a stationary condition of capital and population implies no stationary state of human improvement. There would be as much scope as ever for all kinds of mental culture, and moral and social progress; as much room for improving the Art of Living, and much more likelihood of its being improved, when minds ceased to be engrossed by the art of getting on. Even the industrial arts might be as earnestly and as successfully cultivated, with this sole difference, that instead of serving no purpose but the increase of wealth, industrial improvements would produce their legitimate effect, that of abridging labour. Hitherto it is questionable if all the mechanical inventions yet made have lightened the day's toil of any human being. They have enabled a greater population to live the same life of drudgery and imprisonment, and an increased number of manufacturers and others to make fortunes. They have increased the comforts of the middle classes. But they have not yet begun to effect those great changes in human destiny, which it is in their nature and in their futurity to accomplish. Only when, in addition to just institutions, the increase of mankind shall be under the deliberate guidance of judicious foresight, can the conquests made from the powers of nature by the intellect and energy of scientific discoverers, become the common property of the species, and the means of improving and elevating the universal lot.

DOCUMENT 3.6

FROM JOHN RUSKIN, *UNTO THIS LAST: FOUR ESSAYS ON THE FIRST PRINCIPLES OF POLITICAL ECONOMY* (1862)

THERE IS NO WEALTH BUT LIFE. LIFE, INCLUDING ALL ITS POW-
ers of love, of joy, and of admiration. That country is the richest which nourishes the greatest number of noble and happy human beings; that man is richest who, having perfected the functions of his own life to the utmost, has also the widest helpful influence, both personal and by means of his possessions, over the lives of others.

[...]

"The greatest number of human beings noble and happy." But is the nobleness consistent with the number? Yes, not only consistent with it, but essential to it. The maximum of life can only be reached by the maximum of virtue. In this respect the law of human population differs wholly from that of animal life. The multiplication of animals is checked only by want of food, and by the hostility of races; the population of the gnat is restrained by the hunger of the swallow, and that of the swallow by the scarcity of gnats. Man, considered as an animal, is indeed limited by the same laws: hunger, or plague, or war, are the necessary and only restraints upon his increase,—effectual restraints hitherto,—his principal study having been how most swiftly to destroy himself, or ravage his dwelling-places, and his highest skill directed to give range to the famine, seed to the plague, and sway to the sword. But, considered as other than an animal, his increase is not limited by these laws. It is limited only by the limits of his courage and his love. Both of these *have* their bounds; and ought to have: his race has its bounds also; but these have not yet been reached, nor will be reached for ages.

In all the ranges of human thought I know none so melancholy as the speculations of political economists on the population question. It is proposed to better the condition of the labourer by giving him higher wages. "Nay," says the economist, "if you raise his wages, he will either drag people down to the same point of misery at which you found him, or drink your wages away." He will. I know it. Who gave him this will? [. . .] Either these poor are of a race essentially different from ours, and unredeemable (which, however often implied, I have heard none yet openly say), or else by such care as we have ourselves received, we may make them continent and sober as ourselves—wise and dispassionate as we are—models arduous of imitation. "But," it is answered, "they cannot receive education." Why not? That is precisely the point at issue. Charitable persons suppose the worst fault of the rich is to refuse the people meat; and the people cry for their meat, kept back by fraud, to the Lord of Multitudes. Alas! it is not meat of which the refusal is cruelest, or to which the claim is validest. The life is more than the meat. The rich not only refuse food to the poor; they refuse wisdom; they refuse virtue; they refuse salvation.

[. . .]

I hope for another end, though not, indeed, from any of the three remedies for over-population commonly suggested by economists.

These three are, in brief—Colonization; Bringing in of waste lands; or Discouragement of Marriage.

The first and second of these expedients merely evade or delay the question. It will, indeed, be long before the world has been all colonized, and its deserts all brought under cultivation. But the radical question is not how much habitable land is in the world, but how many human beings ought to be maintained on a given space of habitable land.

Observe, I say, *ought* to be, not how many *can* be. Ricardo, with his usual inaccuracy, defines what he calls the "natural rate of wages" as "that which will maintain the labourer." Maintain him! yes; but how?—the question was instantly thus asked of me by a working girl, to whom I read the passage. I will amplify her question for her. "Maintain him, how?" As, first, to what length of life? Out of a given number of fed persons how many are to be old—how many young; that is to say, will you arrange their maintenance so as to kill them early—say at thirty or thirty-five on the average, including deaths of weakly or ill-fed children?—or so as to enable them to live out a natural life? You will feed a greater number, in the first case, by rapidity of succession; probably a happier number in the second: which does Mr. Ricardo mean to be their natural state, and to which state belongs the natural rate of wages?

[. . .]

Leaving these questions to be discussed, or waived, at their pleasure, by Mr. Ricardo's followers, I proceed to state the main facts bearing on that probable future of the labouring classes which has been partially glanced at by Mr. Mill. That chapter[1] and the preceding one differ from the common writing of political economists in admitting some value in the aspect of nature, and expressing regret at the probability of the destruction of natural scenery. But we may spare our anxieties, on this head. Men can neither drink steam, nor eat stone. The maximum of population on a given space of land implies also the relative maximum of edible vegetable, whether for men or cattle; it implies a maximum of pure air; and of pure water. Therefore: a maximum of wood, to transmute the air, and of sloping ground, protected by herbage from the extreme heat of the sun, to feed the streams. All England may, if it so chooses, become one manufacturing town; and Englishmen, sacrificing themselves to the good of general humanity, may live diminished lives in the midst of noise, of darkness, and of deadly exhalation. But the world cannot become a factory, nor a mine. No amount of ingenuity will ever make iron digestible by the million, nor substitute hydrogen for wine. [. . .]

Nor need our more sentimental economists fear the too wide spread of the formalities of a mechanical agriculture. The presence of a wise population implies the search for felicity as well as for food; nor can any population reach its maximum but through that wisdom which "rejoices" in the habitable parts of the earth. [. . .] The desire of the heart is also the light of the eyes. No scene is continually and untiringly loved, but one rich by joyful human labour; smooth in field; fair in garden; full in orchard; trim, sweet, and frequent in homestead; ringing with voices of vivid existence. No air is sweet that is silent; it is only sweet when full of low currents of under sound—triplets of birds, and murmur and chirp of insects, and deep-toned words of men, and wayward trebles of childhood. As the art of life is learned, it will be found at last that all lovely things are also necessary:—the wild flower by the wayside, as well as the tended corn; and the wild birds and creatures of the forest, as well as the tended cattle; because man doth not live by bread only, but also by the desert manna; by every wondrous word and unknowable work of God.

NOTE

1   See document 3.5.

DOCUMENT 3.7

FROM ANNIE BESANT, *THE LAW OF POPULATION AND ITS RELATION TO SOCIALISM* (1886)

DURING THE PAST WINTER REFERENCES TO OVER-POPULATION HAVE been plentiful in the columns of the daily and weekly metropolitan press. [...] The unanimity with which they now cry out "over-population is the cause of poverty" is only paralleled with the unanimity with which they denounced Mr Bradlaugh and myself[1] when we alleged ten years ago that over-population is a—not the—cause of poverty, and when we recommended limitation of the family in addition to radical changes in the present system. [...] Now the press is eager to get rid of the consequences of its own action, and State-aided emigration is the pet nostrum of the political quacks of the hour. They shut their eyes to the fact that underfed weaklings are not fitted for the hardships of a pioneer's life; that emigration sufficient to relieve the distress is a physical impossibility; that no country in the world is ready to receive our outcast poor; that the slums of all the great seaboard towns in America, Australia and New Zealand are crowded with hapless immigrants. Emigration is no remedy for poverty. This problem of ours has to be solved on our own soil; and the only solution is a fundamental change in the social system, which shall transform individual into communal holding of land and capital. [...]

[...]

How great is the multiplicative power of man may be judged [. . .] by taking the actual rate of increase in the population, and adding to that the numbers killed off by preventable causes. [. . .] The amount of infanticide and of adult murder that go on in this country are appalling. A large number of infants are born of diseased parents, and quickly wither away; and it is no uncommon thing among the higher and middle classes to find children suffering from the pre-marital vices of their father. A great many are killed off by ignorant feeding and clothing, and by insanitary home-conditions. To take a specific instance, the death-rate of children, under one year of age, born in the poor quarter of Glasgow is just three times as great as that of children born in the rich quarter; that is, two-thirds of the children of the Glasgow poor are murdered within a year of their birth. [. . .] The reason why they die so quickly is not far to seek; their mothers are underfed and overworked and live in badly-drained over-crowded houses; they transmit to their children a low rate of vitality; the children themselves are insufficiently tended, are taken out in all weathers bareheaded, barenecked, barearmed; they die of exposure, of want of suitable food, of too little fresh pure air, and of too many effluvia. The waste of human life is appalling; and yet more appalling is it to think that if all these of the present generation had struggled up into manhood and womanhood there would be thrice as many middle-aged poor as there are now, the struggle for existence would be thrice as bitter, the distress thrice as great, the families thrice as numerous.

[. . .]

Socialism declares that land and capital—that is, the natural agents and means of production—ought to be national, not private property. What antagonism is there between this and the law of population?

[. . .] That Socialists should grasp this law of population and understand its bearings appears to me, as a Socialist, to be of vital importance. [. . .] the success of Socialism would imply an enormous increase in the means of subsistence *available to the majority*, and consequently an enormous leap forward of the population. [. . .] Unless a reasonable ratio is maintained between produces and non-productive consumers, the precious leisure of the workers, to which so many longing eyes are bent, will be as far off as ever.

[. . .]

The practical settlement of the matter, so far as the birth-rate is concerned, is very likely to come from the female citizens of the State. The Socialist woman, highly educated, personally free and industrially independent, with hopes and duties which pass beyond the circle of the home, while she will not refuse the happiness of the wife and the mother, will by no means consent to be nothing more than the bearer and nurse of children through all the best years of her life. [. . .] Woman, mistress of her own destiny, will no longer consent to satisfy only that part of her nature she holds in common with the lower animals. Woman, like man, has intellectual faculties, yearnings towards art, aspirations towards science, passion for truth; crushed out of these have been in her past, but they shall burgeon out in her future, and shall develop into full stature of human intellect and human achievement. Womanhood in the future shall have its Beethoven and its Wagner, its Michel Angelo and its Murillo, its Clifford and its Huxley, its Milton and its Shakspere [sic]. And the realisation of these possibilities, O women my sisters, depends on the triumph of Socialism which will give us equality and independence, and the practice of conjugal prudence which will give us physical freedom.

NOTE

1 In 1877, Charles Bradlaugh and Besant, in a case that became notorious, were tried for obscenity for republishing a book encouraging contraception.

DOCUMENT 3.8

FROM JOHN MAYNARD KEYNES, *THE ECONOMIC CONSEQUENCES OF THE PEACE* (1919)

AFTER 1870 THERE WAS DEVELOPED ON A LARGE SCALE AN UNPRECedented situation, and the economic condition of Europe became during the next fifty years unstable and peculiar. The pressure of population on food, which had already been balanced by the accessibility of supplies from America, became for the first time in recorded history definitely reversed. As numbers increased, food was actually easier to secure. Larger proportional returns from an increasing scale of production became true of agriculture as well as industry. With the growth of the European population there were more emigrants on the one hand to till the soil of the new countries, and, on the other, more workmen were available in Europe to prepare the industrial products and capital goods which were to maintain the emigrant populations in their new homes, and to build the railways and ships which were to make accessible to Europe food and raw products from distant sources. Up to about 1900 a unit of labour applied to industry yielded year by year a purchasing power over an increasing quantity of food. It is possible that about the year 1900 this process began to be reversed, and a diminishing yield of Nature to man's effort was beginning to reassert itself. But the tendency of cereals to rise in real cost was balanced by other improvements; and—one of many novelties—the resources of tropical Africa then for the first time came into large employ, and a great traffic in oil-seeds began to bring to the table of Europe in a new and cheaper form one of the essential foodstuffs of mankind. In this economic Eldorado, in this economic Utopia, as the earlier economists would have deemed it, most of us were brought up.

That happy age lost sight of a view of the world which filled with deep-seated melancholy the founders of our Political Economy. Before the eighteenth century mankind entertained no false hopes. To lay the illusions which grew popular at that age's latter end, Malthus disclosed a Devil. For half a century all serious economical writings held that Devil in clear prospect. For the next half century he was chained up and out of sight. Now perhaps we have loosed him again.

What an extraordinary episode in the economic progress of man that age was which came to an end in August, 1914! [. . .] The projects and politics of militarism and imperialism, of racial and cultural rivalries, of monopolies, restrictions, and exclusion, which were to play the serpent to this paradise, were little more than the amusements [. . .] and appeared to exercise almost no influence at all on the ordinary course of social and economic life, the internationalization of which was nearly complete in practice.

It will assist us to appreciate the character and consequences of the Peace which we have imposed on our enemies, if I elucidate a little further some of the chief unstable elements, already present when war broke out, in the economic life of Europe.

I. POPULATION

In 1870 Germany had a population of about 40,000,000. By 1892 this figure had risen to 50,000,000, and by June 30, 1914, to about 68,000,000. In the years immediately preceding the war the annual increase was about 850,000, of whom an insignificant proportion emigrated. This great increase was only rendered possible by a far-reaching transformation of the economic structure of the country. From being agricultural and mainly self-supporting, Germany transformed herself into a vast and complicated industrial machine, dependent for its working on the equipoise of many factors outside Germany as well as within. Only by operating this machine, continuously and at full blast, could she find occupation at home for her increasing population and the means of purchasing their subsistence from abroad. The

German machine was like a top which to maintain its equilibrium must spin ever faster and faster.

In the Austro-Hungarian Empire, which grew from about 40,000,000 in 1890 to at least 50,000,000 at the outbreak of war, the same tendency was present in a less degree, the annual excess of births over deaths being about half a million, out of which, however, there was an annual emigration of some quarter of a million persons.

To understand the present situation, we must apprehend with vividness what an extraordinary centre of population the development of the Germanic system had enabled Central Europe to become. Before the war the population of Germany and Austria-Hungary together not only substantially exceeded that of the United States, but was about equal to that of the whole of North America. In these numbers, situated within a compact territory, lay the military strength of the Central Powers. But these same numbers—for even the war has not appreciably diminished them —if deprived of the means of life, remain a hardly less danger to European order.

European Russia increased her population in a degree even greater than Germany—from less than 100,000,000 in 1890 to about 150,000,000 at the outbreak of war; and in the year immediately preceding 1914 the excess of births over deaths in Russia as a whole was at the prodigious rate of two millions per annum. This inordinate growth in the population of Russia, which has not been widely noticed in England, has been nevertheless one of the most significant facts of recent years.

The great events of history are often due to secular changes in the growth of population and other fundamental economic causes, which, escaping by their gradual character the notice of contemporary observers, are attributed to the follies of statesmen or the fanaticism of atheists. Thus the extraordinary occurrences of the past two years in Russia, that vast upheaval of Society, which has overturned what seemed most stable—religion, the basis of property, the ownership of land, as well as forms of government and the hierarchy of classes—may owe more to the deep influences of expanding numbers than to Lenin or to Nicholas; and the disruptive powers of excessive national fecundity may have played a greater part in bursting the bonds of convention than either the power of ideas or the errors of autocracy.

DOCUMENT 3.9

FROM ALDOUS HUXLEY, "WHAT IS HAPPENING TO OUR POPULATION?" NASH'S PALL MALL MAGAZINE 93 (APRIL 1934)

POPULATION IS NOT STABLE, BUT VARIES BOTH IN QUALITY AND QUANtity. In Great Britain, for example, there are now more than twice as many people as there were at the beginning of the last century; and this quantitative change has been accompanied by qualitative changes, some for the better, some distinctly for the worse.

[...]

Many significant changes in the quality of populations are the result of changes made in the prevailing social environment. Thus, improvements in housing, sanitation, diet and medical services result in improved health and, indirectly, in better opportunities for all to live well and virtuously. Again, education alters and, to some extent, improves men's ways of thinking and feeling. And so on with all the other environmental changes which we call "social reforms." [...]

Aldous Huxley, "What Is Happening to Our Population?" Reproduced from *Complete Essays by Aldous Huxley*, published by Ivan R. Dee. © James Sexton, 2001. Reproduced by arrangement with Ivan R. Dee.

But the complexity of society and of human nature is such that it is often very difficult to foresee the results of a given social change. [...] The way in which admirable reforms may produce evil as well as good is well illustrated by the recent history of mental deficiency. In 1908 there were in England and Wales 156,000 mental deficients. In 1929 the Mental Deficiency Committee estimated the number at 300,000. Twenty-five years ago there were between four and five half-wits to every thousand of population; today there are between eight and nine.

Some of this apparent increase is probably due to the fact that the later committee did its work more thoroughly than the Royal Commission of 1908. It looked harder and therefore found more. But when all the necessary discounts have been made, there is still good reason to believe that the number of defectives has increased, within a generation, to an alarming extent.

This increase is primarily due to a decline in infant mortality—a decline which has affected every class of society, including that from which most defectives spring. This, in its turn, is due to improved sanitation and the wholesale establishment of Maternity and Child Welfare Centres. Mentally deficient children who, in the past, would have died in the cradle are now enabled to reach maturity. An environmental change for the better has resulted, among other things, in a hereditary change for the worse.

[...]

If conditions remain what they are now, and if the present tendency continues unchecked, we may look forward in a century or two to a time when a quarter of the population of these islands will consist of half-wits. What a curiously squalid and humiliating conclusion to English history!

What is the remedy for the present deplorable state of affairs? It consists, obviously, in encouraging the normal and super-normal members of the population to have larger families and in preventing the sub-normal from having any families at all.

[...]

As regards quantitative changes in population, the facts are these. During the nineteenth century the population in Europe, America and to some extent Asia increased at an (historically speaking) abnormal rate. In most countries the rate of increase has recently declined; so much so, that it looks as though population would soon become stable, or would even diminish.

[...]

As for the economic advantages of a large population, these certainly exist. The trouble is that nobody knows at what point they cease to be advantages and become disadvantages. Economists agree that there is such a thing as the *optimum* population of a country. [. . .] In practice, however, it seems impossible to decide whether a given country is, for economic purposes, over-populated or under-populated. This being so, we had better drop the idea of an economic optimum and try to judge the population problem by other standards. Man is not merely economic; he is a mind as well as a stomach. How has the great nineteenth-century increase of population affected him as a mental animal?

The most obvious difference between England today and England in, say, 1750, is a difference in looks. Thinly populated and only slightly urbanised, England was then a very beautiful country. Thickly populated and excessively urbanised, it now reveals itself to the majority of its inhabitants as an extremely ugly country. Town planners promise that this state of things can be remedied; and, obviously, by spending a vast amount of money, we can undo a good deal of the fatal work of the nineteenth century. But can we undo it all? I doubt it. Suppose (which is impossible) that every house in London could be transformed into an architectural masterpiece; London would still contain vast acres of pure dreariness. Repeat even a masterpiece a million times; the result is six hundred square miles of oppressive monotony.

Increase of population has had other distressing results, which I have no time to describe. But I have said enough to make my point clear. The population may or may not have reached an economic *optimum*; there is no means of deciding. That it has gone beyond the aesthetic *optimum* is certain. It has probably also passed the political *optimum*.

A final word about the probable effects of certain temporary fluctuations in population, now beginning to manifest themselves. During the war years—in effect, from 1915 to 1920—the birth-rate declined sharply in all the belligerent countries. The greatest decline was in France, where the number of births, during this five-year period, amounted to only about half the average. A similar, but less marked, decline was recorded in England and Germany. In the United States, however, nothing of the kind occurred. The immigration figures in 1914 were among the highest on record, and as the fertility of these immigrants was very great, the American birth-rate during all the war years remained high.

From 1934 to 1939 the number of young people entering industry in England, Germany and especially France will be considerably less than in ordinary years. This means that, if other things remain equal, unemployment should decline. In France it is possible that it may temporarily disappear altogether.

All governments in power during this period will obviously take credit for this decline. "Alone we did it," they will say in loud self-admiration; whereas it was the non-existent fathers of the war years who did it—or rather, poor devils, who didn't. The automatic decline in unemployment may be expected to achieve, among other things, the consolidation of Nazi power in Germany.

DOCUMENT 3.10

FROM JOSUÉ DE CASTRO, "THE CYCLE OF THE CRAB" (1937)

THE SILVA FAMILY LIVES IN THE MANGROVES OF THE CITY OF RECIFE, in a *mocambo* that the chief of the family built when they arrived.[1] The family comes from the *sertão*.[2] They descended from Cariri, in the drought area, haunted by hunger. They made a short stop in the wetland, to try the work in the sugarcane mills, but it is impossible to live with the wages of that area, without having the right to plant anything but cane.[3] That is, without having at least the resource of the *xiquexique* or the *macambira*, in the *sertão*, when the grip of hunger caught them.[4]

At that time, rumors spread in the hinterland that the government had created a Ministry to defend the workers' rights and that, with the tutors of law, city life was wonderful, because workers earned as much as they needed to kill the hunger. The Silvas heard this story, completely believed it, and decided to descend to the city to enjoy the advantages that the good government offered to the poor.

When arriving, the family saw that situation was different. There was no doubt that the city was nice, with many palaces and streets swarming with

---

Josué de Castro, "The Cycle of the Crab" (1937). Translation © Federico Ferretti, reproduced by permission of the translator.

cars. But the worker's life was hard as usual. There was a lot of things for the eyes, very little for the belly. *Caboclo* Zé Luis da Silva did not want to desist.[5] He adapted himself: "When there is no solution, one has already resolved." He entered the urban struggle for life with all of his forces, but his forces were not enough for making his family live with a house, clothes, and food. There were houses only over 80,000 reais, 150 reais were needed for food, and salaries did not reach 5,000 reais per day.

Tight circumstances began. There was only one way to have relief: going to the mangrove. In the mangrove, one does not pay the house, eats crabs, and walks almost naked. The mangrove is a paradise. It does not have the pink and light-blue colors of the Heaven, but it has the dark color of the mud, the paradise of the crabs. In the mangroves, land does not belong to anybody. It belongs to the tide. When it raises, spreads, and stretches itself, it floods the entire land, but when it lowers and decreases, it leaves the highest bumps uncovered. Over one of these, *caboclo* Zé Luis built his *mocambo*. The walls are built on mangroves and are pressed mud. The roof is made by straw, dried grass, and other materials that the waste provides. Everything is freely found in basic partnership with nature.

The mangrove is an old friend. It gives everything, house and food: *mocambo* and crab. Now, when the *caboclo* goes to work in the morning, the rest of the family is already awake. The children push the trunk, open the door, and go to the mangrove. They wash their eyes' gunk with muddy water, they pee and poop right there, then they completely inter their arms in the mud to catch crabs. With their arms and legs sunk in the mud, the Silvas have their sustenance guaranteed. While Zé Luis works, he is relieved, because he has left his family within their own food, sunk in the mud swarming with crabs and blue crabs.

The Capibaribe mangroves are the crab's paradise. If land was done for men, with everything which served him, then the mangrove was done for the crab. There, everything is, was, or will be crab, including the mud and the people who live in it. The mud mixed with urine, excrements and other remains that the tide brings, when it is not yet crab, will become it. Crabs come into the world in this matter and live in it, they grow up eating the mud, fattening up with its waste, transforming the mud into the white slim flesh of their legs and the greenish gelatine of their sticky viscera. On the other side, people live off of crabs, sucking their legs and licking their skulls until they are clean like a glass. With their mud-made meat they make the human flesh of their bodies and that of their children. They are hundreds of thousands of citizens, all made up of crab flesh. What their body rejects is sent back as a remain to the mangrove mud to become crabs again.

In this stagnant-water-like calm, identified and embedded with the cycle of the crab, the Silvas are living their resolved life, like one of the steps of a wonderful cycle. All members of the Silva family live within this cycle until the end, until the day of their death. That day, their pious neighbors will bring that mud-made dead body to the Santo Amaro cemetery, where it will follow the steps of the worm and the flower. These steps are too poetic, too replete with a poetry that the mangrove would not carry out: that day, it is only apparently that the cycle of the crab stops. Yet the relatives who remain piously spread their tears across the mangroves to feed the mud which feeds again the cycle of the crab.

NOTES

1. *Mocambos* [or *mucambos*] are informal settlements, similar to the Brazilian favela, which are self-constructed by destitute people, generally of Afro-Brazilian or Indian-Brazilian descent.
2. The *sertão* is the hinterland of northeastern Brazil (diminutive of *Desertão*, that is, "big desert"), a region that is famous for the periodical and devastating droughts that render it one of the poorest regions in Brazil still today.
3. Fighting against the prohibition of laborers keeping small parcels of land to plant for self-consumption was a key point for Castro's geographies of hunger all his life and a theme that is still debated in critical literature on food and development.
4. *Macambira* are sort of cactuses and wild plants of the *sertão*.
5. *Caboclo* is a very common word, in Brazil, to indicate a person of mixed ancestry, normally Indian and European, typically belonging to the lowest social strata.

4

THE POPULATION BOMB

IN THE THREE DECADES AFTER WORLD WAR II, DEBATES ABOUT THE interrelationships between population, resource availability, and environmental issues reached their peak—which has been framed as "the Malthusian moment." What was at stake? How did the argument about the human population's interrelationship with the environment change?

The Malthusian moment was framed in the context of aspirations for a global community of planning, progress, and peace as symbolized by the foundation of the United Nations. We can note several important elements that were new at this time. Most importantly, fears were raised of imminent and potentially catastrophic food supply problems due to rapid population growth. The centrality of American intellectuals to this discourse changed the locus of debate from Europe to the other side of the Atlantic. Of course, Benjamin Franklin had been an important interlocutor in these debates before Malthus, but it was only now that Americans took intellectual leadership of the discussion. If this was a fairly conventional Malthusian issue, two elements of its construction as a "problem" were novel. First, as well as being a problem of food supply, scholars and public intellectuals believed excess population and the agricultural demands it made would cause a breakdown of the ecological systems on which humanity relied. Second, in raising these issues of "Green Malthusianism," the call was for ways to head ecological disaster off at the pass. This was seen as the role of the United Nations and was also the rationale for the food aid packages of the 1950s. Food aid was often tied to the implementation of contraception policies, and the whole was framed in the context of the Cold War as a means by which to prevent the poverty that was seen to prefigure the collapse of democracies into communist regimes. It was in this context that framing demographic-environmental maladjustment as a "population bomb" became common currency. Scholars such as the philosopher Bertrand Russell were among the many who paralleled atomic bombs with a population bomb and suggested the two were intimately interconnected. As a language of bombs, breakdowns, and disasters intimates, while the content of this Malthusian moment was in many ways conventional, its rhetoric was more highly strung. And yet for all the talk of catastrophe, we should not overlook that the jeremiads also offered clear strategies to build new political and social constellations where environmental consciousness, active conservation, and demographic responsibility forged ways out of the alleged impasse.

There were influential critics of the notion of a political and ecological population bomb. The architect and futuristic speculator Buckminster Fuller, for example, advocated technology as the force that would square the circle between population growth and resource needs on a finite planet. Lines of skeptical response suggested that human ingenuity coupled to political and economic planning and reallocation made the population bomb just so much scaremongering. For example, the Scottish agronomist John Boyd Orr, who was the first director general of the Food and Agriculture Organization of the United Nations in the 1940s, laid out a clear platform whereby technological advances by land, by sea, and by chemical manipulation could circumvent Malthusian catastrophe if there was sufficient global will and cooperation, clear echoes of William Godwin's ruminations in 1820.

Forceful pushback was also offered on behalf of the so-called developing nations from the 1940s by the Indian political theorist and economist Radhakamal Mukerjee, who advocated global-scale reallocation of underutilized lands in areas such as Australia to the purportedly overpopulated nations to allow a form of planned, reverse settler colonialism. Likewise, the Brazilian economist Josué de Castro claimed in his bestselling 1952 book, *The Geopolitics of Hunger*, that "it is not overpopulation which creates famines, but famine which creates overpopulation" to counter the neo-Malthusian framing of poverty as a natural phenomenon rather than a manifestation of the global politics of food distribution. This line of argument came to be common currency as scholars from the Global South built new arguments about the interconnection of population, resources, and the environment. Thus, Mahmood Mamdani, an exiled Ugandan intellectual, frames an argument with startling verbal and conceptual similarities to that just cited from Castro, albeit from a more directly doctrinal Marxist standpoint, suggesting that poverty is a creation of imperialist asymmetries of power and opportunity not of an excess of population over resource availability. Amartya Sen's unraveling of famine as more readily explicable in terms of failures in entitlement in emergent capitalist markets than in terms of a lack of resources per se (specifically, Malthus's core resource of food) both was less radical and would prove far more influential to the political and economic analysis of food-population interactions.

The high-water mark of the Malthusian moment came in the 1960s and 1970s. Paul Ehrlich's iconic 1968 tract, *The Population Bomb*, has been called "the most famous population treatise since Malthus" and would sell three million copies. The rhetoric could appear downright hysterical by this time, as in the notorious opening to Ehrlich's book reprinted here. And yet for all the headline-grabbing apocalyptic assertions that have stayed in the public mind and often been ridiculed as quasi-astrological predictions that went awry, Ehrlich also developed important new dimensions to the discussion of population and the natural environment. Above all, he brought a biologist's precision to the notion of "environment" and chronicled in detail how increasing anthropogenic demands on the physical resources of the earth could lead to ecological breakdown. He chronicled the use of the physical environment as a sink for pollution and speculated, in ways that look forward to debates in the twenty-first century, that using the atmosphere as a sink could deleteriously change climatic norms. In short, Ehrlich's prognostications cannot always be dismissed, and hysteria is not his only tone. Infamously, his collaborator Garrett Hardin sought to pursue the ethical and political consequences of population growth drawing on environmental resources. For Hardin, coercive systems were the only way to prevent ecosystem collapse through overuse, an interesting turn of events in the face of the democratic boosterism of the postwar period. Hardin's argument that freedom to breed was intolerable also had clear resonances with the eugenic arguments of the interwar years about selective breeding, but economists such as Elinor Ostrom have worked to patiently unpick his framing of the commons in theoretical terms and through real-world examples.

Hardin pioneered ideas of a "lifeboat ethics," whereby some countries would be left to flounder because their population-resource situation was deemed beyond redemption; this was global planning with a harder (indeed holocaustic) edge. These concepts were picked up in US policy-making circles, a notable example being William and Paul Paddock's lurid 1967 book, whose thesis was admirably summarized by its title, *Famine 1975! America's Decision: Who Will Survive?* Paul Paddock had worked in the foreign office of the US government, and the book trailed the idea that the United States would have to engage in "food triage," allowing some nations to collapse into starvation. The judgment of Washington would decide which of the global suitors received wheat and leave the others to an Iliad of woes. More measured, but showing the penetration of these ideas directly into government, was a 1974 pamphlet issued by the House of Representatives titled *Malthus and America*. In the light of recent scarcity issues from the OPEC oil crisis, its authors were clear that the American people and their government needed to look to the most basic question of survival versus demographic-cum-ecological Armageddon, a question not just for the poor nations of the globe but one on their very doorstep.

Three main lines of counter neo-Malthusian argument emerged. First, within the ecological-environmental community from which Ehrlich and Hardin hailed, there were voices seeking to complicate any notion that the total size of the population was the major factor leading to ecosystem stress. Perhaps the most important tool for making this point was one that, as the biologist and public intellectual Barry Commoner made clear, was itself pioneered by Ehrlich and his colleague John Holdren, the so-called IPAT equation. IPAT (in longhand notation, $I = P \times A \times T$) stated that the total human impact (I) on the environment was a function of population size (P), affluence or consumption levels (A), and technology (T), the latter being a variable that could increase or decrease per capita impacts. Commoner's work in the wake of the galvanizing moment that was the 1970 Earth Day sought to develop a quantitative proof that ecologically insensitive technologies were the root cause of America's burgeoning environmental problems, not population growth (T, not P). It is worth adding that, whatever their disagreements, Ehrlich shared ground with Commoner as he would go on to frame the United States as a nation of "super-consumers" whose ecological footprint (or, in the terms of IPAT, their affluence function, A) was far higher than that of the more rapidly growing populations of the developing world. Commoner spliced his ecological analysis together with political arguments for global social cooperation, for recognition of overpopulation in the developing world as a legacy of colonialism, and for watering down the evangelical tone of US laissez-faire capitalism.

Second, from within the tradition of UN-sponsored agrarian and technological research came the so-called Green Revolution to boost crop yields as a way to address the supply side of the population-food problem. Norman Borlaug was the icon of this movement, and his 1970 speech accepting the Nobel Peace Prize is representative of his credo. The work of the Green Revolution began in the 1940s, but it bore fruit as a public and political platform at just the moment when Ehrlich and colleagues were center stage. Borlaug's is anything but a Panglossian optimism; he repeatedly noted the qualified gains agronomy had managed to produce and framed them as allowing the breathing space in which economic, social, and contraceptive change could adjust the demand side of population growth and rising affluence. Concerning the ecological impacts of the Green Revolution, he was far less voluble, although that would be an important point of contention between ecological-population pessimists and optimists of the Green Revolution.

Finally, Julian Simon represented a bold counterthrust that sought to scotch the entire notion of a population, resource, and environment "problem." With an eye for provocation the equal of Ehrlich's, Simon argued that resources were neither scarce nor finite. If they were scarce, prices would be going up, which they weren't; as resources were not "things" but capabilities created by the interaction of humans with their environment, people could create new resources by their ingenuity. As he would put it in a celebrated book, people were not a drain on the world but its "ultimate resource," who by their innovation created resources. And if resources were not finite, the notion that they were being outstripped by the very entity that created them—mankind—was incoherent. Famously, Simon and Ehrlich made a bet about whether resource prices would rise or fall in the 1980s. When Julian Simon won the bet in 1990, this was symptomatic of a decade of changing attitudes toward ecologically inflected neo-Malthusianism. In the United States, the Reagan administration moved away from ecological pessimism, and in parallel, the 1984 United Nations' International Conference on Population declared population to be "neutral" rather than negative to economic and social development, a judgment that still guides the United Nations' approach to population today. Taken together, these fragments were indicative of the end of the Malthusian moment.

What had this Malthusian moment achieved? We can frame this by comparing its approach to the linkage of population, resources, and the environment with Malthus's moment a century and a half earlier. First, the Malthusian moment discernibly changed the concept of "resources," seeing the ecological, biophysical, and even (tentatively) atmospheric systems of the globe as resources to be conserved in the face of potential shortages. Where Malthus only saw food as a limited resource, the debate from the 1940s to the 1980s significantly expanded the terms of the debate and presaged the need for an environmental economics. Second, the debates around IPAT show that what was meant by "population" was notably nuanced in the Malthusian moment. Where Malthus and most conventional Malthusian discourse had only looked to population size, population density, and rates of population growth, the ecological tenor of debate between scholars such as Ehlrich and Commoner made affluence and technological change key issues because they inflected the relationship between a population and its resource usage. From very different angles, that was a rare point on which Ehlrich and Simon shared common ground. Third, there was a keen awareness that scientific, demographic, ecological, and agronomic questions were unavoidably folded together with a range of political issues such as democracy versus autocracy and the legacies of colonial (mis)rule. In sum, all these developments created a far more sophisticated debate about the relationship between population, resources, and the environment that belied the often shrill and superficial tone in which it was conducted.

DOCUMENT 4.1

FROM WILLIAM VOGT, *THE ROAD TO SURVIVAL* (1948)

CONSERVATION IS NOT GOING TO SAVE THE WORLD. NOR IS CONTROL of populations. Economic, political, educational, and other measures also are indispensable; but unless population control and conservation are included, other means are certain to fail. A world organization devoted to search for economic and political solutions that ignores the ecological is as helpless as a bird with one wing. Indeed, it may force the human race deeper into the mire.

[. . .]

Ecological health, for the world, requires, above all, two things: (1) That renewable resources be used to produce as much wealth as possible on a sustained-yield basis. We must use these resources well to support as high a living standard as possible; and we must not exhaust them, as there is no substitute. (2) We must adjust our demand to the supply, either by accepting less per capita (lowering our living standards) or by maintaining less people. Since our civilization cannot survive a drastic lowering of standards, we cannot escape the need for population cuts.

[. . .]

Effective conservation has been made impossible, in many parts of the world, by man's failure to recognize the indispensability of scientific treatment.

When a man is sick, he usually goes to a highly trained general practitioner who may send him to an orthopedist, psychiatrist, specialist in eye-ear-nose-and-throat diseases, specialist in circulatory diseases, genito-urinary or gastro-intestinal diseases, etc. A sick river valley is vastly more complicated than a sick man, if only because the man is one of the most important parts of it; diagnosis and treatment of the illness should, in many cases, require the particular skills of climatologists, pedologists, hydrologists, botanists, zoologists, agronomists, soil conservationists, foresters, grazing experts, sociologists, economists, etc. In some parts of the world the sick valley may be subjected to the blundering management of a lawyer. In the United States we are likely to turn it over to an Army engineer. Is it any wonder that, on all continents, flood peaks are steadily rising?

[...]

If the democratic way of life has any long-range justification, it must prove that it has survival value. This, I am convinced, it can do. Better than any other system of government that now exists, it can bring to all its people the realization that their lives and their civilization are profoundly shaped by their environment. The town meeting, the grange, the garden club, the women's organization, the soil-conservation district, are all inevitably influenced by environmental impacts. Their recognition of this relationship, their development of a program leading ever more rapidly to a more favorable relationship, may give democracy the survival value it has certainly lacked through most of the past hundred and fifty years. We have been skidding down the road toward national suicide by destroying the environment that permits our survival; a reversal of our direction is unthinkable in any but democratic terms. Here may well be the most fruitful opportunity democracy has ever had.

[...]

International control of resource exploitation, in order to protect technologically retarded nations, is indispensable. Latin-American countries should be shielded against conscienceless exploitation by North American fishermen and lumbermen. Colonial lands should be placed under an ecological trusteeship, just as the treatment of "natives" is safeguarded. International bodies of scientists should make periodic evaluations of land use, insist on sustained-yield practices, and hold trustees responsible for resource destruction. The United Nations, and associated organizations, should maintain an ecological commission, cutting across organization lines, to assay the influence of all

UN activities on the relationship between human beings and their indispensable environment.

[. . .]

All possible conservation measures are futile unless human breeding is checked. It is obvious that fifty years hence the world cannot support three billion people at any but coolie standards—for most of them. One-third of an acre cannot decently feed a man, let alone clothe him and make possible control of the hydrologic cycle. When numbers mount, land abuse, as has been shown, mounts with them. Unless population increases can be stopped, we might as well give up the struggle.

A primary need is a completely new approach to contraception. [. . .] If the United States had spent two billion dollars developing such a contraceptive, instead of the atom bomb, it would have contributed far more to our national security while, at the same time, it promoted a rising living standard for the entire world.

[. . .]

Population "experts" say that, given time, populations will level off and stabilize themselves. To this the obvious answer is, *there is not time*. The modern world has gone down twice—and only extraordinary measures can keep it from going down again.

DOCUMENT 4.2

FROM RADHAKAMAL MUKERJEE, "POPULATION THEORY AND POLITICS" (1941)

AT THE BOTTOM OF THE EXPANSION OF POPULATION IS ALSO THE racial myth that the elite people, pure and undefiled, should multiply to an unlimited extent to achieve world mastery. [...] Thus the economic yardstick of optimum population less and less serves as the end of economic activity; the definition of optimum population itself becomes a political decision. [...] Accordingly, the true optimum of population is the integral optimum which is based on a harmonious co-ordination of the optima in the successive levels of ecology, economy, and state [...]

At the successive levels, a basic principle which determines population growth and a norm for population control emerges: (1) the demographic principle of probability as it applies to vitality, health, average expectation of life, and the norm of maximum longevity—which measure biological fitness; (2) the ecological principle of balance and vital solidarity of the region, and the norm of maximum use and conservation of resources which measure the ecological fitness of the community on a continuing basis; (3) the economic principle of equi-marginal utilities that governs occupational balance and full employment, and the norm of maximum average income—which measure

---

Radhakamal Mukerjee, "Population Theory and Politics," *American Sociological Review* 6, no. 6 (1941): 784–93. © American Sociological Association.

economic efficiency; and (4) the sociological principle of cultural selection and control governing the choice of individual and collective ends, and the norm of power and prestige of the organized state and culture—which measure national security.

The notion of the integral optimum population has an immense significance for the war and peace of to-day. It focuses attention on the claims for Lebensraum of the "dissatisfied" nations as well as on the demogenic oppositions and pressures that arise out of an exaggerated stress on historical or political factors, racial doctrines and natural geographic or economic advantages or handicaps. The development of a social optimum population in one country is indissolubly tied up with peaceful or hostile economic and political relations with its neighbors. A planned pursuit of population and economic autarchy in one country, without considering its long-run effects on the standard of living, is inconsistent with international economic cooperation, which alone can assure an improvement of the standards of living of all peoples through a better balance between population movements and developments of resources. A nation pitching its optimum population high with an eye towards a future war not merely contributes towards the lowering of its own and other peoples' standards of living but also establishes a vicious circle of unemployment and conscription, armament production and accumulation of war material and "cannon fodder" from which there may be no escape except war itself. This is, indeed, one of the moot questions of the age: whether nations that complain about living space for their present populations should use political stimulants to increase numbers regardless of resources. Aggression is the outcome of sheer population pressure or of confidence of greater numerical strength in a regime of universal conscription, and it may be both military, as in the case of imperialistic expansion of the Axis Powers, and economic, as in the case of Germany and Japan, whose methods of economic bargaining and penetration into the territories of their less effectively organized neighbors are aided by political pressure and greatly depress the standards of living of the latter. Countries belonging to the same order of civilization should show a similarity in the fertility trend governed by social and cultural selection, and to manipulate it by premiums and subsidies or by the propagation of a gospel of racial superiority is to commit overt aggression. Now that there are no longer large empty spaces in the world waiting for occupation, the right to claim new lands as outlets for surplus population is inconsistent with a population-encouraging state policy however camouflaged it may be by the doctrine of the divine mission of a superior race or culture. The right to claim new lands as outlets for surplus population must rest rather on the deliberate policy of the nation to check excess fertility and reduce population pressure by birth control and social pressure and propaganda. Freedom of emigration is, indeed, intimately bound up with a planned policy of restriction of numbers of the more crowded nations, since, otherwise, migration would accelerate population increase and the open spaces would be occupied by the culturally inferior and faster growing peoples until the whole earth would have no "standing room."

To prevent nations from following a predatory demographic and economic policy is, however, a matter of both international mindedness and education and of international security, justice, and readjustment. On the other side, the denial to the less favored and crowded countries of foreign markets by fiscal protection and of opportunities for emigration by restrictionist policy depresses their standards of living or prevents a normal rise in comforts. The use of the dual weapon of commercial protection and exclusion of immigrants by America and the European colonial powers withholds equality of opportunity for the less favored nations and pushes back their economic optimum. Such have been the effects of the U.S.A. immigration quota laws, the Smoot-Hawley tariff, the British Imperial Ottawa pacts, and abandonment of the gold standard. To ban Japanese emigration altogether in countries which are under-populated and undeveloped but are not unappropriated, and then, as they produce manufactured goods at home for foreign markets at competitive prices, to shut these out on the plea that the lower wage costs in Japan sabotage international standards of living, is economically indefensible and politically dangerous. No doubt an optimum population fixed with reference to the man-land ratio of a distant future by the European colonial powers, who in the meanwhile keep vast empty lands in Australasia, South Asia, or Africa as their exclusive preserves, trenches on the economic optimum of neighboring Asiatics on the other side of the Pacific and Indian Oceans. This occupation of millions of square miles of productive land which are thrown out of use pushes back the world optimum and is all the more unjust as the major portion of these lands lies in the monsoon and tropical zones where only the Asiatics can work and thrive as do the white peoples in the temperate zone. Similarly, a political adjustment which destroys or checkmates the economic integrity and reduces the economic optimum of a region through the diminution of territory and of accustomed markets and outlets for surplus population, works against a realistic optimum population. This was the blunder of the Treaty of Versailles which, for the sake of liberating some peoples who had never been able to find their way to liberty, trenched upon the economic opportunities of several nations and the possibilities of the creation of larger economic unions that could have insured the optimum.

[. . .] So long as the richer powers practise exclusion they must recognize the justice of the case of the poorer peoples. On the remedy of this injustice, indeed, largely depends the economic integration of mankind. Only in a more liberal world economy can the self-defeating and immaterial ends of modern nationalist policies be reconciled with the vital and material ends of improvement in the standard of living of individuals as judged by these individuals. Where there are "two Europes" and two worlds with dual standards of living and different minimum scales of consumption by individuals, there cannot be peace; nor can there be peace where nations value numbers from the stand point of political or military power; nor where race and color prejudice dams the rolling tide of migration from the world's heaviest zones of population pressure from spilling over into neighboring and vast open spaces.

[. . .]

More and more, population growth will bring in its wake severe and increasing economic pressure for an increasing number of nations. In south and eastern Asia in particular, where the population increased from 550 millions in 1800, about the same as Europe's present population, to about 1010 millions today, the terrific population pressure on the land—more than half the human race being confined to an area which is about only 13.6 percent of the globe surface—and increasing misery would impel vast migratory movements and conflicts between oriental and oriental. As we cross the middle of this century, the disparity of population rates of increase between the white and colored populations of the world and the congestion in Europe and in south and eastern Asia as contrasted with the emptiness of the New World would profoundly aggravate the present instability of the international equilibrium.

The momentous phase in world history associated with the Industrial and Commercial Revolution and the phenomenal expansion of the white peoples who increased from only about 155 millions in 1770 to about 730 millions today, and their acquisition, control, and exploitation of resources of the different continents outside Europe, will now be over. White humanity conjured up the spectre of the Yellow Peril in the closing decades of the nineteenth century. The Yellow Peril has not materialized nor will it materialize in the

West in the coming decades. There seems to be little possibility that the yellow peoples may swamp the children of the Eur-Americans in the future. But the White Peril to the colored inhabitants in Africa, Asia, and Oceania will be revived as one or other of the white peoples will expand and explode. Highly industrialized nations of the temperate regions whose populations unduly expand must seek to secure a larger place in the sun for obtaining a supply of raw materials and finding markets for their manufactured goods. It is in this manner that both population balance and balance of occupations of particular peoples will play an important role in world politics through favoring imperialistic or peaceful policies. Though their economic lives will interlock, differences in rates of growth of population in Europe, eastern North America and southern and eastern Asia—the favored regions where the world's population will show a heavier and heavier concentration—will provoke differential population pressures and economic and military aggressions, especially in Asia, where 1300 millions will find their way blocked for agricultural colonization in the open spaces of the New World inhabited by about only one fourth of their number. Neither morality nor economic intercourse nor physical force will be able to bar the entry of the flowing millions into the empty lands which cannot be worked by the western Europeans. This would be as necessary for the equalization of the world's standards of living as for meeting the world demand for an annual extension of 20 million acres of new land; 12 million acres for the increase of the white population and 8 million acres for the increase of the oriental population.

Birth control among the overcrowded countries and freedom of migration into the new and unoccupied lands under the control of the fortunate powers thus emerge as the necessary dual prelude to world peace. Without birth control, migration cannot alleviate the evils of over-population in the emigration country nor can it increase the rate of population growth in the new country without threatening it with the burden of misery of the old land with its cry for *Lebensraum*. Birth control could prevent areas of dense population and economic advantage from becoming areas of abject misery or of explosive energy. Planned migration under an international code would at the same time offer opportunities of toil and thrift to the land-hungry peoples and remove a real obstacle to world cooperation. By facilitating the utilization of vast and untapped agricultural and industrial resources, it would also help to wipe out the present chronic world shortage of food and essential materials, while any danger of racial friction and outbreaks might be minimized by planned land settlement of migrants in the open spaces who would largely be subsistence farmers and would require little of public assistance and spoon-feeding. Such groups of agricultural pioneers and settlers could be appropriately derived from overpopulated but climatically similar regions whence they would import suitable crops and work-animals, agricultural practices and institutions. Thus, migration and population problems are inextricably bound up with each other for their solution and the solution should be sought internationally in the interests of world peace. The twofold complementary program of birth control and "open door" adopted by the contrasted regions of the earth from the standpoint of welfare of the international economic community would alone accelerate the trend towards world optimum population and productivity, since the economic exploitation of the pioneer and immature zones will add to the aggregate purchasing power of humanity and thus increase both wealth and employment for the industrial millions of the crowded manufacturing zones of the earth. Thus, the Occident and the Orient, the Old and the New World, may approach equality in the supply of resources and essential materials and in the plane of living in a juster and more rational world economy.

War or peace depends largely on the acceptance of certain universal and objective criteria in respect of material and cultural standards of living by the nations; it also depends on the statesmanship of each which can co-ordinate a national with an international optimum population policy so as to bring about an approximation of the national standards of living and conditions of security and guarantee a minimum standard for all peoples. Such coordination rests on a simultaneous combination of the qualitative and the quantitative optima in population planning by each country. Population planning by each great nation according to the notion of the integral optimum will then be the cornerstone of world peace, because social justice and world peace are one and indivisible.

DOCUMENT 4.3

FROM JOHN BOYD ORR, *THE WHITE MAN'S DILEMMA* (1953; 1965 ED.)

CONSIDERATION OF FUTURE FOOD REQUIREMENTS AND THE COLOSSAL rate of growth of population has raised again the spectre of Malthus.

[...]

Vogt, an authority on soil erosion, advocates drastic measures in his book *The Road to Survival*. He suggests that the elimination of preventable disease, and the sending of food, or means of increasing food production, to countries suffering from food shortage, should be stopped until disease and famine have reduced numbers to the level those countries can support. Then they should be kept down by a vigorous policy of birth-control. But today the people of these countries, who outnumber the well-fed in the world by two to one, will not die quietly.

[...]

It is evident, from what we have seen of present population trends and inadequate world food supplies, that even with the most optimistic expectations of birth-control it will be necessary to more than double present food production. We can apply science in many ways to achieve the increase.

1. Urgent action is needed to reverse the process of soil erosion. This is a task well within the power of modern engineering. The destructive forces of river

waters liable to flood can be harnessed and transformed into electricity, while the controlled outflow can be used for irrigation. In parts of the world where there is a heavy periodic rainfall, such as the monsoons, followed by a long dry season, rain can be stored in reservoirs and used for irrigation during the drought. Such engineering projects, coupled with improving methods of agriculture in semi-arid areas, reforestation of denuded hills, and planting of trees as windbreaks, can put an end to soil erosion and reclaim areas which were once cultivated and are now deserts. [. . .]

2. So far we have considered only engineering projects. Agricultural science, if applied to the land already under cultivation, could alone double the world food supply. In Western Europe, where the humus content of the soil is preserved, and balanced fertilizers are used, the yield of wheat averages about 22 cwt. an acre. On the best farms it is over 30 cwt. In most other regions, including America and Australia, the average is little more than half Europe's. In India and Pakistan, using fertilizers, especially nitrogen, by extension of the practice of composting and green manuring to put humus into the ground, and also by use of better seeds, the yield could be substantially increased. On demonstration plots and on well-managed estates, where these and. other improved methods are applied, the yield is about 50% higher than on land with similar conditions where they are not yet applied. [. . .]

3. If the farmers and fishermen should fail to feed the world, we could call in the chemists, who can synthesize nearly all the constituents except the minerals, of which there is no shortage. [. . .] It is in fact possible to produce food without farm crops. The energy yielding constituents of food are produced by the plants through harnessing solar energy. Only a small fraction of the energy which reaches the earth is converted into food for human beings and animals. [. . .]

[. . .]

Modern science has the answer to Malthus, but it has to be applied on a world scale. Much of the industrial output now devoted to armaments would need to be diverted for the purpose. And so we come back to the fundamental question, upon the answer to which the future of mankind depends. Will governments co-operate to apply science to promote the welfare of the peoples of the world, or, in rival groups, apply it to their mutual destruction? If moral and ethical principles were the guide to foreign policy there is no doubt what the answer would be. The aggression of hunger and poverty, which causes the premature death of two thirds of the world, is a greater menace to health and happiness than the cold-war aggression of either Communism or Capitalism. Apart from moral principles, intelligent self-interest should induce the highly industrialized countries to co-operate in abolishing hunger and poverty; for these are a growing threat to the security of the prosperous third of the world, a proportion, moreover, steadily dwindling since the poorer populations grow at double the rate.

DOCUMENT 4.4

FROM PAUL EHRLICH, *THE POPULATION BOMB* (1968)

PROLOGUE:

The battle to feed all of humanity is over. In the 1970's the world will undergo famines—hundreds of millions of people are going to starve to death in spite of any crash programs embarked upon now. At this late date nothing can prevent a substantial increase in the world death rate, although many lives could be saved through dramatic programs to "stretch" the carrying capacity of the earth by increasing food production. But these programs will only provide a stay of execution unless they are accompanied by determined and successful efforts at population control. Population control is the conscious regulation of the numbers of human beings to meet the needs, not just of individual families, but of society as a whole.

[...]

Our position requires that we take immediate action at home and promote effective action worldwide. We must have population control at home, hopefully through a system of incentives and penalties, but by compulsion if

---

Paul Ehrlich, *The Population Bomb* (1968), © 1968, 1971. Used by permission of Ballantine Books, an imprint of Random House, a division of Penguin Random House LLC. All rights reserved.

voluntary methods fail. We must use our political power to push other countries into programs which combine agricultural development and population control. And while this is being done we must take action to reverse the deterioration of our environment before population pressure permanently ruins our planet. The birth rate must be brought into balance with the death rate or mankind will breed itself into oblivion. We can no longer afford merely to treat the symptoms of the cancer of population growth; the cancer itself must be cut out. Population control is the only answer.

[...]

THE PROBLEM:

I have understood the population explosion intellectually for a long time. I came to understand it emotionally one stinking hot night in Delhi a couple of years ago. My wife and daughter and I were returning to our hotel in an ancient taxi. The seats were hopping with fleas. The only functional gear was third. As we crawled through the city, we entered a crowded slum area. The temperature was well over 100, and the air was a haze of dust and smoke. The streets seemed alive with people. People eating, people washing, people sleeping. People visiting, arguing, and screaming. People thrusting their hands through the taxi window, begging. People defecating and urinating. People clinging to buses. People herding animals. People, people, people, people. As we moved slowly through the mob, hand horn squawking, the dust, noise, heat, and cooking fires gave the scene a hellish aspect. Would we ever get to our hotel? All three of us were, frankly, frightened. It seemed that anything could happen—but, of course, nothing did. Old India hands will laugh at our reaction. We were just some overprivileged tourists, unaccustomed to the sights and sounds of India. Perhaps, but since that night I've known the feel of overpopulation.

[...]

A Dying Planet

Our problems would be much simpler if we needed only to consider the balance between food and population. But in the long view the progressive deterioration of our environment may cause more death and misery than any conceivable food-population gap. And it is just this factor, environmental deterioration, that is almost universally ignored by those most concerned with closing the food gap.

It is fair to say that the environment of every organism, human and nonhuman, on the face of the Earth has been influenced by the population explosion of Homo sapiens. [. . .] Ecologists—those biologists who study the relationships of plants and animals with their environments—are especially concerned about these changes. They realize how easily disrupted are ecological systems (called ecosystems), and they are afraid of both the short- and long-range consequences for these ecosystems of many of mankind's activities.

Environmental changes connected with agriculture are often striking. For instance, in the United States we are paying a price for maintaining our high level of food production. [. . .] The history of similar deterioration in other parts of the world is clear for those who know how to read it. It stretches back to the cradles of civilization in the Middle East, where in many places deserts now occupy what were once rich and productive farmlands. In this area the process of destruction goes on today, still having, as in the past, ecologically incompetent use of water resources as a major feature. A good example is the building of dams on the Nile, preventing the deposit of nutrient-rich silt that used to accompany annual floods of the river. As almost anyone who remembers his high school geography could have predicted, the result has been a continuing decrease in the productivity of soils in the Nile Delta. [. . .]

Plans for increasing food production invariably involve large-scale efforts at environmental modification. These plans involve the "inputs" so beloved of the agricultural propagandist—especially fertilizers to enrich soils and pesticides to discourage our competitors. Growing more food also may involve the clearing of forests from additional land and the provision of irrigation water. There seems to be little hope that we will suddenly have an upsurge in the level of responsibility or ecological sophistication of persons concerned with increasing agricultural output. I predict that the rate of soil deterioration will accelerate as the food crisis intensifies. Ecology will be ignored more and more as things get tough. It is safe to assume that our use of synthetic pesticides, already massive, will increase. In spite of much publicity, the intimate relationship between pesticides on the one hand and environmental deterioration on the other is not often recognized. This relationship is well worth a close look. One of the basic facts of population biology—that branch of biology that deals with groups of organisms—is that the simpler an ecosystem is, the more unstable it is. [. . .] Man, however, is a simplifier of complex ecosystems and a creator of simple ecosystems.

[. . .]

All of the junk we dump into the atmosphere, all of the dust, all of the carbon dioxide, have effects on the temperature balance of the Earth. Air pollution affects how much of the sun's heat reaches the surface of the Earth and how much is radiated back into space. And it is just this temperature balance that causes the changes in the atmosphere that we call "the weather."

Concern about this problem has been greatly increased by the prospect of supersonic transports. Most people have been opposing this project on the basis that the "sonic booms" generated will drive half the people in the country out of their skulls while benefiting almost no one. But ecologists, as usual, have been looking at the less obvious. Supersonic transports will leave contrails high in the stratosphere, where they will break up very slowly. A lid of ice crystals gradually will be deposited high in the atmosphere, which might add to the "greenhouse effect" (prevention of the heat of the Earth from radiating back into space). On the other hand, they may produce a greater cooling than heating effect because of the sun's rays which they reflect back into space. One way or another, you can bet their effect will not be "neutral." The greenhouse effect is being enhanced now by the greatly increased level of carbon dioxide in the atmosphere. In the last century our burning of fossil fuels raised the level some 15%. The greenhouse effect today is being countered by low-level clouds generated by contrails, dust, and other contaminants that tend to keep the energy of the sun from warming the Earth in the first place.

At the moment we cannot predict what the overall climatic results will be of our using the atmosphere as a garbage dump. We do know that very small changes in either direction in the average temperature of the Earth could be very serious. With a few degrees of cooling, a new ice age might be upon us, with rapid and drastic effects on the agricultural productivity of the temperate regions. With a few degrees of heating, the polar ice caps would melt, perhaps raising ocean levels 250 feet. Gondola to the Empire State Building, anyone?

In short, when we pollute, we tamper with the energy balance of the Earth. The results in terms of global climate and in terms of local weather could be catastrophic. Do we want to keep it up and find out what will happen? What do we gain by playing "environmental roulette"?

[. . .]

I have just scratched the surface of the problem of environmental deterioration, but I hope that I have at least convinced you that subtle ecological effects may be much more important than the obvious features of the problem. The causal chain of the deterioration is easily followed to its source. Too many cars, too many factories, too much detergent, too much pesticide, multiplying contrails, inadequate sewage treatment plants, too little water, too much carbon dioxide—all can be traced easily to *too many people.*

DOCUMENT 4.5

FROM GARRETT HARDIN, "THE TRAGEDY OF THE COMMONS" (1968)

IT IS FAIR TO SAY THAT MOST PEOPLE WHO ANGUISH OVER THE POPUlation problem are trying to find a way to avoid the evils of overpopulation without relinquishing any of the privileges they now enjoy. They think that farming the seas or developing new strains of wheat will solve the problem—technologically. I try to show here that the solution they seek cannot be found. The population problem cannot be solved in a technical way, any more than can the problem of winning the game of tick-tack-toe.

[...]

We can make little progress in working toward optimum population size until we explicitly exorcize the spirit of Adam Smith in the field of practical demography. In economic affairs, *The Wealth of Nations* (1776) popularized the "invisible hand," the idea that an individual who "intends only his own gain," is, as it were, "led by an invisible hand to promote [...] the public interest." Adam Smith did not assert that this was invariably true, and perhaps neither did any of his followers. But he contributed to a dominant tendency

---

Garrett Hardin, "The Tragedy of the Commons," *Science* 162, no. 3859 (1968): 1243–48. Reproduced by Permission of the American Association for the Advancement of Science.

of thought that has ever since interfered with positive action based on rational analysis, namely, the tendency to assume that decisions reached individually will, in fact, be the best decisions for an entire society. If this assumption is correct it justifies the continuance of our present policy of laissez-faire in reproduction. If it is correct we can assume that men will control their individual fecundity so as to produce the optimum population. If the assumption is not correct, we need to reexamine our individual freedoms to see which ones are defensible.

The rebuttal to the invisible hand in population control is to be found in a scenario first sketched in a little-known pamphlet in 1833 by a mathematical amateur named William Forster Lloyd (1794–1852).[1] We may well call it "the tragedy of the commons" [. . .]

The tragedy of the commons develops in this way. Picture a pasture open to all. It is to be expected that each herdsman will try to keep as many cattle as possible on the commons. Such an arrangement may work reasonably satisfactorily for centuries because tribal wars, poaching, and disease keep the numbers of both man and beast well below the carrying capacity of the land. Finally, however, comes the day of reckoning, that is, the day when the long-desired goal of social stability becomes a reality. At this point, the inherent logic of the commons remorselessly generates tragedy.

As a rational being, each herdsman seeks to maximize his gain. Explicitly or implicitly, more or less consciously, he asks, "What is the utility to me of adding one more animal to my herd?" This utility has one negative and one positive component.

1) The positive component is a function of the increment of one animal. Since the herdsman receives all the proceeds from the sale of the additional animal, the positive utility is nearly +1.

2) The negative component is a function of the additional overgrazing created by one more animal. Since, however, the effects of overgrazing are shared by all the herdsmen, the negative utility for any particular decision-making herdsman is only a fraction of −1.

Adding together the component partial utilities, the rational herdsman concludes that the only sensible course for him to pursue is to add another animal to his herd. And another; and another. [. . .] But this is the conclusion reached by each and every rational herdsman sharing a commons. Therein is the tragedy. Each man is locked into a system that compels him to increase his herd without limit—in a world that is limited. Ruin is the destination toward which all men rush, each pursuing his own best interest in a society that believes in the freedom of the commons. Freedom in a commons brings ruin to all.

[. . .]

In an approximate way, the logic of the commons has been understood for a long time, perhaps since the discovery of agriculture or the invention of private property in real estate. But it is understood mostly only in special cases which are not sufficiently generalized. Even at this late date, cattlemen leasing national land on the western ranges demonstrate no more than an ambivalent understanding, in constantly pressuring federal authorities to increase the head count to the point where overgrazing produces erosion and weed-dominance. Likewise, the oceans of the world continue to suffer from the survival of the philosophy of the commons. Maritime nations still respond automatically to the shibboleth of the "freedom of the seas." Professing to believe in the "inexhaustible resources of the oceans," they bring species after species of fish and whales closer to extinction.

The National Parks present another instance of the working out of the tragedy of the commons. At present, they are open to all, without limit. The parks themselves are limited in extent there is only one Yosemite Valley—whereas population seems to grow without limit. The values that visitors seek in the parks are steadily eroded. Plainly, we must soon cease to treat the parks as commons or they will be of no value to anyone.

[. . .]

In a reverse way, the tragedy of the commons reappears in problems of pollution. Here it is not a question of taking something out of the commons, but of putting something in—sewage, or chemical, radioactive, and heat wastes into water; noxious and dangerous fumes into the air; and distracting and unpleasant advertising signs into the line of sight. The calculations of utility are much the same as before. The rational man finds that his share of the cost of the wastes he discharges into the commons is less than the cost of purifying his wastes before releasing them. Since this is true for everyone, we are locked into a system of "fouling our own nest," so long as we behave only as independent, rational, free-enterprisers.

The tragedy of the commons as a food basket is averted by private property, or something formally like it. But the air and waters surrounding us cannot readily be fenced, and so the tragedy of the commons as a cesspool must be prevented by different means, by coercive laws or taxing devices that make it cheaper for the polluter to treat his pollutants than to discharge them untreated. We have not progressed as far with the solution of this problem as we have with the first. [. . .]

The pollution problem is a consequence of population. It did not much matter how a lonely American frontiersman disposed of his waste. "Flowing water purifies itself every 10 miles," my grandfather used to say, and the myth was near enough to the truth when he was a boy, for there were not too many people. But as population became denser, the natural chemical and biological recycling processes became overloaded, calling for a redefinition of property rights.

[. . .]

The tragedy of the commons is involved in population problems in another way. In a world governed solely by the principle of "dog eat dog"—if indeed there ever was such a world—how many children a family had would not be a matter of public concern. Parents who bred too exuberantly would leave fewer descendants, not more, because they would be unable to care adequately for their children. David Lack[2] and others have found that such a negative feedback demonstrably controls the fecundity of birds. But men are not birds, and have not acted like them for millenniums, at least.

If each human family were dependent only on its own resources; if the children of improvident parents starved to death; *if*, thus, overbreeding brought its own "punishment" to the germ line—*then* there would be no public interest in controlling the breeding of families. But our society is deeply committed to the welfare state, and hence is confronted with another aspect of the tragedy of the commons.

In a welfare state, how shall we deal with the family, the religion, the race, or the class (or indeed any distinguishable and cohesive group) that adopts overbreeding as a policy to secure its own aggrandizement? To couple the concept of freedom to breed with the belief that everyone born has an equal right to the commons is to lock the world into a tragic course of action.

Unfortunately this is just the course of action that is being pursued by the United Nations.

[. . .]

Perhaps the simplest summary of this analysis of man's population problems is this: the commons, if justifiable at all, is justifiable only under conditions of low-population density. As the human population has increased, the commons has had to be abandoned in one aspect after another. [. . .] Every new enclosure of the commons involves the infringement of somebody's personal liberty. Infringements made in the distant past are accepted because no contemporary complains of a loss. It is the newly proposed infringements that we vigorously oppose; cries of "rights" and "freedom" fill the air. But what does "freedom" mean? When men mutually agreed to pass laws against robbing, mankind became more free, not less so. Individuals locked into the logic of the commons are free only to bring on universal ruin; once they see the necessity of mutual coercion, they become free to pursue other goals. I believe it was Hegel who said, "Freedom is the recognition of necessity."[3]

The most important aspect of necessity that we must now recognize, is the necessity of abandoning the commons in breeding. No technical solution can rescue us from the misery of overpopulation. Freedom to breed will bring ruin to all. At the moment, to avoid hard decisions many of us are tempted to propagandize for conscience and responsible parenthood. The temptation must be resisted, because an appeal to independently acting consciences selects for the disappearance of all conscience in the long run, and an increase in anxiety in the short. The only way we can preserve and nurture other and more precious freedoms is by relinquishing the freedom to breed, and that very soon. "Freedom is the recognition of necessity"—and it is the role of education to reveal to all the necessity of abandoning the freedom to breed. Only so, can we put an end to this aspect of the tragedy of the commons.

NOTES

1 *Two Lectures on the Checks to Population* (1833).
2 Lack was the British biologist who developed "Lack's principle" about the size of bird clutch sizes.
3 While true to Hegel's arguments in *The Philosophy of Right* (1820), this form of words appears to be from Friedrich Engels's characterization of Hegel.

DOCUMENT 4.6

FROM COMMITTEE ON AGRICULTURE, HOUSE OF REPRESENTATIVES, *MALTHUS AND AMERICA: A REPORT ABOUT FOOD AND PEOPLE* (1974)

THE PURPOSE OF THIS REPORT IS TO INFORM YOU AND TO MAKE YOU think about the food-population equation.

We mean to first inform the Congress and the public about the existence of problems that rank in enormity and complexity with none other in the history of the human species.

Then we seek to begin to define more precisely some of the basic questions that Americans must answer, one way or another, right now or soon.

The Subcommittee found as many scholars and thinkers have already discovered that the problems occasioned by the growth of humanity are indeed most diverse. The Subcommittee found that there isn't even a single problem, much less a single answer, for nearly uncountable variations of the numerology

---

Committee on Agriculture, House of Representatives, *Malthus and America: A Report about Food and People*, © US Government Printing Office, reprinted under section 105 of the Copyright Act.

of people as compounded by rising affluence and inflation throughout a world being molded or remolded by technology that both cures and sickens us all.

The unrelenting growth of the numerical mass of human beings in our world "lily pond" forces all of us to an intellectual state where we must ask ourselves:

"What is it doing to our ethical and moral standards?"

"What is it doing to the earth's 'commons' otherwise known as our environment?

"What is it doing to our political, social, and cultural system?"

"What is it doing to both our standard and our style of life?"

"What is it doing to the national strength and safety of our great republic?"

"Do we humans live, as has been popularly noted, in a 'spaceship earth' or are we Americans luckily adrift in a 'lifeboat' surrounded by a sea of hungry people as described by Garrett Hardin?"

"Will you and I as American citizens some day have to participate in the choice of 'Food Triage'[1] similar to that facing a combat surgeon in war?"

"Or can we putt with a clear conscience on a golf green fertilized by ammonia that could be used to grow wheat in Bihar?"

"Are we Americans the ants of the world . . . or are we the grasshoppers . . . or does the answer to that question depend on whether we talk about grain or about metals?"

"What then should be our export and import priorities in terms of agriculture, in terms of foreign policy, and yes, in terms of humanitarian ideals . . . and how do we select those priorities while avoiding what Secretary Butz[2] has identified as apocalyptic nonsense?"

"Is the great historian Arnold Toynbee[3] right when he says 'The wartime austerity was temporary; the future austerity will be perennial, and it will become progressively more severe'?"

"Or is there, as Elliot Janeway[4] says, 'Bad news on the food front but not for America'?"

"And, oh yes, is this report and these hearings and theorems set forth in current public dialogue an echo from the grave of Thomas Malthus or is it merely another cry of 'wolf' that can be mastered by the magic of science and the adaptability of man?"

Think about it, Congress.

Think about it, America.

[...]

The principal constraint on efforts to expand world food supplies during the final years of this century may well be water and climate, rather than land. In many regions of the world fertile agricultural land is still available, provided that water can be found to make it productive, but most of the rivers that lend themselves to damming and to irrigation have already been developed. [...]

Climatic trends can cause radically different consequences in various countries. A temperature change of a degree or two downward in the latitudes above 40° north in North America may not sound very impressive, but such a change could completely eliminate wheat and corn production in growing districts of Canada during the deterioration. At the same time in some areas of the United States the wheat and corn crop yields could increase.

[...]

Ecological implications of highly intensive food production efforts must be considered. New signs of agricultural stress appear almost daily as the growing demand for food presses against our ecosystem's finite capacities. Interventions by early agricultural men were local in effect, but the technological intrusions of modern agriculture often have global consequences. Efforts to expand the food supply, either by expanding the area under cultivation or intensifying cultivation through the use of agricultural chemicals and irrigation, bring with them troublesome and disturbing ecological consequences. Accelerating soil loss, problems caused by irrigation and eutrophication of streams and lakes due to increased use of chemical fertilizers are pressing ecological dangers associated with efforts to increase food production. Enlarging livestock herds for food and draft power has caused overgrazing and the inevitable erosion that follows. Nature requires centuries to create topsoil and man can destroy it in only a few years. Deforestation has been followed by erosion in many parts of the world.

[...]

Building quietly and ominously these days is a voice that will rock the world in our lifetime, and that voice articulates the world food and people equation [...] and it is to our blessed land of abundance from across the threshold of scarcity that this voice cries.

Will Americans discover too late that Thomas Malthus is a 200-year-old alarmist whose time has finally arrived?

The Subcommittee concludes that unless present trends in population growth and food production are significantly altered, a food crisis that will have the potential to affect everyone from every walk of life will hit with more impact than the energy crisis of 1973–74. Unfortunately most of the citizens of this and every country of the world are yet unaware of the phenomenal problem that looms on the horizon, and if the hearings held by the Subcommittee and this followup report can serve to make people at least aware of what the statistics show we are headed for, our goal will have been achieved. Americans, who heretofore have been rather complacent about this subject, inasmuch as abundant food supplies have been available at low prices in years past and since the growth rate of our population has slowed considerably, cannot afford to sit idly by thinking that this problem does not affect us. Did you ever stop to think, for example, what the effects on our national security would be if, say, the governments of three or four major countries collapsed due to a shortage of food, resulting in riots in the streets and an overthrow of the government? Can we live in peace in a whole world neighborhood of sick and hungry people?

This United States of America, comprising approximately 5 to 6 percent of the world's population, consumes more than 40 percent of the world's resources. The demand for food, like the demand for oil, metals, minerals, and other resources, is obviously going to skyrocket, and that rocket is going to be fueled by fires of inflation and joblessness.

[. . .] Our country has, throughout its history, operated our political and social systems within the perimeters of abundance and has seldom had to cope with the politics of scarcity. But last summer, Americans were forced to cope with scarcities and found it none too pleasant. Price controls were applied to beef. Export controls were set on soybeans. Import restrictions on nearly all commodities were lifted. Humanitarian food shipments under Title II of Public Law 480, our Food for Peace program, were suspended.

[. . .]

[. . .] the Subcommittee is certain that the U.S. Government can no longer afford to take a piecemeal approach to food policy as we have done in past years. The problem with the piecemeal approach is that it never allows for all of the pieces to really be put together and thus have never solved the puzzle. What is needed is an integrated social policy approach in the formulation, debate, and implementation of the policy position to be taken by the United States. An integrated social policy approach sees the issue of food in terms of its relationship to the other elements of socio-economic-political development in a highly interdependent world. Income distribution, health care systems, literacy programs, land reform in the agricultural sector, employment policies in the industrial sector, encouragement of savings among the poor, and the possibility of political participation by all sectors—these are some of the elements which give people a stake in society and thus motivates them to do something for the sake of society and for themselves, namely to have smaller families. Additionally, issues such as world prices (inflation), trade, preferential tariffs, international money structures, et cetera, should be taken into consideration. In other words, the issue is much broader than just a question of food supply and demand or population, and all factors which might conceivably enter into the picture as previously stated should be discussed.

[. . .]

Will America allow a food shortage to surprise us such as we allowed the energy crisis to do this year, and only then react *after* we find people standing in line from 7 a.m. to 9 a.m. on Tuesday and Thursday mornings waiting to get into their local grocery store to buy a limited quantity of food? The Department Operations Subcommittee sincerely hopes not.

The answers aren't easy, but the price of inaction will be cruel.

Think about it, Congress.

Think about it, America.

NOTES

1. Food triage is a concept popularized by William and Paul Paddock in *Famine 1975! America's Decision: Who Will Survive?* (1967).
2. Earl Butz was secretary of agriculture under Presidents Richard Nixon and Gerald Ford.
3. Arnold Joseph Toynbee is best known for a twelve-volume project, *A Study of History* (1934–1961).
4. Eliot Janeway was an American economist and journalist who was influential with President Lyndon Johnson and nicknamed "Calamity Janeway" for his economic pessimism.

DOCUMENT 4.7

FROM BARRY COMMONER, "A BULLETIN DIALOGUE ON *THE CLOSING CIRCLE*: RESPONSE" (1972)

I DISCOVERED, DURING EARTH WEEK 1970,[1] THAT MANY OF THE VIEWS about the origins of the environmental crisis held by different Earth Week participants were contradictory and that some lacked scientific support. In particular, I was struck with the sharp contrast between the unalloyed conviction of Ehrlich, Hardin and others that the numerous assaults on the environment "can be traced easily to *too many people*" (Ehrlich, "The Population Bomb," emphasis in the original),[2] and the absence of any firm, especially numerical, supporting data for this conclusion.

In the last few years, together with a number of colleagues, I have tried to assemble and analyze the available data regarding the roles of several factors—population size, affluence and technology—that might influence the way in which the productive system of the United States affects the environment. In the course of that work it became increasingly evident that changes in productive technology since World War II have played an important role

---

Barry Commoner, "A Bulletin Dialogue on *The Closing Circle*: Response," *Bulletin of the Atomic Scientists* 28, no. 5 (1972): 17, 42–56. Reproduced by permission of the Educational Foundation for Nuclear Science.

in the development of the environmental crisis. I began to write and speak about some of the examples that we had studied: how the use of more nitrogen fertilizer on less land (the displacement of land by fertilizer) has intensified the environmental impact of agriculture; how the conversion of the prewar car into today's high-powered monsters transformed a means of transportation into a smog generator; how the substitution of detergents for soap has worsened environmental quality. I found that the numerical size of such technological changes (for example the more than tenfold increase in the annual use of inorganic nitrogen fertilizer since 1945) was much larger than the concurrent increase in population (about 42 per cent), and on these grounds suggested that it might be wrong to conclude that the environmental crisis is exclusively, or even chiefly, the result of population growth.

[...]

Early in 1971, together with my colleagues Michael Corr and Paul Stamler, I wrote an article on this problem for "Environment" (April 1971).[3] We began our considerations with a helpful statement published earlier by Ehrlich and Holdren.[4] We said "Dr Paul Ehrlich provides the following statement regarding these several related factors:"

> Pollution can be said to be the result of multiplying three factors: population size, per capita consumption, and an "environmental impact" index that measures, in part, how wisely we apply the technology that goes with consumption.

We paraphrased this relationship as follows:

> Population size × per capita consumption × environmental impact per unit of production = level of pollution.

We then pointed out that:

> If we are to take effective action, we will need a more detailed guide than the equation offers. To begin with, we must know the relative importance of the three factors on the left side of the equation.

Our article then goes on to discuss the relative value of these factors in the United States since 1946 (as revealed in the available statistical tables) and to point out that the technology factor (environmental impact per unit of production) appears to have increased more than the other two factors.

[...]

The conclusion which Ehrlich and Holdren ascribe to me (i.e., that population increase amounts to one fifth or less of the increases in pollution level) is accurate.

[...]

In a way this statement provides the clearest expression of the gulf which separates Ehrlich's view of the global population problem and my own. He takes the position that ecological catastrophe is inevitable if the peoples of the developing countries—or, for that matter, of the industrialized ones—are left to regulate population growth by their own self-determined actions, following the course taken by the developed countries (as described by the demographic transition). [. . .] According to Ehrlich, population growth is governed by the automatic mechanism made famous by Malthus. [. . .] Ehrlich believes, apparently, that human society today is in the grip of an automatic clash between population and resources, and that no self-motivated human effort [. . .] can possibly prevent catastrophe.

My view is different. I believe that population control is generated within a given society by a series of complex interactions in which improved well-being and social security motivated people to reduce fertility voluntarily, and that, subject to short-term fluctuations, this phenomenon (demographic transition) can achieve long-term population stability. Ehrlich's view stresses the inevitable clash between two biological processes: growth of population and the slower increase of food supply. My view stresses the effects of social action to improve living conditions. [. . .]

To put the difference between us more bluntly. This, after all being the year 1972, Ehrlich's advice is to "look after yourself and your friends and enjoy what little time you have left." While I believe that, today and into the future, human society (as distinct from "yourself and your friends") can be organized as a stable, ongoing, humane civilization—by powerful, sustained social action to remove the economic and political barriers that keep people and whole nations in poverty.

[...]

In my view, the environmental crisis involves very grave and complex social problems that ought to be resolved by public decision and not determined by the force of private agreements among scientists as to which issues are to be openly debated and which are to be hidden from public view. As I have pointed out in *The Closing Circle*,[5] these issues confront the American people with two alternative (but not mutually exclusive) paths toward a solution: a reduction in the population sufficient to render tolerable the environmental degradation due to ecologically faulty technology, or social action to correct counter-ecological technologies and to change the economic measures which generate them. Population control (as distinct from voluntary, self-initiated control of fertility), no matter how disguised, involves some measure of political repression, and would burden the poor nations with the social cost of a situation—overpopulation—which is the current outcome of their previous exploitation, as colonies, by wealthy nations. And as I have also taken pains to point out, the alternative means of resolving the environmental crisis by improvement of productive technology would require sweeping and basic changes in the private enterprise system in a nation such as the United States. Now, I know of no scientific principle which can tell us how much to rely on population control and how much on technological change (and the required economic controls) in order to reduce environmental impact. The choice between these paths is clearly a political one, not a matter of science.

NOTES

1 Earth Day is an annual event on April 22 raising environmental awareness. The first Earth Day was that in 1970, referred to here by Commoner.
2 Commoner here cites the last line of document 4.4.
3 Barry Commoner, Michael Corr, and Paul J. Stamler, "The Causes of Pollution," *Environment* 13, no. 3 (1971): 2–19.
4 Commoner here refers to John Holdren, an American scientist and global environmental analyst. A close collaborator with Ehrlich, Holdren was a participant in the Ehrlich-Simon bet of 1980. He later became assistant to the president for science and technology for President Barack Obama.
5 Commoner is referring to his most famous book, *The Closing Circle: Nature, Man, and Technology* (1971).

DOCUMENT 4.8

FROM MAHMOOD MAMDANI, "THE IDEOLOGY OF POPULATION CONTROL" (1976)

THE PRINCIPAL EXPLANATION FOR INDIA'S CONTINUING POVERTY advanced by bourgeois social science over the last decade has been the theory of overpopulation, particularly in its neo-Malthusian version. [. . .] The left critique of neo-Malthusian thought has sought to argue that its very presentation of the problem has been *ideological*. [. . .]

A critique at the level of ideology, however, is only a first step. Though a necessary step, it must be followed by a *scientific* explanation of what is a real phenomenon: the rising rates of natural increase in population in most backward capitalist countries. It is the purpose of this essay to contribute to the development of such an explanation and thereby deepen the critique of neo-Malthusian thought as well as attempt a redefinition of what has been called the "population problem."

A scientific explanation is possible only if a phenomenon is located in its specificity, in this case both social and historical. Birth rates are not territorially

---

Mahmood Mamdani, "The Ideology of Population Control," *Economic and Political Weekly* 11, no. 31/33 (1976): 1141, 1143, 1145, 1147–48. Reproduced by permission of the author.

specific as much as specific to particular social groups. Anybody familiar with the demography of a town or a village knows that the reproductive practice of land labourers is different from that of the landlords and of the petty bourgeois from that of the proletarian or the unemployed. Reproductive behaviour is not a natural but a social phenomenon. Territorial birth rates or rates of natural increase are an abstraction that do not advance as much as mystify our understanding. Secondly, this same behaviour is neither idiosyncratic nor accidental but is substantially *reproduced* over time. The "population problem" would only exist if there was a certain uniformity over time of the reproductive behaviour of social groups. In other words, our concern with reproductive behaviour is not in its individuality, as a subjective phenomenon, but as one both social and objective. The question that must be posed then is: What are the *social relations* that underlie these practices? Furthermore, the social relations themselves did not always exist but were historically created. The very relations must then be understood in their historical specificity.

[...] What we hope to show is, one, that it is not high population growth that explains India's poverty but the contrary, and two, that this poverty itself is not a natural but a historical phenomenon: its reproduction cannot be understood unless we analyse it as the result of social relations which themselves must be placed in the context of a system of oppression, imperialism.

[...]

The decision by a couple located within the working peasantry or the appropriated masses to have a number of children is essentially a rational decision, a judgement of their social environment. Rationality does not exist in the abstract; it is concrete, the product of a particular social and historical context. The pitfall of neo-Malthusian liberalism is precisely its "rationalism," that it assumes a universal rationality and forgets that in a class society there exists class rationality.

The demand for population control may be rational in one class situation, but not necessarily in another. The "rationalism" of the neo-Malthusian *universalises* the situation and thus the rationality of a particular class: what is good for the bourgeoisie is good for all!

Ideological thought is not simply false. It is thought that presents an aspect of reality as reality and obscures the relation between the aspect and the totality. The specific historical relation between high rates of population growth in particular social groups and their social oppression is obscured. How a problem is defined greatly affects the formulation of the solution. When the phenomenon is defined as the "population problem," its core assertion is that people are poor because they are too many. Exploitation is reduced to poverty and the explanation of poverty become the poor themselves!

DOCUMENT 4.9

FROM AMARTYA SEN, "FAMINES AS FAILURES OF EXCHANGE ENTITLEMENTS" (1976)

THE APPROACH OF "FOOD AVAILABILITY DECLINE," WHICH I WILL call FAD [. . .] attributes the causation of famines to a sharp decline in the availability of food supply in the region in question. This is the common element of the approach, though the *manifestations* of famines can be explained in one of several distinct ways. Also, the *causation* of the sudden decline of food supply can also be explained in many different ways. Frequently enough, FAD goes with a Malthusian theory of population.

[. . .]

FAD works best when much of the food eaten by a family happens to be grown by it without the need of exchange. In an exchange economy, however, one has to look at the terms of exchange, and while food availability clearly will be an important influence on these terms, there are also other factors involved. [. . .] The crucial fact is that in an exchange economy the "distribution" of a particular commodity is the result of exchange, and whether a family has something to eat depends on what it can sell and the prices that are fetched by what it can sell in comparison with the prices of food. An economy in a state of comparative tranquillity may develop a famine if there is a sudden shake up of the system of rewards for exchange of labour, commodities and other possessions. A sharp revision of "exchange entitlements" can precipitate a famine even when there is no over-all shortage of food. It is this type of causation that the approach of the "failure of exchange entitlements" (FEE for short) is aimed at capturing.

[...]

It can be argued that FEE-type famines have a special relevance for developing countries at early stages of modernisation and growth. In a primitive economy based on family labour or communal labour prior to the development of the wage system, famines resulting from failures in exchanging labour cannot arise. In so far as exchange of commodities is also limited and people eat what they themselves grow, the role of other failures of exchange entitlements is also remote. Famines based on FAD can, of course, take place, but the relevance of FEE-type famines grows only as the economy becomes more exchange-orientated and in particular as labour emerges as another "commodity" to be bought and sold in the market. Failures of exchange entitlements are also less likely in socialist economies, or in advanced capitalist economies, since a system of employment guarantee in the former and entitlements to "unemployment benefits" in the latter, tend to rule out large-scale starvation resulting from, inability to exchange one's ware. It is perhaps worth remarking in this context that the absence of famines in the economically advanced countries is almost certainly due to the altered system of exchange entitlements through "social security" rather than due to the average level of national prosperity as such.

In contrast an exchange economy based on wage labour, without a system of unemployment benefits and related measures of social security, is particularly susceptible to famines of the FEE-type. A recent example was the 1974 famine in Bangladesh. The flood that destroyed the crop did reduce the availability of food, but the sharp decline in employment and the failure of exchange entitlement of labour was immediate, and the famine was made severe by that.

[...] There are reasons to think that the "exchange entitlements" approach is particularly important after wage labour emerges in the process of development and before social security measures become common. Expansion of commodity exchanges in general also contributes to this. The "food availability" approach—no matter how relevant for medieval famines—is not robust enough to permit a serious analysis of modern famines.

[...]

The Bengal Famine of 1943—the greatest famine of the century—can be viewed both in terms of "food availability decline" (FAD) as well as that of "failures of exchange entitlements" (FEE). [. . .] I have tried to present the contrast between the two approaches as applied to the Bengal Famine, and have argued that the FAD approach works very badly in this case, while the FEE approach works much better. [. . .] it emerges that the food availability per capita in Bengal in 1943 was not substantially different from availabilities in previous years. [. . .] More recently, the FAD interpretation of the Bengal Famine has been frequently cited in the outbursts of alarm about the "world food crisis." [. . .] The factual basis of this diagnosis of the Bengal Famine seems eminently questionable.

DOCUMENT 4.10

FROM NORMAN BORLAUG, "THE GREEN REVOLUTION, PEACE, AND HUMANITY" (1970)

CIVILIZATION AS IT IS KNOWN TODAY COULD NOT HAVE EVOLVED, NOR can it survive, without an adequate food supply. Yet food is something that is taken for granted by most world leaders despite the fact that more than half of the population of the world is hungry. Man seems to insist on ignoring the lessons available from history.

[. . .]

In the misty, hazy past, as the Mesolithic Age gave way to the Neolithic, there suddenly appeared in widely separated geographic areas the most highly successful group of inventors and revolutionaries that the world has ever known. This group of Neolithic men and women, and in all probability largely the latter, domesticated all the major cereals, legumes, and root crops, as well as all of the most important animals that to this day remain man's principal source of food. [. . .] The invention of agriculture, however, did not permanently emancipate man from the fear of food shortages, hunger, and famine. Even in prehistoric times population growth often must have threatened or

---

Normal Borlaug, "The Green Revolution, Peace, and Humanity," Nobel Prize Lecture (1970), copyright © The Norwegian Nobel Institute. Reproduced with permission of the Norwegian Nobel Institute.

exceeded man's ability to produce enough food. Then, when droughts or outbreaks of diseases and insect pests ravaged crops, famine resulted.

[. . .]

But today we should be far wiser; with the help of our Gods and our science, we must not only increase our food supplies but also insure them against biological and physical catastrophes by international efforts to provide international granaries of reserve food for use in case of need. And these food reserves must be made available to all who need them—and before famine strikes, not afterwards. Man can and must prevent the tragedy of famine in the future instead of merely trying with pious regret to salvage the human wreckage of the famine, as he has so often done in the past. We will be guilty of criminal negligence, without extenuation, if we permit future famines. Humanity cannot tolerate that guilt.

[. . .]

Perhaps no one in recent times has more pungently expressed the interrelationship of food and peace than Nobel Laureate Lord John Boyd Orr,[1] the great crusader against hunger and the first director-general of the Food and Agriculture Organization, with his famous words, "You can't build peace on empty stomachs."[2] These simple words of wisdom spoken twenty-one years ago are as valid today as when they were spoken. They will become even more meaningful in the future as world population skyrockets and as crowding, social pressures, and stresses increase. To ignore Lord Orr's admonition would result in worldwide disorders and social chaos, for it is a fundamental biological law that when the life of living organisms is threatened by shortage of food they tend to swarm and use violence to obtain their means of sustenance.

It is a sad fact that on this earth at this late date there are still two worlds, "the privileged world" and "the forgotten world." The privileged world consists of the affluent, developed nations, comprising twenty-five to thirty percent of the world population, in which most of the people live in a luxury never before experienced by man outside the Garden of Eden. The forgotten world is made up primarily of the developing nations, where most of the people, comprising more than fifty percent of the total world population, live in poverty, with hunger as a constant companion and fear of famine a continual menace.

When the Nobel Peace Prize Committee designated me the recipient of the 1970 award[3] for my contribution to the "green revolution," they were in effect, I believe, selecting an individual to symbolize the vital role of agriculture and food production in a world that is hungry, both for bread and for peace.

[...]

The term "The Green Revolution" has been used by the popular press to describe the spectacular increase in cereal-grain production during the past three years. Perhaps the term "green revolution," as commonly used, is premature, too optimistic, or too broad in scope. Too often it seems to convey the impression of a general revolution in yields per hectare and in total production of all crops throughout vast areas comprising many countries. Sometimes it also implies that all farmers are uniformly benefited by the breakthrough in production.

[...]

Never before in the history of agriculture has a transplantation of high-yielding varieties coupled with an entirely new technology and strategy been achieved on such a massive scale, in so short a period of time, and with such great success. The success of this transplantation is an event of both great scientific and social significance. Its success depended upon good organization of the production program combined with skillful execution by courageous and experienced scientific leaders.

[...]

In summarizing the accomplishments of the green revolution during the past three years, I wish to restate that the increase in cereal production, rice, maize, and wheat, especially in wheat, has been spectacular and highly significant to the welfare of millions of human beings. It is still modest in terms of total needs. Recalling that fifty percent of the present world population is undernourished and that an even larger percentage, perhaps sixty-five percent, is malnourished, no room is left for complacency. It is not enough to prevent the currently bad situation from getting worse as population increases. Our aim must be to produce enough food to eradicate all present hunger while at the same time striving to correct malnutrition. To eliminate hunger now in the developing nations, we would need to expand world cereal production by thirty percent. If it were, however, as simple as increasing the total world production by thirty percent, regardless of where the production is to be expanded, it could be accomplished rather rapidly by expanding it in the United States, Canada, Australia, Argentina, and Russia. But this would not necessarily solve the hunger problem of the developing world because their weak economies will not permit them to expand their food imports by thirty percent. Worse still, even if present production could be expanded rapidly by thirty percent in the developing countries—which I believe is possible based on recent progress of the green revolution—so as theoretically to eliminate hunger, the hunger problem as it now exists still would not be solved. There remains the unsolved social-economic problem of finding effective ways to distribute the needed additional food to the vast underprivileged masses who have little or no purchasing power. This is still the great unsolved problem with which the economists, sociologists, and political leaders must now come to grips.

[...]

The green revolution has won a temporary success in man's war against hunger and deprivation; it has given man a breathing space. If fully implemented, the revolution can provide sufficient food for sustenance during the next three decades. But the frightening power of human reproduction must also be curbed; otherwise the success of the green revolution will be ephemeral only.

Most people still fail to comprehend the magnitude and menace of the "Population Monster." In the beginning there were but two, Adam and Eve. When they appeared on this earth is still questionable. By the time of Christ, world population had probably reached 250 million. But between then and now, population has grown to 3.5 billion. Growth has been especially fast since the advent of modern medicine. If it continues to increase at the estimated present rate of two percent a year, the world population will reach 6.5 billion by the year 2000. Currently, with each second, or tick of the clock, about 2.2 additional people are added to the world population. The rhythm of increase will accelerate to 2.7, 3.3, and 4.0 for each tick of the clock by 1980, 1990, and 2000, respectively, unless man becomes more realistic and preoccupied about this impending doom. The ticktock of the clock will continually grow louder and more menacing each decade. Where will it all end?

Malthus signaled the danger a century and a half ago. But he emphasized principally the danger that population would increase faster than food supplies. In his time he could not foresee the tremendous increase in man's food production potential. Nor could he have foreseen the disturbing and destructive physical and mental consequences of the grotesque concentration of human beings into the poisoned and clangorous environment of pathologically hypertrophied megalopoles. Can human beings endure the strain? Abnormal stresses and strains tend to accentuate man's animal instincts and provoke irrational and socially disruptive behavior among the less stable individuals in the maddening crowd.

We must recognize the fact that adequate food is only the first requisite for life. For a decent and humane life we must also provide an opportunity for good education, remunerative employment, comfortable housing, good clothing, and effective and compassionate medical care. Unless we can do this, man may degenerate sooner from environmental diseases than from hunger.

And yet, I am optimistic for the future of mankind, for in all biological populations there are innate devices to adjust population growth to the carrying capacity of the environment. Undoubtedly, some such device exists in man, presumably *Homo sapiens*, but so far it has not asserted itself to bring into balance population growth and the carrying capacity of the environment on a worldwide scale. It would be disastrous for the species to continue to increase our human numbers madly until such innate devices take over. It is a test of the validity of *sapiens* as a species epithet.

NOTES

1 See document 4.3.
2 In 1945, John Boyd Orr was elected a member of Parliament in the United Kingdom. In 1946, the House of Commons discussed the "World Food Situation," and Boyd Orr said, "[W]e cannot build peace on empty stomachs" (*Hansard*, May, 31, 1946, vol. 423, cols. 1490–1578).
3 Borlaug was the recipient of the 1970 Nobel Peace Prize; this is the text of his Nobel Lecture on that occasion.

DOCUMENT 4.11

FROM ELINOR OSTROM, *GOVERNING THE COMMONS* (1990)

HARDLY A WEEK GOES BY WITHOUT A MAJOR NEWS STORY ABOUT THE threatened destruction of a valuable natural resource. In June of 1989, for example, a *New York Times* article focused on the problem of overfishing in the Georges Bank about 150 miles off the New England coast. Catches of cod, flounder, and haddock are now only a quarter of what they were during the 1960s. Everyone knows that the basic problem is overfishing; however, those concerned cannot agree how to solve the problem. Congressional representatives recommend new national legislation, even though the legislation already on the books has been enforced only erratically. Representatives of the fishers argue that the fishing grounds would not be in such bad shape if the federal government had refrained from its sporadic attempts to regulate the fishery in the past. The issue in this case—and many others—is how best to limit the use of natural resources so as to ensure their long-term economic viability. Advocates of central regulation, of privatization, and of regulation by those involved have pressed their policy prescriptions in a variety of different arenas.

Elinor Ostrom, *Governing the Commons: The Evolution of Institutions for Collective Action* (Cambridge: Cambridge University Press, 1990), excerpts from the introduction. Reproduced with permission of Cambridge University Press through PLSclear.

Similar situations occur on diverse scales ranging from small neighborhoods to the entire planet. The issues of how best to govern natural resources used by many individuals in common are no more settled in academia than in the world of politics. Some scholarly articles about the "tragedy of the commons" recommend that "the state" control most natural resources to prevent their destruction; others recommend that privatizing those resources will resolve the problem. What one can observe in the world, however, is that neither the state nor the market is uniformly successful in enabling individuals to sustain long-term, productive use of natural resource systems. Further, communities of individuals have relied on institutions resembling neither the state nor the market to govern some resource systems with reasonable degrees of success over long periods of time.

[. . .] Since Garrett Hardin's challenging article in *Science* (1968), the expression "the tragedy of the commons" has come to symbolize the degradation of the environment to be expected whenever many individuals use a scarce resource in common. To illustrate the logical structure of his model, Hardin asks the reader to envision a pasture "open to all." He then examines the structure of this situation from the perspective of a rational herder. Each herder receives a direct benefit from his own animals and suffers delayed costs from the deterioration of the commons when his and others' cattle overgraze. Each herder is motivated to add more and more animals because he receives the direct benefit of his own animals and bears only a share of the costs resulting from overgrazing.

[. . .]

Instead of there being a single solution to a single problem, I argue that many solutions exist to cope with many different problems. Instead of presuming that optimal institutional solutions can be designed easily and imposed at low cost by external authorities, I argue that "getting the institutions right" is a difficult, time-consuming, conflict-invoking process. It is a process that requires reliable information about time and place variables as well as a broad repertoire of culturally acceptable rules. New institutional arrangements do not work in the field as they do in abstract models unless the models are well specified and empirically valid and the participants in a field setting understand how to make the new rules work.

Instead of presuming that the individuals sharing a commons are inevitably caught in a trap from which they cannot escape, I argue that the capacity of individuals to extricate themselves from various types of dilemma situations *varies* from situation to situation.

[...]

To open up the discussion of institutional options for solving commons dilemmas, I want now to present a [...] [scenario] in which the herders themselves can make a binding contract to commit themselves to a cooperative strategy that they themselves will work out. [...] The herders [...] must now negotiate prior to placing animals on the meadow. During negotiations, they discuss various strategies for sharing the carrying capacity of the meadow and the costs of enforcing their agreement. Contracts are not enforceable, however, unless agreed to unanimously by the herders. Any proposal made by one herder that did not involve an equal sharing of the carrying capacity and of enforcement costs would be vetoed by the other herder in their negotiations. Consequently, the only feasible agreement—and the equilibrium of the resulting game—is for both herders to share equally the sustainable yield levels of the meadow and the costs of enforcing their agreement. [...]

The key difference [...] is that the participants themselves design their own contracts [...] in light of the information they have at hand. The herders, who use the same meadow year after year, have detailed and relatively accurate information about carrying capacity. They observe the behavior of other herders and have an incentive to report contractual infractions. Arbitrators may not need to hire monitors to observe the activities of the contracting parties. The self-interest of those who negotiated the contract will lead them to monitor each other and to report observed infractions so that the contract is enforced. [...]

A self-financed contract-enforcement game is no panacea. Such institutional arrangements have many weaknesses in many settings. The herders can overestimate or underestimate the carrying capacity of the meadow. Their own monitoring system may break down. [...] A myriad of problems can occur in natural settings, as is also the case with the idealized central-regulation or private-property institutions.

The structure of the institutional arrangements that one finds in natural settings is, of course, far more complicated than the structure of any of the extremely simple games presented here for discussion. What I attempt to do with these simple games is to generate different ways of thinking about the mechanisms that individuals may use to extricate themselves from commons dilemmas—ways different from what one finds in much of the policy literature.

DOCUMENT 4.12

FROM JULIAN SIMON, "RESOURCES, POPULATION, ENVIRONMENT: AN OVERSUPPLY OF FALSE BAD NEWS" (1980)

IN SEPTEMBER 1977 *NEWSWEEK* REPORTED THAT "MORE THAN 100,000 West Africans perished of hunger" in the Sahel between 1968 and 1973 because of drought.[1] Upon inquiry, the writer of the account, Peter Gwynne, informed me that the estimate came from Kurt Waldheim's message to the United Nations' Desertification Conference.[2] I therefore wrote to Waldheim asking for the source of the estimate. [. . .]

[The answer was] a one-page memo written for the United Nations by Helen Ware, an Australian expert on African demography, who was a visiting fellow at the University of Ibadan in March 1975 when she wrote it. From calculations of the normal death rate for the area, together with "the highest death rate in any group of nomads" during the drought, she estimated "an absolute, and most improbable, upper limit [of] a hundred thousand. Even as a maximum [this estimate] represents an unreal limit."

Julian Simon, "Resources, Population, Environment: An Oversupply of False Bad News," *Science* 208, no. 4451 (1980): 1431–37. Reproduced by permission of the American Association for the Advancement of Science.

Ware's statement, which makes nonsense of Waldheim's well-publicized assessment, was on page one of a document written for the United Nations well before the Desertification Conference. Apparently it was the only calculation the United Nations had, and it was grossly misinterpreted.

[...]

This is an example of a common phenomenon: Bad news about population growth, natural resources, and the environment that is based on flimsy evidence or no evidence at all is published widely in the face of contradictory evidence.

[...]

Here are some other examples of publicized, false, bad news and the unpublicized, good-news truth: *Statement*: The food situation in less developed countries is worsening. "Serious World Food Gap Is Seen Over the Long Run" is a typical *New York Times* headline. Perhaps most influential in furthering that idea was Paul Ehrlich's best-selling book *The Population Bomb*, which begins: "The battle to feed all of humanity is over. In the 1970's the world will undergo famines-hundreds of millions of people are going to starve to death"[3]

[...]

Fact: Per capita food production has been increasing at roughly 1 percent yearly—25 percent during the last quarter century. Even in less-developed countries food production has increased substantially. World food stocks are high now, and even India has large amounts of food in storage. In the United States farmers are worrying about disaster from too much food.

[...]

At the heart of all these models is simply an arithmetical truth: When considering the ratio (total income)/persons and assuming the numerator (income) to be fixed, an increase in the denominator (persons) implies a decrease in income per capita. That is, an added child with all sharing a given amount of goods means there is less to go around. As Wilfred Beckerman[4] remarked, the instant a calf is born, per capita income and wealth go up, but the instant a child is born, per capita income and wealth go down. [...]

Once the children grow up, however, and become producers as well as consumers, their impact on per capita income reverses. Eventually the income of other people is higher because of the additional children. [...] But this takes more than the 25 or 30 years covered by the well-known models.

Another point of view: The main new element in my model for more-developed countries (MDC's) is the contribution of additional people to increasing productivity. This occurs partly through larger markets and economies of scale. But more important are an additional person's contributions to increased knowledge and technical progress. People bring not only mouths and hands into the world but also heads and brains. The source of improvements in productivity is the human mind, and the human mind is seldom found apart from the human body. This is an old idea, going back at least as far as William Petty:

> As for the Arts of Delight and Ornament, they are best promoted by the greatest number of emulators. And it is more likely that one ingenious curious man may rather be found among 4 million than 400 persons.... And for the propagation and improvement of useful learning, the same may be said concerning it as above-said concerning... the Arts of Delight and Ornaments....[5]

Population growth and productivity increase are not independent forces running a race. Rather, additional persons cause technological advances by inventing, adapting, and diffusing new productive knowledge.

[...] The result is that additional persons, instead of being a permanent drag, lead to an increase in per worker output starting 30 to 70 years after birth—that is, 10 to 50 years after entry into the labor force. (Economics can therefore be a cheerful science rather than the dismal science Malthus thought it to be.)

[...]

Statement: The supplies of natural resources are finite. This apparently self-evident proposition is the starting point and the all-determining assumption of such models as *The Limits to Growth*[6] and of much popular discussion.

Response: Incredible as it may seem at first, the term "finite" is not only inappropriate but is downright misleading in the context of natural resources, from both the practical and the philosophical points of view. As with so many of the important arguments in this world, this one is "just semantic." Yet the semantics of resource scarcity muddle public discussion and bring about wrongheaded policy decisions.

A definition of resource quantity must be operational to be useful. It must tell us how the quantity of the resource that might be available in the future could be calculated. But the future quantities of a natural resource such as copper cannot be calculated even in principle, because of new lodes, new methods of mining copper, and variations in grades of copper lodes; because copper can be made from other metals; and because of the vagueness of the boundaries within which copper might be found—including the sea, and other planets. Even less possible is a reasonable calculation of the amount of future services of the sort we are now accustomed to get from copper, because of recycling and because of the substitution of other materials for copper, as in the case of the communications satellite.

Even the total weight of the earth is not a theoretical limit to the amount of copper that might be available to earthlings in the future. Only the total weight of the universe—if that term has a useful meaning here—would be such a theoretical limit, and I don't think anyone would like to argue the meaningfulness of "finite" in that context.

[. . .]

In summary, because we find new lodes, invent better production methods, and discover new substitutes, the ultimate constraint upon our capacity to enjoy unlimited raw materials at acceptable prices is knowledge. And the source of knowledge is the human mind. Ultimately, then, the key constraint is human imagination and the exercise of educated skills. Hence an increase of human beings constitutes an addition to the crucial stock of resources, along with causing additional consumption of resources.

NOTES

1. *Newsweek*, September 19, 1977, 80.
2. At this time, Waldheim was secretary-general of the United Nations.
3. These are the opening lines of Ehrlich's "Prologue" to *The Population Bomb* (1968); see document 4.4.
4. Beckerman was a British economist and skeptic about environment economics.
5. Petty was a seventeenth-century politician arithmetician whose work was closely allied with that of John Graunt; see document 1.4. This quote is from "Another Essay in Political Arithmetick" (1682).
6. *The Limits to Growth* was a 1972 report by a group of economists known as the Club of Rome about the outcomes of a computer simulation on the interrelations of population and resource availability. Modeling finite resources against ongoing population increase, the simulation inevitably predicted a Malthusian collapse of population when resources were exhausted.

5

THE MALTHUS WARS TODAY

IN RECENT DECADES, POPULATION HAS BECOME A LESS POTENT SOURCE of political and ecological anxieties. Students of demography no longer regularly appear on prime-time television chat shows as did Paul Ehrlich. Congressional committees rarely print suggestions for global food triage or warn of the spectre of US scarcity. This does not mean that the debate about the nexus between population, resources, and the natural environment has shuffled off this mortal coil, merely that it has changed its form and tone.

An extensive literature emerged in the 1990s that frames the demographic-ecological nexus as a new population bomb. Concerned with the threat population may pose in conjunction with ecological limits to political security and stability, updating the Cold War concerns of the 1950s, this work uses the language of bombs, collapse, and incendiarism in an updated version of the Ehrlich's imagery. The core of these arguments is interconnectedness: population, food, resources, ecosystems, and climate change are seen as tied together to imperil social, political, and economic stability. These ideas gained considerable traction in political circles, notably within the US government and particularly within the foreign and intelligence services. Most influential in government circles was Robert Kaplan's 1994 essay for *The Atlantic*, "The

Coming Anarchy," while Jared Diamond's "collapse" hypothesis galvanized a more general audience.

What are the key arguments and how have they changed since the Malthusian moment? Three main elements can be discerned. First, the fear is of systems' collapse, that is, the total breakdown of governmental structures on which complex societies rely. The anxiety, then, is not now with a political flip from capitalism to communism but with the creation of power vacuums by violent political convulsions. This argument was taken furthest by Diamond, whose book *Collapse* (2005) took a wide range of examples across time and space to argue that a combination of population growth and resource scarcity was a recurrent constellation leading to sudden, dramatic civilizational decay. Diamond applied this with an explicitly Malthusian gloss to understand the Rwandan Genocide of 1994. Second, much of the discussion no longer pertains to population sizes and growth rates, instead turning to demographic structure. Indeed, new population bombs are primarily envisaged as caused by age structures. Many scholars have attempted to show that having a large male cohort in the age range 15 to 30 years creates a "youth bulge," which correlates with higher levels of protest, rebellion, and social incendiarism. Both the Arab Spring of 2011 and the events of 9/11 have been explained in terms of cohorts of disenfranchised men who are radicalized by dint of demographic disempowerment. In mirror fashion, the aging populations of the developed world have been seen to create other demographic pressure points, notably a dependency ratio that is unsustainable for the active, working-age population and the connected tensions surrounding the need to recruit large cohorts of immigrant labor. Global locations where these two regimes butt against each other are seen as having the volcanic potential of demographic tectonic plates meeting, with the US-Mexico border and the Mediterranean face-off of Europe and Africa being oft-cited "hotspots." As this implies, the locus of fears about population-resource breakdowns has changed. In the era of Ehrlich and Hardin, concern centered on Asia and in particular on India as the world's largest but also potentially most fragile democracy in a Cold War context (something Besant had also prefigured a century earlier). In the decades either side of the new millennium, the demographic-security rubric has focused on Europe and North America but most particularly on Africa. This is most apparent in Kaplan's lurid framing of Sierra Leone as the Dickensian ghost of West African collapse in the present and the harbinger of global collapse in the future. Rwanda's experiences have also been a key site for contestation about how to understand contemporary resource, population, and political interactions.

Unsurprisingly, there has been considerable pushback against this new "security demographic," with two lines of response being notable. First, detailed scholarship has suggested the extent to which the historical, cultural, and political details of the societies being discussed by the likes of Diamond have been caricatured or simplified to make the collapse argument persuasive. A whole volume of essays—*Questioning Collapse* (2009)—was produced to refute the collapse hypothesis, with the American anthropologist Christopher Taylor, for example, seeking to show how Diamond's Malthusian reading of the Rwandan Genocide can be complicated by recourse to anthropological inquiries into the religio-political culture of the nation stretching back over centuries to precolonial times. Diamond penned a furiously critical review of the book in *Nature*, which led to Cambridge University Press as the publisher publicly backing the scholarly credentials of its authors. Clearly, the intellectual temperature around the nexus of population, resources, and the environment can still reach boiling point from time to time!

The point made by the contributors to *Questioning Collapse* is equally applicable to other theorists of this ilk; smooth feedback loop diagrams of new population bombs strip the cultural and historical complexity out of the realities of political change. They also, in a critique that echoes Hazlitt and Godwin on Malthus, naturalize what are irreducibly social and political events. This leads to the second response to the idea of new population bombs represented here by radical feminist work, by indigenous views of the population-environment nexus, and by intersectional race-gender approaches. One of the main reasons for the mutation in global demographic discussion in the era after Ehrlich and Simon is the championing of women's reproductive rights and, separately, a feminist critique of neo-Malthusianism, the former being enshrined in the 1974 and 1994 UN conference on population in Bucharest and Cairo, respectively, a moment represented in this collection by the statement of the Committee on Women, Population, and the Environment. Obviously, the role of women in population-resource debates is not "new" to the final decades of the twentieth century. Indeed, going back a century and more, Annie Besant, Margaret Sanger, and Marie Stopes, among others, led a very different global movement titled "Malthusian" that sought to give women control over their reproductive destiny via contraception. But the extent of the feminist critique of population, resource, and environment arguments is new. This critique suggests that new population bombs encourage a coercive politics that disempowers women politically and reproductively and replaces social understandings of resource dilemmas with false naturalizations. Feminism asks who benefits from these fictions. Do they pander to a military-industrial complex in need of new foes to stay relevant and play well to an intelligence community looking for resources and power? From this perspective, it is imperative that the political, social, and gendered underpinnings of population-environment interactions are understood rather than being dismissed, as Diamond (or indeed Malthus) might do, as mere feathers floating on the surface.

The intersections of gender with race and indigeneity have offered further lines of argument. If, for example, Native American populations have a different conception of what a "population" includes, being not just humans but also animals, fish, and trees, there is no real trinity of population, resources, and the environment as the Western logics predominantly encoded in this book assume. Instead, population is an interconnected web whose preservation depends upon respect and the extension of "personhood" to the environment and all its inhabitants. Furthermore, the discourse of population tends to encode racial assumptions that are tied together with a geographical imaginary of the south as both colored and (dangerously) fecund. From this perspective, environmental and racial justice are intersectional qualities that cannot be attained separately one from the other. All such arguments raise the possibility that the very categories of a Western, male, and white epistemology both make the population-resource-environment nexus and predetermine our failure to unpick the problems and tensions of that nexus.

If measures of environmental quality and climatic change are one element in the feedback loops being posited by proponents and critics of security demographics, they form the core of the distinct but overlapping discussion of population in the age of climate change/the Anthropocene that forms the other main new direction in the debate over the past few decades. As long ago as 1968, Ehrlich asked whether our tendency to litter the globe with atmospheric "junk" could alter climate. A generation later, this speculative aside has become a major area of inquiry, seeking to model how population is interlinked with global climate change. As such, where Ehrlich's attention to "the environment" might be seen as primarily ecological or ecosystemic with a small climatic element, the balance of scrutiny has now switched to the atmospheric and then beyond that to how anthropogenically driven temperature changes will interact with other climatic systems (notably oceans) to change the habitability of the earth. This is by no means something where one simple variable—population size—is correlated with another—carbon dioxide—and a causal connection is assumed. On the contrary, models look not just at population size but also at the key drivers of twenty-first-century demographic change, such as household size, age of population, and urbanization, showing how each trend will have discernible and often contradictory impacts on global climatic regimes. The impetus to undertake this work can be connected back to the security demographic: governments fear that population change will interact with climate change via resource and food demands, each of which will push our biophysical reliance on the earth beyond its limits. This is the doomsday scenario of a possible "perfect storm" of ecological, resource, and demographic interactions.

There are fundamental lineages between perfect storm arguments and those that kicked off the Malthus wars two centuries earlier. How have the debates of the past few decades changed our understanding of the connection of population, resources, and the environment? First, the nature of the object of study called "population" has mutated. We saw in part 4 how the debates of the postwar era nuanced the analysis by moving beyond demographic totals and growth rates to consider technology and affluence as key co-variables in determining the environmental impact of a population. Recent decades have taken this need to nuance the discussion of population further by considering the age and gender structure of a population, its rates of urbanization, and its household size and structure as key variables in its impact on the environment. Relatedly, arguments that feminist, indigenous, and racialized knowledges need to be taken seriously in framing what population is, in what sense it may be a "problem," and what it is to analyze its intersections with the environment have gained increasing traction. Taking some of the key tools of demographers and critical social scientists into account, then, has changed how the population-resource nexus is framed. Second, the nature of the concern about what ceilings or thresholds population increase (in whatever form) might overtop in planetary biophysical systems has changed. Where Ehrlich and colleagues were focused on ecosystem services, recent decades have attended to the atmosphere and unintended anthropogenic forcing of global and smaller-scale climatic regimes. Reciprocal causations between a population size, structure, and distribution, on the one hand, and secular climatic changes and shorter-term alterations in weather variability and extreme events, on the other hand, are at the core of current debates. To understand these interactions, there has been a strong drive to build complex feedback models and to quantify population-environment interactions. Of course, such ambitions are in a direct lineage from Malthus's logic of ratios, but their sophistication is an order of magnitude greater even than that which was exhibited in the debates of the mid-twentieth century, whose limits to growth models look remarkably crude today. Clearly, the intellectual sophistication, conceptual rigor, numerical ambition, and political sensitivities of debates around population, resources, and the natural environment remain as vibrant today as they were in either Malthus's moment of the 1790s or the Malthusian moment of the postwar era.

DOCUMENT 5.1

FROM JESSICA TUCHMAN MATHEWS, "REDEFINING SECURITY" (1989)

GLOBAL DEVELOPMENTS NOW SUGGEST THE NEED FOR BROADENING [the] definition of national security to include resource, environmental and demographic issues. [...]

Moreover, for the first time in its history, mankind is rapidly—if inadvertently—altering the basic physiology of the planet. Global changes currently taking place in the chemical composition of the atmosphere, in the genetic diversity of species inhabiting the planet, and in the cycling of vital chemicals through the oceans, atmosphere, biosphere and geosphere, are unprecedented in both their pace and scale. If left unchecked, the consequences will be profound and, unlike familiar types of local damage, irreversible.

Population growth lies at the core of most environmental trends. [...] The relationship linking population levels and the resource base is complex. Policies, technologies and institutions determine the impact of population growth. These factors can spell the difference between a highly stressed, degraded environment and one that can provide for many more people. [...]

[...]

Jessica Tuchman Mathews, "Redefining Security," *Foreign Affairs* 68, no. 2 (Spring 1989): 162–77. Reproduced by permission from the Council on Foreign Relations.

Environmental decline occasionally leads directly to conflict, especially when scarce water resources must be shared. Generally, however, its impact on nations' security is felt in the downward pull on economic performance and, therefore, on political stability. The underlying cause of turmoil is often ignored; instead governments address the poverty and instability that are its results.

If such resource and population trends are not addressed, as they are not in so much of the world today, the resulting economic decline leads to frustration, resentment, domestic unrest or even civil war. Human suffering and turmoil make countries ripe for authoritarian government or external subversion. Environmental refugees spread the disruption across national borders. Haiti, a classic example, was once so forested and fertile that it was known as the "Pearl of the Antilles." Now deforested, soil erosion in Haiti is so rapid that some farmers believe stones grow in their fields, while bulldozers are needed to clear the streets of Port-au-Prince of topsoil that flows down from the mountains in the rainy season. While many of the boat people who fled to the United States left because of the brutality of the Duvalier[1] regimes, there is no question that—and this is not widely recognized—many Haitians were forced into the boats by the impossible task of farming bare rock. Until Haiti is reforested, it will never be politically stable.

A different kind of environmental concern has arisen from mankind's new ability to alter the environment on a planetary scale. [. . .] The lesson is this: current knowledge of planetary mechanisms is so scanty that the possibility of surprise, perhaps quite nasty surprise, must be rated rather high. The greatest risk may well come from a completely unanticipated direction. We lack both crucial knowledge and early warning systems.

[. . .] The human species already consumes or destroys 40 percent of all the energy produced by terrestrial photosynthesis, that is, 40 percent of the food energy potentially available to living things on land. While that fraction may be sustainable, it is doubtful that it could keep pace with the expected doubling of the world's population. Human use of 80 percent of the planet's potential productivity does not seem compatible with the continued functioning of the biosphere as we know it. The expected rate of species loss would have risen from perhaps a few each day to several hundred a day. The pollution and toxic waste burden would likely prove unmanageable. Tropical forests would have largely disappeared, and arable land, a vital resource in a world of ten billion people, would be rapidly decreasing due to soil degradation. In short, sweeping change in economic production systems is not a choice but a necessity.

[. . .]

Reflecting on the discovery of atomic energy, Albert Einstein noted "everything changed." And indeed, nuclear fission became the dominant force—military, geopolitical, and even psychological and social—of the ensuing decades. In the same sense, the driving force of the coming decades may well be environmental change. Man is still utterly dependent on the natural world but now has for the first time the ability to alter it, rapidly and on a global scale. Because of that difference, Einstein's verdict that "we shall require a substantially new manner of thinking if mankind is to survive"[2] still seems apt.

NOTES

1 François and Jean-Claude Duvalier were father and son authoritarian presidents of Haiti from 1957 to 1986.
2 This is often ascribed to Einstein's 1949 essay "Why Socialism?" from the first issue of *Monthly Review*. I cannot find that it is in this text.

DOCUMENT 5.2

FROM ROBERT D. KAPLAN, "THE COMING ANARCHY" (1994)

WEST AFRICA IS BECOMING THE SYMBOL OF WORLDWIDE DEMOgraphic, environmental, and societal stress, in which criminal anarchy emerges as the real "strategic" danger. Disease, overpopulation, unprovoked crime, scarcity of resources, refugee migrations, the increasing erosion of nation-states and international borders, and the empowerment of private armies, security firms, and international drug cartels are now most tellingly demonstrated through a West African prism. West Africa provides an appropriate introduction to the issues, often extremely unpleasant to discuss, that will soon confront our civilization.

[...]

Sierra Leone is a microcosm of what is occurring, albeit in a more tempered and gradual manner, throughout West Africa and much of the underdeveloped world: the withering away of central governments, the rise of tribal and regional domains, the unchecked spread of disease, and the growing pervasiveness of war. West Africa is reverting to the Africa of the Victorian

---

Robert D. Kaplan, "The Coming Anarchy: How Scarcity, Crime, Overpopulation, Tribalism, and Disease Are Rapidly Destroying the Social Fabric of Our Planet," *Atlantic Monthly*, February 1994. Reproduced with permission from Atlantic Media, Inc.

atlas. It consists now of a series of coastal trading posts, such as Freetown and Conakry, and an interior that, owing to violence, volatility, and disease, is again becoming, as Graham Greene once observed, "blank" and "unexplored." However, whereas Greene's vision implies a certain romance, as in the somnolent and charmingly seedy Freetown of his celebrated novel *The Heart of the Matter*,[1] it is Thomas Malthus, the philosopher of demographic doomsday, who is now the prophet of West Africa's future. And West Africa's future, eventually, will also be that of most of the rest of the world.

[...]

For a while the media will continue to ascribe riots and other violent upheavals abroad mainly to ethnic and religious conflict. But as these conflicts multiply, it will become apparent that something else is afoot, making more and more places like Nigeria, India, and Brazil ungovernable.

Mention The Environment or "diminishing natural resources" in foreign-policy circles and you meet a brick wall of skepticism or boredom. To conservatives especially, the very terms seem flaky. Public-policy foundations have contributed to the lack of interest, by funding narrowly focused environmental studies replete with technical jargon which foreign-affairs experts just let pile up on their desks.

It is time to understand The Environment for what it is: the national-security issue of the early twenty-first century. The political and strategic impact of surging populations, spreading disease, deforestation and soil erosion, water depletion, air pollution, and, possibly, rising sea levels in critical, overcrowded regions like the Nile Delta and Bangladesh—developments that will prompt mass migrations and, in turn, incite group conflicts—will be the core foreign-policy challenge from which most others will ultimately emanate, arousing the public and uniting assorted interests left over from the Cold War. In the twenty-first century water will be in dangerously short supply in such diverse locales as Saudi Arabia, Central Asia, and the southwestern United States. A war could erupt between Egypt and Ethiopia over Nile River water. Even in Europe tensions have arisen between Hungary and Slovakia over the damming of the Danube, a classic case of how environmental disputes fuse with ethnic and historical ones. The political scientist and erstwhile Clinton adviser Michael Mandelbaum has said, "We have a foreign policy today in the shape of a doughnut—lots of peripheral interests but nothing at the center." The environment, I will argue, is part of a terrifying array of problems that will define a new threat to our security, filling the hole in Mandelbaum's doughnut and allowing a post–Cold War foreign policy to emerge inexorably by need rather than by design.

Our Cold War foreign policy truly began with George F. Kennan's famous article, signed "X," published in *Foreign Affairs* in July of 1947. [. . .] It may be that our post–Cold War foreign policy will one day be seen to have had its beginnings in an even bolder and more detailed piece of written analysis: one that appeared in the journal International Security. The article, published in the fall of 1991 by Thomas Fraser Homer-Dixon, who is the head of the Peace and Conflict Studies Program at the University of Toronto, was titled "On the Threshold: Environmental Changes as Causes of Acute Conflict." Homer-Dixon has, more successfully than other analysts, integrated two hitherto separate fields—military-conflict studies and the study of the physical environment.

In Homer-Dixon's view, future wars and civil violence will often arise from scarcities of resources such as water, cropland, forests, and fish. Just as there will be environmentally driven wars and refugee flows, there will be environmentally induced praetorian regimes—or, as he puts it, "hard regimes." Countries with the highest probability of acquiring hard regimes, according to Homer-Dixon, are those that are threatened by a declining resource base yet also have "a history of state [read 'military'] strength." Candidates include Indonesia, Brazil, and, of course, Nigeria. Though each of these nations has exhibited democratizing tendencies of late, Homer-Dixon argues that such tendencies are likely to be superficial "epiphenomena" having nothing to do with long-term processes that include soaring populations and shrinking raw materials. Democracy is problematic; scarcity is more certain.

Indeed, the Saddam Husseins of the future will have more, not fewer, opportunities. In addition to engendering tribal strife, scarcer resources will place a great strain on many peoples who never had much of a democratic or institutional tradition to begin with. [. . .] Homer-Dixon writes, ominously, "Neo-Malthusians may underestimate human adaptability in today's environmental-social system, but as time passes their analysis may become ever more compelling."

NOTE

1 Greene's novel was published in 1948.

DOCUMENT 5.3

FROM JARED DIAMOND, *COLLAPSE: HOW SOCIETIES CHOOSE TO FAIL OR SUCCEED* (2005)

EAST AFRICA'S PEOPLE [...] OVERWHELMED US, WITH THEIR FRIENDLIness, warmth to our children, colorful clothes—and their sheer numbers. To read in the abstract about "the population explosion" is one thing; it is quite another thing to encounter, day after day, lines of African children along the roadside, many of them about the same size and age as my sons, calling out to passing tourist vehicles for a pencil that they could use in school. The impact of those numbers of people on the landscape is visible even along stretches of road where the people are off doing something else. In pastures the grass is sparse and grazed closely by herds of cattle, sheep, and goats. One sees fresh erosion gullies, in whose bottoms run streams brown with mud washed down from the denuded pastures.

[...]

Jared Diamond, *Collapse: How Societies Choose to Fail or Succeed* (2005), excerpt from chap. 10, "Malthus in Africa: Rwanda's Genocide." © 2005 by Jared Diamond. Used by permission of Viking Books, an imprint of Penguin Publishing Group, a division of Penguin Random House LLC. All rights reserved.

In recent decades, Rwanda and neighboring Burundi have become synonymous in our minds with two things: high population, and genocide. [...]

The usual accounts of the genocides in Rwanda and Burundi portray them as the result of pre-existing ethnic hatreds fanned by cynical politicians for their own ends. [...] But there is also evidence that other considerations contributed as well. [...] Especially puzzling, if one believes that there was nothing more to the genocide than Hutu-versus-Tutsi ethnic hatred fanned by politicians, are events in northwestern Rwanda. There, in a community where virtually everybody was Hutu and there was only a single Tutsi, mass killings still took place—of Hutu by other Hutu.

[...] these facts illustrate why we need to search for other contributing factors in addition to ethnic hatred.

To begin our search, let's again consider Rwanda's high population density that I mentioned previously. Rwanda (and Burundi) was already densely populated in the 19th century before European arrival, because of its twin advantages of moderate rainfall and an altitude too high for malaria and the tsetse fly. Rwanda's population subsequently grew, albeit with ups and downs, at an average rate of over 3% per year, for essentially the same reasons as in neighboring Kenya and Tanzania (New World crops, public health, medicine, and stable political borders). By 1990, even after the killings and mass exilings of the previous decades, Rwanda's average population density was 760 people per square mile, higher than that of the United Kingdom (610) and approaching that of Holland (950). But the United Kingdom and Holland have highly efficient mechanized agriculture, such that only a few percent of the population working as farmers can produce much of the food for everyone else, plus some surplus food for export. Rwandan agriculture is much less efficient and unmechanized; farmers depend on handheld hoes, picks, and machetes; and most people have to remain farmers, producing little or no surplus that could support others.

As Rwanda's population rose after independence, the country carried on with its traditional agricultural methods and failed to modernize, to introduce more productive crop varieties, to expand its agricultural exports, or to institute effective family planning. Instead, the growing population was accommodated just by clearing forests and draining marshes to gain new farmland, shortening fallow periods, and trying to extract two or three consecutive crops from a field within one year. [...] By 1985, all arable land outside of national parks was being cultivated. As both population and agricultural production increased, per-capita food production rose from 1966 to 1981 but then dropped back to the level where it had stood in the early 1960s. That, exactly, is the Malthusian dilemma: more food, but also more people, hence no improvement in food per person.

[. . .] By the late 1980s famines began to reappear. In 1989 there were more severe food shortages resulting from a drought, brought on by a combination of regional or global climate change plus local effects of deforestation.

[. . .]

Even before 1994, Rwanda was experiencing rising levels of violence and theft, perpetrated especially by hungry landless young people without off-farm income. When one compares crime rates for people of age 21–25 among different parts of Rwanda, most of the regional differences prove to be correlated statistically with population density and per-capita availability of calories: high population densities and worse starvation were associated with more crime.

[. . .]

I'm accustomed to thinking of population pressure, human environmental impacts, and drought as ultimate causes, which make people chronically desperate and are like the gunpowder inside the powder keg. One also needs a proximate cause: a match to light the keg. In most areas of Rwanda, that match was ethnic hatred whipped up by politicians cynically concerned with keeping themselves in power. [. . .]

[. . .] it is justifiable to reject the simplistic view that population pressure was the single cause of the Rwandan genocide. Other factors did contribute [. . .]: regardless of the order of their importance, those other factors included Rwanda's history of Tutsi domination of Hutu, Tutsi large-scale killings of Hutu in Burundi and small-scale ones in Rwanda, Tutsi invasions of Rwanda, Rwanda's economic crisis and its exacerbation by drought and world factors (especially by falling coffee prices and World Bank austerity measures), hundreds of thousands of desperate young Rwandan men displaced as refugees into settlement camps and ripe for recruitment by militias, and competition among Rwanda's rival political groups willing to stoop to anything to retain power. Population pressure joined with those other factors.

Finally, one should not misconstrue a role of population pressure among the Rwandan genocide's causes to mean that population pressure automatically leads to genocide anywhere around the world. To those who would object that there is not a necessary link between Malthusian population pressure and genocide, I would answer, "Of course!" Countries can be over-populated without descending into genocide, as exemplified by Bangladesh (relatively free of large-scale killings since its genocidal slaughters of 1971) as well as by the Netherlands and multi-ethnic Belgium, despite all three of those countries being more densely populated than Rwanda. Conversely, genocide can arise for ultimate reasons other than overpopulation, as illustrated by Hitler's efforts to exterminate Jews and Gypsies during World War II, or by the genocide of the 1970s in Cambodia, with only one-sixth of Rwanda's population density.

Instead, I conclude that population pressure was one of the important factors behind the Rwandan genocide, that Malthus's worst-case scenario may sometimes be realized, and that Rwanda may be a distressing model of that scenario in operation. Severe problems of overpopulation, environmental impact, and climate change cannot persist indefinitely: sooner or later they are likely to resolve themselves, whether in the manner of Rwanda or in some other manner not of our devising, if we don't succeed in solving them by our own actions. In the case of Rwanda's collapse we can put faces and motives on the unpleasant solution; I would guess that similar motives were operating, without our being able to associate them with faces, in the collapses of Easter Island, Mangareva, and the Maya. [. . .] Similar motives may operate again in the future, in some other countries that, like Rwanda, fail to solve their underlying problems. They may operate again in Rwanda itself, where population today is still increasing at 3% per year, women are giving birth to their first child at age 15, the average family has between five and eight children, and a visitor's sense is of being surrounded by a sea of children.

DOCUMENT 5.4

FROM JACK A. GOLDSTONE, "THE NEW POPULATION BOMB: THE FOUR MEGATRENDS THAT WILL CHANGE THE WORLD" (2010)

FORTY TWO YEARS AGO, THE BIOLOGIST PAUL EHRLICH WARNED IN *The Population Bomb* that mass starvation would strike in the 1970s and 1980s, with the world's population growth outpacing the production of food and other critical resources. Thanks to innovations and efforts such as the "green revolution" in farming and the widespread adoption of family planning, Ehrlich's worst fears did not come to pass. In fact, since the 1970s, global economic output has increased and fertility has fallen dramatically, especially in developing countries.

[. . .]

But twenty-first-century international security will depend less on how many people inhabit the world than on how the global population is composed and distributed: where populations are declining and where they are growing,

---

Jack A. Goldstone, "The New Population Bomb: The Four Megatrends That Will Change the World," *Foreign Affairs* 89, no. 1 (January/February 2010): 31–43. Reproduced by permission from the Council on Foreign Relations.

which countries are relatively older and which are more youthful, and how demographics will influence population movements across regions. [...]

[There are] four historic shifts that will fundamentally alter the world's population over the next four decades: the relative demographic weight of the world's developed countries will drop by nearly 25 percent, shifting economic power to the developing nations; the developed countries' labor forces will substantially age and decline, constraining economic growth in the developed world and raising the demand for immigrant workers; most of the world's expected population growth will increasingly be concentrated in today's poorest, youngest, and most heavily Muslim countries, which have a dangerous lack of quality education, capital, and employment opportunities; and, for the first time in history, most of the world's population will become urbanized, with the largest urban centers being in the world's poorest countries, where policing, sanitation, and health care are often scarce.

Taken together, these trends will pose challenges every bit as alarming as those noted by Ehrlich. Coping with them will require nothing less than a major reconsideration of the world's basic global governance structures.

[...]

According to the research of Richard Cincotta and other political demographers, countries with younger populations are especially prone to civil unrest and are less able to create or sustain democratic institutions. And the more heavily urbanized, the more such countries are likely to experience Dickensian poverty and anarchic violence. In good times, a thriving economy might keep urban residents employed and governments flush with sufficient resources to meet their needs. More often, however, sprawling and impoverished cities are vulnerable to crime lords, gangs, and petty rebellions. Thus, the rapid urbanization of the developing world in the decades ahead might bring, in exaggerated form, problems similar to those that urbanization brought to nineteenth-century Europe. Back then, cyclical employment, inadequate policing, and limited sanitation and education often spawned widespread labor strife, periodic violence, and sometimes—as in the 1820s, the 1830s, and 1848—even revolutions.

International terrorism might also originate in fast-urbanizing developing countries (even more than it already does). With their neighborhood networks, access to the Internet and digital communications technology, and concentration of valuable targets, sprawling cities offer excellent opportunities for recruiting, maintaining, and hiding terrorist networks.

[...]

Averting this century's potential dangers will require sweeping measures. [...] today's population bomb is the product less of absolute growth in the world's population than of changes in its age and distribution. Policymakers must therefore adapt today's global governance institutions to the new realities of the aging of the industrialized world, the concentration of the world's economic and population growth in developing countries, and the increase in international immigration.

During the Cold War, Western strategists divided the world into a "First World," of democratic industrialized countries; a "Second World," of communist industrialized countries; and a "Third World," of developing countries. [...] Unfortunately, because they ignore current global demographic trends, these views will be obsolete within a few decades. A better approach would be to consider a different three-world order, with a new First World of the aging industrialized nations of North America, Europe, and Asia's Pacific Rim (including Japan, Singapore, South Korea, and Taiwan, as well as China after 2030, by which point the one-child policy will have produced significant aging); a Second World comprising fast-growing and economically dynamic countries with a healthy mix of young and old inhabitants (such as Brazil, Iran, Mexico, Thailand, Turkey, and Vietnam, as well as China until 2030); and a Third World of fast-growing, very young, and increasingly urbanized countries with poorer economies and often weak governments.

To cope with the instability that will likely arise from the new Third World's urbanization, economic strife, lawlessness, and potential terrorist activity, the aging industrialized nations of the new First World must build effective alliances with the growing powers of the new Second World and together reach out to Third World nations. Second World powers will be pivotal in the twenty-first century not just because they will drive economic growth and consume technologies and other products engineered in the First World; they will also be central to international security and cooperation. The realities of religion, culture, and geographic proximity mean that any peaceful and productive engagement by the First World of Third World countries will have to include the open cooperation of Second World countries.

[...]

Never since 1800 has a majority of the world's economic growth occurred outside of Europe, the United States, and Canada. Never have so many people in those regions been over 60 years old. And never have low-income countries' populations been so young and so urbanized. But such will be the world's demography in the twenty-first century. The strategic and economic policies of the twentieth century are obsolete, and it is time to find new ones.

DOCUMENT 5.5

FROM JOHN BEDDINGTON, "PROFESSOR SIR JOHN BEDDINGTON'S SPEECH AT SDUK 09" (2009)

[L]AST YEAR IS THE LOWEST LEVEL OF RESERVES THAT WE HAVE HAD as a proportion of our consumption in years, since 1970 and actually since records were taken of this sort.

[...]

That means that we've got somewhere like reserves of around 14% of our consumption, that implies, give or take, 38 or 39 days of food reserves if we don't grow any more.

[...] Is that a problem? Well the answer is yes it is going to be a problem. We saw the food spike last year; prices going up by something in the order of 300%, rice went up by 400%, we saw food riots, we saw major issues for the poorest in the world, in the sense that the organisations like the World Food Programme did not have sufficient money to buy food on the open market and actually use it to feed the poorest of the poor.

John Beddington, "Professor John Beddington's Speech at SDUK 09," 2009, https://www.gren.org.uk/resources/Beddington%27sSpeechatSDUK09.pdf. Contains public sector information licensed under the Open Government Licence v3.0.

So this is a major problem. You can see the catastrophic decline in those reserves, over the last five years or so, indicates that we actually have a problem; we're not growing enough food, we're not able to put stuff into the reserves. And so what I expect to occur is significant volatility in food prices with the consequent problems for the poorest.

So, what are the drivers? I am going to go through them now very briefly.

First of all, population growth. World population grows by six million every month—greater than the size of the UK population every year. Between now and . . . I am going to focus on the year 2030 and the reason I am going to focus on 2030 is that I feel that some of the climate change discussions focusing on 2100 don't actually grip. In 2100, I would be 155 years of age, my grandchildren would be fairly substantial and it doesn't kind of grip. But by 2030 (I won't say how old I will be then but older than I am now by 21 years, the acute amongst you will deduce), I hope my grandchildren will start to have children and I think 2030 focuses it. I am going to look at 2030 because that's when a whole series of events come together.

By 2030, looking at population terms, you are looking at the global population increasing from a little over six billion at the moment to about eight billion. What is actually happening to that extra population?

First of all, there is a second trend which is to do with population, which is urbanisation. [. . .] for the first time in 2009, the urban population exceeded the rural population. And [. . .] round about by 2030, the urban population is going to be substantially greater than the rural population: major issues for land use, major issues for providing that large urban population with food, with water and with energy. But the population will be distributed very differently to anything we've seen before. So, urbanisation is the second trend.

Now, the other trend which is actually good [. . .] is that, despite global recession, significant proportions of the developing world are actually moving out of what would be abject poverty and we are seeing a creation of what you might think of as middle class, particularly in India and China. Now that lifting from poverty is part of the Millennium Development Goals, we wish to see the world out of poverty, but as the world moves out of poverty, consumption patterns change.

[. . .] in particular, we are going to see an increase in the demand for food. Looking at the demand for food, you are going to see major changes but particularly in the demand for livestock—meat and dairy. Now, this is not the West that is doing this. This is largely coming from the developing world as they move from very, very simple diets based on very simple agricultural products to more complex agricultural products, including livestock. [These are] perfectly reasonable and legitimate aims for countries moving out of abject poverty.

Quite clearly, there are issues to the individual, within the UK, about to what extent one eats high production diets, for example like large steaks. Someone gave me an indication that a steak meal has used as much carbon as actually driving a large Range Rover from London to Birmingham, so the next time you're sitting down to your steak and chips, ponder that!

By 2030, the demand for food is going to be increased by about 50%. Can we do it? One of the questions. There is a major food security issue by 2030. We've got to somehow produce 50% more by that time.

The second issue I want to focus on is the availability of fresh water. [. . .] the fresh water available per head of the world population is around 25% of what it was in 1960. To give you some idea of this; there are enormous potential shortages in certain parts of the world. China for example, two weeks ago, was actually involved in seeding clouds to address a drought in China. China has something like 23% of the world's population and 11% of the world's water. [. . .] One in three people are already facing water shortages and the total world demand for water is predicted to increase by 30% by 2030. So, we've got food—expectation of demand increase of 50% by 2030, we've got water—expectation of demand increase of 30% by 2030. And in terms of what it looks like, we have real issues of global water security.

[. . .]

Now, the third one [issue] I want to focus on is energy and, driven by the population increase that I talked about, the urbanisation I talked about and indeed the movement out of poverty, the expectation is that primary energy demand is going to increase. [. . .] [E]nergy demand is actually increasing and going to hit something of the order of a 50% increase, again by 2030.

Now, if that were not enough . . . those are three things that are coming together. What will the world be like when that happens? But we also have, of course, the issue of climate change. [. . .]

[. . .]

The other area that really worries me in terms of climate change and the potential for positive feedbacks and also for interactions with food is ocean acidification. [. . .] This is actually simple physics and chemistry. Knowing the level of CO_2 in the atmosphere, knowing the level of interaction that will occur with the ocean with that level of CO_2 in the atmosphere, this is what is going to happen. [. . .]

[. . .]

So, this is cheerful stuff, isn't it? What I have said, which I guess is why I have been talking to the media a bit, is I have coined the point that we have got to deal with increased demand for energy, increased demand for food, increased demand for water, and we've got to do that while mitigating and adapting to climate change. And we have but 21 years to do it.

And there are still enormous uncertainties remaining. Let me just focus on some of these which are actually relevant to the agendas of food, water and energy security. The Sahelian drought has been going for some time, when will it break? How significant will the CO_2 and rainfall changes we know the climate change models are going to predict affect Africa and Asia. The monsoons, hugely important for feeding vast parts of the developing world and making them viable, will they weaken or strengthen? We don't know. What is the effect of glacial melt? We can see some effects of it but we are going to get events which drive major climate events in our world.

[. . .]

Now, as I say, not exactly an optimistic picture. Are we all doomed? Is there any hope? Whenever I interview, people always mention Thomas Malthus and am I now a second Thomas Malthus? Not quite because I am reasonably optimistic. I think [the] key thing here is we've got to recognise there is a problem and the reason I raise the food, the water security issues is that they are going to be hitting very early. Climate change is there and is a major issue, but we've got to work on these problems in an interrelated way. We talked about biofuels. Biofuels was a reasonable attempt to try and make transport greener. But there are significant problems in the use of food stocks for biofuels on food security issues. We can't ignore that. We can't ignore food, we can't ignore water, we can't ignore energy demands. What the world of 2030 will look like if we don't mitigate these things?

First of all, with demand significantly exceeding supply, the poorest will suffer. Prices of food, prices of energy and water prices will go up. Water in particularly is currently a free good. With the urbanisation we are seeing, it is unimaginable that water will be free to the poor farmers of the world. The cities will have more purchasing power and more political power, which will add to the fact that we will move more populations to migrate to the cities due to water shortage and so on.

So are there any grounds for optimism? I think the grounds for optimism are that we recognise we have a problem, we have enormous ingenuity, the ability to generate solutions to that.

[. . .]

I think that what is needed [. . .] is a really coordinated group of scientific advisers that can actually say things that are not helpful, that actually are incredibly inconvenient to policy makers. We need that. [. . .] We need to move forward in a cooperative way; cooperation and not competition is the way.

I will leave you with some key questions. Can nine billion people be fed? Can we cope with the demands in the future on water? Can we provide enough energy? Can we do it, all that, while mitigating and adapting to climate change? And can we do all that in 21 years time? That's when these things are going to start hitting in a really big way. We need to act now. We need investment in science and technology, and all the other ways of treating very seriously these major problems. 2030 is not very far away.

DOCUMENT 5.6

FROM JOEL E. COHEN, "POPULATION AND CLIMATE CHANGE" (2010)

THE INTERACTIONS BETWEEN CLIMATE AND THE HUMAN POPULATION depend on economics and culture. I find it useful to visualize these interactions by means of a regular tetrahedron with a triangular base and a point on top. The three corners of the base refer to economics, the environment, and culture. The vertex refers to population. If you are an economist, or anthropologist, or ecologist, please feel free to rotate the tetrahedron to put your field at the top. [...]

[...]

Climate changes will affect people's health, mortality, and migration directly and, through effects on livelihood, indirectly. Relman et al. (2008, xii) warned, "The warming of the Earth is already contributing to the worldwide burden of disease and premature deaths, and is anticipated to influence the transmission dynamics and geographic distribution of malaria, dengue, tick-borne diseases, cholera, and other diarrheal diseases."[1] Dyson (2005) warned of the possibility of "several negative changes occurring simultaneously and to cumulative adverse effect."[2] However, specifying the

---

Joel E. Cohen, "Population and Climate Change," *Proceedings of the American Philosophical Society* 154, no. 2 (2010): 158–82. Reprinted with permission of the American Philosophical Society.

consequences more precisely is "impossible because simply not enough is known about what exactly will happen in terms of changing biophysical conditions and how the populations of the future will be able to cope with these changes. . . . [A]ssessment of likely future vulnerability is very difficult and probably presents the biggest research gap for assessing the dangers associated with climate change" (Lutz 2009).[3]

[. . .]

To review, the four broad dimensions [. . .] interact with one another in all directions and on many time-scales. From 2010 to 2050, the human population is likely to grow bigger, more slowly, older, and more urban. It is projected that by 2050 more than 2.6 billion people (almost 94% of global urban growth) will be added to the urban population in today's developing countries. That works out to 1.26 million additional urban people in today's developing countries every week from 2010 to 2050.

Humans alter the climate by emitting greenhouse gases, by altering planetary albedo, and by altering atmospheric components. Between 1900 and 2000, humans' emissions of carbon into the atmosphere increased fifteenfold, while the numbers of people increased less than fourfold. Population growth alone, with constant rates of emissions per person, could not account for the increase in the carbon emissions to the atmosphere. The world economy grew sixteenfold in the twentieth century, accompanied by enormous increases in the burning of gas, oil, and coal. In the last quarter of the twentieth century, population grew much faster in developing countries than in high-income countries, and, compared with population growth, the growth of carbon emissions to the atmosphere was even faster in developing countries than in high-income countries. The ratio of emissions-to-population growth rates was 2.8 in developing countries compared with 1.6 in high-income countries. Emissions of CO_2 and other greenhouse gases are influenced by the sizes and density of settlements, the sizes of households, and the ages of householders. Between 2010 and 2050, these demographic factors are anticipated to change substantially. Therefore demography will play a substantial role in the dynamics of climate changes.

Climate changes affect many aspects of the living environment, including human settlements, food production, and diseases. These changes will affect poor people more severely than rich, and poor nations more severely than rich. Yet not enough is known to predict quantitatively many details that will matter enormously to future people and other species.

Three kinds of responses are related to demographic issues that affect climate changes: universal secondary education, voluntary contraception and maternal health services, and smarter urban design and construction. These responses may prevent, reduce, or ameliorate the impacts of climate changes. They are as relevant to rich countries as to poor, though in ways that are as different as are rich countries and poor. They are desirable in their own right because they improve the lives of the people they affect directly; and they are desirable for their beneficial effects on the larger society and globe. They are effective responses to the twin challenges of reducing poverty and reducing greenhouse gas emissions.

NOTES

1. David Relman, Margaret Hamburg, Eileen Choffnes, and Alison Mack, *Global Climate Change and Extreme Weather Events: Understanding the Contributions to Infectious Disease Emergence* (Washington, DC: National Academies Press, 2008).
2. Tim Dyson, "On Development, Demography and Climate Change: The End of the World as We Know It?" *Population and Environment* 27 (2005): 117–49.
3. Wolfgang Lutz, "What Can Demographers Contribute to Understanding the Link between Population and Climate Change?" *Popnet Population Network Newsletter* 41 (2009/2010): 1–2.

DOCUMENT 5.7

FROM BRIAN O'NEILL ET AL., "GLOBAL DEMOGRAPHIC TRENDS AND FUTURE CARBON EMISSIONS" (2010)

STATISTICAL ANALYSES OF HISTORICAL DATA SUGGEST THAT POPULA-tion growth has been one driver of emissions growth over the past several decades and that urbanization, aging, and changes in household size can also affect energy use and emissions. Demographers expect major changes in these dimensions of populations over the coming decades. Global population could grow by more than 3 billion by mid-century, with most of that difference accounted for by growing urban populations. Aging will occur in most regions, a result of declines in both fertility and mortality, and is expected to be particularly rapid in regions like China that have recently experienced sharp falls in fertility. The number of people per household is also declining as populations age and living arrangements shift away from multigeneration households toward nuclear families.

Brian C. O'Neill, Michael Dalton, Regina Fuchs, Leiwen Jiang, Shonali Pachauri, and Katarina Zigova, "Global Demographic Trends and Future Carbon Emissions," *Proceedings of the National Academy of Sciences* 107, no. 41 (2010): 17521–26. Reproduced with the permission of the National Academy of Sciences.

Despite these expectations, explicit analysis of the effect of demographic change on future emissions has been extremely limited. Early exploratory analyses considered only population size or total numbers of households and used simple multiplicative models that did not account for important relationships between population and economic and technological factors. Furthermore, these early models used little or no regional disaggregation, an important consideration given that, with some exceptions including the United States, population growth tends to be highest where per capita emissions are lowest.

More recently, a large emissions scenario literature has developed that informs a wide range of climate change analysis and related policy discussions. [. . .] Although nearly all scenarios include assumptions about future population growth, none has explicitly investigated the separate effect of demographic influences on emissions, with the exception of a few studies at the country level.

Here, we assess the global implications of demographic change by developing a set of economic growth, energy use, and emissions scenarios using an energy–economic growth model, the Population-Environment-Technology model (PET).

[. . .]

Results show that the effects of changes in population composition can have a significant influence on emissions in particular regions, separate from the effect of changes in population size. Aging can reduce emissions in the long term by up to 20%, particularly in industrialized country regions. Aging affects emissions in the PET model primarily through its influence on labor supply. In the model, aging populations are associated with lower labor productivity or labor force participation rates at older ages, which (ceteris paribus) leads to slower economic growth. In contrast, urbanization can lead to an increase in projected emissions by more than 25%, particularly in developing country regions, also mainly through effects on labor supply. The higher productivity of urban labor evident in the household surveys implies that urbanization tends to increase economic growth. Although other studies find that, controlling for income, urban living can be more energy efficient, survey data for urban households include income effects and therefore result in increased emissions.

[. . .]

Results also show that if population were to follow the low path rather than the medium in the B2 scenario,[1] emissions would decrease significantly, with a global reduction of 1.4 GtC/y[2] in 2050 and 5.1 GtC/y in 2100. However, if population were to follow the high projection rather than the medium, global emissions would be increased by 1.7 GtC/y in 2050 and 7.3 GtC/y in 2100.

[. . .] Our results also show that reduced population growth could make a significant contribution to global emissions reductions. Several analyses have estimated how much emissions would have to be reduced by 2050 to meet long-term policy goals such as avoiding warming of more than 2°c or preventing a doubling of CO_2 concentrations through implementation of a portfolio of mitigation measures. [. . .] Our estimate that following a lower population path could reduce emissions 1.4–2.5 GtC/y by 2050 is equivalent to 16–29% of the emission reductions necessary to achieve these goals. [. . .] By the end of the century, the effect of slower population growth would be even more significant, reducing total emissions from fossil fuel use by 37–41% across the two scenarios.

NOTES

1. The authors here refer to that of the 2007 report of the Intergovernmental Panel for Climate Change.
2. GtC/y = billion tons of carbon per year.

DOCUMENT 5.8

FROM PAUL J. CRUTZEN, "GEOLOGY OF MANKIND" (2002)

FOR THE PAST THREE CENTURIES, THE EFFECTS OF HUMANS ON THE global environment have escalated. Because of these anthropogenic emissions of carbon dioxide, global climate may depart significantly from natural behaviour for many millennia to come. It seems appropriate to assign the term "Anthropocene" to the present, in many ways human-dominated, geological epoch, supplementing the Holocene—the warm period of the past 10–12 millennia. The Anthropocene could be said to have started in the latter part of the eighteenth century, when analyses of air trapped in polar ice showed the beginning of growing global concentrations of carbon dioxide and methane. This date also happens to coincide with James Watt's design of the steam engine in 1784.

[...]

The rapid expansion of mankind in numbers and per capita exploitation of Earth's resources has continued apace. During the past three centuries, the human population has increased tenfold to more than 6 billion and is expected to reach 10 billion in this century. The methane-producing cattle

---

Paul J. Crutzen, "Geology of Mankind," *Nature* 415, no. 23 (2002): 23. Reproduced by permission of Springer Nature © 2002.

population has risen to 1.4 billion. About 30–50% of the planet's land surface is exploited by humans. Tropical rainforests disappear at a fast pace, releasing carbon dioxide and strongly increasing species extinction. Dam building and river diversion have become commonplace. More than half of all accessible fresh water is used by mankind. Fisheries remove more than 25% of the primary production in upwelling ocean regions and 35% in the temperate continental shelf. Energy use has grown 16-fold during the twentieth century, causing 160 million tonnes of atmospheric sulphur dioxide emissions per year, more than twice the sum of its natural emissions. More nitrogen fertilizer is applied in agriculture than is fixed naturally in all terrestrial ecosystems; nitric oxide production by the burning of fossil fuel and biomass also overrides natural emissions. Fossil-fuel burning and agriculture have caused substantial increases in the concentrations of "greenhouse" gases—carbon dioxide by 30% and methane by more than 100%—reaching their highest levels over the past 400 millennia, with more to follow.

So far, these effects have largely been caused by only 25% of the world population.

[. . .]

Unless there is a global catastrophe—a meteorite impact, a world war or a pandemic—mankind will remain a major environmental force for many millennia. A daunting task lies ahead for scientists and engineers to guide society towards environmentally sustainable management during the era of the Anthropocene. [. . .] At this stage, however, we are still largely treading on *terra incognita*.

DOCUMENT 5.9

FROM JOHAN ROCKSTRÖM ET AL., "PLANETARY BOUNDARIES: EXPLORING THE SAFE OPERATING SPACE FOR HUMANITY" (2009)

HUMAN ACTIVITIES INCREASINGLY INFLUENCE THE EARTH'S CLIMATE and ecosystems. The Earth has entered a new epoch, the Anthropocene, where humans constitute the dominant driver of change to the Earth System. The exponential growth of human activities is raising concern that further pressure on the Earth System could destabilize critical biophysical systems and trigger abrupt or irreversible environmental changes that would be deleterious or even catastrophic for human well-being. This is a profound dilemma because the predominant paradigm of social and economic development remains largely oblivious to the risk of human-induced environmental disasters at continental to planetary scales.

Here, we present a novel concept, planetary boundaries, for estimating a safe operating space for humanity with respect to the functioning of the Earth System. We make a first preliminary effort at identifying key Earth System

---

Johan Rockström, Will Steffen, Kevin Noone, Åsa Persson, F. Stuart Chapin III, Eric Lambin, Timothy M. Lenton, et al., "Planetary Boundaries: Exploring the Safe Operating Space for Humanity," *Ecology and Society* 14, no. 2 (2009): 32. © The authors. Reprinted here under a Creative Commons Attribution-NonCommercial 4.0 International License.

processes and attempt to quantify for each process the boundary level that should not be transgressed if we are to avoid unacceptable global environmental change.

[...]

Land-system change, driven primarily by agricultural expansion and intensification, contributes to global environmental change, with the risk of undermining human well-being and long-term sustainability. [...] Humanity may be reaching a point where further agricultural land expansion at a global scale may seriously threaten biodiversity and undermine regulatory capacities of the Earth System (by affecting the climate system and the hydrological cycle).

As a planetary boundary, we propose that no more than 15% of the global ice-free land surface should be converted to cropland. Because this boundary is a complex global aggregate, the spatial distribution and intensity of land-system change is critically important for the production of food, regulation of freshwater flows, and feedbacks to the functioning of the Earth System. In setting a terrestrial land boundary in terms of changes in cultivated area, we acknowledge the limitations this metric entails given the tight coupling with the other boundaries of P[hosphorus] and N[itrogen] use, rate of biodiversity loss, and global freshwater use.

For humanity to stay within this boundary, cropland should be allocated to the most productive areas, and processes that lead to the loss of productive land, such as land degradation, loss of irrigation water, and competition with land uses such as urban development or biofuel production, should be controlled. Demand-side processes may also need to be managed; these include diet, per capita food consumption, population size, and wastage in the food distribution chain. Agricultural systems that better mimic natural processes (e.g., complex agroecosystems) could also allow an extension of this boundary.

Although the effects of land-system change act as a slow variable that influences other boundaries, such as biodiversity, water, and climate, they can also trigger rapid changes at the continental scale when land-cover thresholds are crossed. For example, conversion of the Amazon rainforest into cultivated or grazing systems may reach a level where an additional small amount of conversion would tip the basin into an irreversible transformation to a semi-arid savanna. At the global scale, if enough high-productivity land is lost to degradation, biofuel production, or urbanization, food production may spread into marginal lands with lower yields and a higher risk of degradation. This may constitute a threshold where a small increment of additional food production may trigger an accelerating increase in cultivated land. [...]

About 12% of the global land surface is currently under crop cultivation. The allowed 3% expansion (approximately 400 Mha) to the level we propose as a land-system boundary will most likely be reached over the coming decades and includes suitable land that is not either currently cultivated or is under forest cover—e.g., abandoned cropland in Europe, North America, and the former Soviet Union and some areas of Africa's savannas and South America's cerrado.

[...]

Our preliminary analysis indicates that humanity has already transgressed three boundaries (climate change, the rate of biodiversity loss, and the rate of interference with the nitrogen cycle). There is significant uncertainty surrounding the duration over which boundaries can be transgressed before causing unacceptable environmental change and before triggering feedbacks that may result in crossing of thresholds that drastically reduce the ability to return within safe levels. [...]

There is little doubt, however, that the complexities of interconnected slow and fast processes and feedbacks in the Earth System provide humanity with a challenging paradox. On the one hand, these dynamics underpin the resilience that enables planet Earth to stay within a state conducive to human development. On the other hand, they lull us into a false sense of security because incremental change can lead to the unexpected crossing of thresholds that drive the Earth System, or significant subsystems, abruptly into states deleterious or even catastrophic to human well-being. The concept of planetary boundaries provides a framework for humanity to operate within this paradox.

DOCUMENT 5.10

COMMITTEE ON WOMEN, POPULATION, AND THE ENVIRONMENT, "WOMEN, POPULATION, AND THE ENVIRONMENT: CALL FOR A NEW APPROACH" (1993)

WE ARE TROUBLED BY RECENT STATEMENTS AND ANALYSES THAT single out population size and growth as a primary cause of global environmental degradation. [. . .]

[. . .]

Moreover, blaming global environmental degradation on population growth helps to lay the groundwork for the re-emergence and intensification of top-down, demographically driven population policies and programs which are deeply disrespectful of women, particularly women of color and their children.

In Southern countries, as well as in the United States and other northern countries, family planning programs have often been the main vehicles for

---

Committee on Women, Population, and the Environment, "Women, Population, and the Environment: Call for a New Approach," *Capitalism, Nature, Socialism* 4, no. 3 (1993): 125–27. Reproduced by permission of Taylor & Francis Ltd. Journal accessible at http://www.tandfonline.com.

dissemination of modern contraceptive technologies. However, because so many of their activities have been oriented toward population control rather than women's reproductive health needs [. . .] [p]opulation programs have frequently fostered a climate where coercion is permissible and racism acceptable.

Demographic data from around the world affirm that improvements in women's social, economic and health status and in general living standards are often keys to declines in population growth rates. We call on the world to recognize women's basic right to control their own bodies and to have access to power, resources, and reproductive health services to ensure that they can do so.

National governments, international agencies and other social institutions must take seriously their obligation to provide the essential prerequisites for women's development and freedom. These include:

1) Resources such as fair and equitable wages, land rights, appropriate technology, education, and access to credit.
2) An end to structural adjustment programs, imposed by the IMF, the World Bank and repressive governments, which sacrifice human dignity and basic needs for food, health and education to debt repayment and "free market," male-dominated models of unsustainable development.
3) Full participation in the decisions which affect our own lives, our families, our communities and our environment, and incorporation of women's knowledge systems and expertise to enrich these decisions.
4) Affordable, culturally appropriate, and comprehensive health care and health education for women of all ages and their families.
5) Access to safe, voluntary contraception and abortion as part of broader reproductive health services which also provide pre- and post-natal care, infertility services, and prevention and treatment of sexually transmitted diseases including HIV and AIDS.
6) Family support services that include child care, parental leave and elder care.
7) Reproductive health services and social programs that sensitize men to their parental responsibilities and to the need to stop gender inequalities and violence against women and children.

8) Speedy ratification and enforcement of the UN Convention on the Elimination of All Forms of Discrimination Against Women as well as other UN conventions on human rights.

People who want to see improvements in the relationship between the human population and the natural environment should work for the full range of women's rights; global demilitarization; redistribution of resources and wealth between and within nations; reduction of consumption rates of polluting products and processes and of non-renewable resources; reduction of chemical dependency in agriculture; and environmentally responsible technology. They should support local, national and international initiative for democracy, social justice and human rights.

DOCUMENT 5.11

FROM BETSY HARTMANN, "POPULATION, ENVIRONMENT AND SECURITY: A NEW TRINITY" (1998)

THE END OF THE COLD WAR HAS FORCED A REDEFINITION OF NATIONAL security in the United States. While "rogue states" such as Iraq have replaced the Soviet Union as the enemy, globalization has ushered in an era of more amorphous threats and environmental problems rank high among them. "Environment and security" are linked in a rapidly growing policy enterprise which involves the US Departments of State and Defense, the CIA, academic research institutes, private foundations and non-governmental organizations.

There are a number of reasons why "environment and security" is an idea whose time has come. Clearly, serious global environmental problems such as ozone depletion, global warming and pollution of the seas require new forms of international cooperation. Whether or not these should be the

---

Betsy Hartmann, "Population, Environment and Security: A New Trinity," *Environment and Urbanization* 10, no. 2 (1998): 113–28, https://journals.sagepub.com/doi/10.1177/095624789801000202. Reproduced with the permission of the author and the International Institute for Environment and Development.

purview of national security agencies is another question, given their tradition of competition, secrecy, and nationalism.

The environment and security field often focuses less on these legitimate concerns, however, than on a supposed causal relationship between population pressures, resource scarcities and intra-state conflict in the South. According to the main architect of this theory, Canadian political scientist Thomas Homer-Dixon, environmentally induced internal conflict, in turn, causes states to fragment or become more authoritarian, seriously disrupting international security.

The scarcity-conflict model is fast becoming conventional wisdom in foreign policy, population and environment circles, popularized and sensationalized by writers such as Robert Kaplan and Paul Kennedy.[1] Top State Department officials have blamed political strife in Haiti, Rwanda and Chiapas, Mexico in large part on population and environmental stresses.

Opportunism no doubt plays a role in making the model a fashionable trend. For the State Department, it is a convenient form of ideological spin control which masks the tragic human consequences of US support for military regimes and Duvalier[2] style dictatorships during the Cold War. For the military, it provides new rationales and missions to legitimize its multi-billion dollar budget. This also means more business for the large aerospace corporations suffering from the loss of Cold War defence contracts. Increasingly, the military-industrial complex is becoming a "military-environmental security complex."

[. . .] The population lobby has seized on it too, for several reasons. As birth rates continue to fall around the globe more rapidly than anticipated, it is hard to sustain the alarmism that fuels popular support or population control. Building an image of an overpopulated, environmentally degraded and violent Third World is politically expedient, especially as it feeds on popular fears that refugees from this chaos will storm our borders.

[. . .]

A psychoanalyst could have a field day with [demographic security theorists'] images of Africa—the dark, impenetrable rainforest as the sub-conscious; fears of women's uncontrolled fertility as a manifestation of sexual repression; Africa as the unknown, the other, the enemy; the US as the superpower superego.

Whatever the reason, these images have infected the US political psyche, helping to shape public opinion if not public policy. That overpopulation was a major cause of the genocide in Rwanda quickly became conventional wisdom in mainstream environmental and foreign policy circles. In a much heralded speech on the environment, former Secretary of State Warren Christopher warned that: "We must not forget the hard lessons of Rwanda, where depleted resources and swollen populations exacerbated the political and economic pressures that exploded into one of this decade's greatest tragedies."[3] Similarly, former Under Secretary of State for Global Affairs Timothy Wirth remarked recently that in Rwanda ". . . there were simply too many people competing for too few resources."[4]

Scholars more familiar with Rwanda's history, and that of neighbouring states, offer a much more complex understanding of the tragic events there. Whilst not denying the existence of demographic and environmental pressures, Peter Uvin, who worked as a development consultant in the region, analyzes the role of economic and political inequalities, institutionalized ethnic prejudice and foreign assistance in generating the conflict.

[. . .]

By over-emphasizing the role of population growth in environmental degradation and violence, the model legitimizes population control as a top priority. [. . .] Viewing population pressure as a security threat creates a false climate of fear and urgency, eroding the progress made by the women's health movement in moving the population establishment away from a narrow focus on fertility reduction to a more comprehensive women's reproductive health and rights perspective at the 1994 UN Population Conference in Cairo. This perspective is likely to be lost if family planning is viewed as the magic bullet to pacify Third World trouble spots and save the environment. [. . .]

This approach to population is part of a larger gender bias and blindness in the environment and security field. [. . .] While the neglect of gender issues could easily lead to policies that reinforce male hegemony and treat women as objects rather than subjects, it also prevents recognition of the leading role women have played in reconciliation efforts such as the peace movement in the Middle East and Somalia and the anti-communalism struggle in India. Women have been at the forefront of attempts at ecological restoration too, such as the Green Belt movement in Kenya and the Chipko movement in India. Rather than targeting women's fertility, it would make more sense to learn from their organizing efforts and engage them in the processes of conflict resolution.

Dehumanizing and depoliticizing refugees: By naturalizing poverty and political violence in the South, the scarcity-conflict model dehumanizes refugees, turning them into faceless invaders fleeing the chaos and environmental degradation they brought upon themselves. This view feeds racism and helps legitimize current US immigration "reforms" that, among other restrictive measures, severely curtail the rights of asylum seekers.

Militarizing sustainability: A particularly pressing issue is what impact the scarcity-conflict model will have on US defence policies. Currently, the Environment and Security Office of the US Department of Defense has a budget of about US$ 5 billion, almost equivalent to that of the civilian Environmental Protection Agency (EPA). [. . .] Isn't it a fundamental contradiction in terms to have the military engaged in "sustainable development" when it is it that has been the cause of so much environmental devastation and who is hardly known for its democratic, participatory and gender-sensitive approach?

[. . .] It may be an ironic outcome of the scarcity-conflict model that environmental groups are, themselves, targeted as security threats when they challenge the control and degradation of natural resources by local élites, governments and transnational corporations.

Anti-environmentalist repression is already occurring in many countries. Witness the violent suppression of the Ogoni people in Nigeria who are trying to protect their lands from destruction by Shell Oil. Sooner or later, when their lands are rendered uninhabitable, they too will probably be written off as resource scarce.

It is time to challenge the population, environment and security trinity before it exercises a firmer hold on public policy and consciousness. Whilst a watchdog role is necessary, it is not sufficient. The integration of progressive social science research with the experiences and activism of environmental, women's, peace and refugee rights movements can create a new and deeper understanding of the forces generating poverty, environmental destruction and violence. Solutions will come not from the barrel of a gun, a spy satellite or coercively imposed contraceptive technologies but from the wisdom and actions of those who have been working long and hard to overcome the scarcity of justice.

NOTES

1 Paul Kennedy is a British historian best known for his 1987 "big picture" history, *The Rise and Fall of the Great Powers*. Here Hartmann is referring to an essay he wrote with Matthew Connelly, "Must It Be the Rest against the West?," *Atlantic Monthly*, December 1994, 61–84.
2 François and Jean-Claude Duvalier were father and son authoritarian presidents of Haiti from 1957 to 1986.
3 Warren Christopher, "American Diplomacy and the Global Environmental Challenges of the 21st Century," speech, Stanford University, Palo Alto, CA, April 9, 1996, reprinted in Woodrow Wilson Center, *Environmental Change and Security Project Report* (Washington, DC: Woodrow Wilson Center, 1997), 81–85.
4 Timothy Wirth, "Population Pressure and the Crisis in the Great Lakes Region of Africa," remarks at the Center for National Policy, December 18, 1996, excerpted in Woodrow Wilson Center, *Environmental Change*, 118.

DOCUMENT 5.12

FROM WINONA LADUKE, *ALL OUR RELATIONS* (1999)

THE LAST 150 YEARS HAVE SEEN A GREAT HOLOCAUST. THERE HAVE been more species lost in the past 150 years than since the Ice Age. During the same time, Indigenous peoples have been disappearing from the face of the earth. Over 2000 nations of Indigenous peoples have gone extinct in the western hemisphere, and one nation disappears from the Amazon rainforest every year.

There is a direct relationship between the loss of cultural diversity and the loss of biodiversity. Wherever Indigenous peoples still remain, there is also a corresponding enclave of biodiversity. Trickles of rivers still running in the Northwest are home to the salmon still being sung back by Native people. The last few Florida panthers remain in the presence of traditional Seminoles, hidden away in the great cypress swamps of the Everglades. Some of the largest patches of remaining prairie grasses sway on reservation lands. One half of all reservation lands in the United States is still forested, much of it old-growth. Remnant pristine forest ecosystems, from the northern boreal forests to the Everglades, largely overlap with Native territories.

Winona LaDuke, *All Our Relations: Native Struggles for Land and Life* (1999; Chicago: Haymarket Books, 2015), excerpt from the introduction. Reproduced with permission of Haymarket Books.

In the Northwest, virtually every river is home to a people, each as distinct as a species of salmon. The Tillamook, Siletz, Yaquina, Alsea, Siuslaw, Umpqua, Hanis, Miluk, Colville, Tututni, Shasta, Costa, and Chetco are all peoples living at the mouths of salmon rivers. One hundred and seven stocks of salmon have already become extinct in the Pacific Northwest, and 89 are endangered. "Salmon were put here by the Creator, and it is our responsibility to harvest and protect the salmon so that the cycle of life continues," explains Pierson Mitchell of the Columbia River Intertribal Fishing Commission. "Whenever we have a funeral, we mourn a loved one, yes, but we are also reminded of the loss of our salmon and other traditional foods," laments Bill Yallup, Sr., the Yakama tribal chairman.

The stories of the fish and the people are not so different. Environmental destruction threatens the existence of both. The Tygh band of the Lower Deschutes River in Oregon includes a scant five families, struggling to maintain their traditional way of life and relationship to the salmon. "I wanted to dance the salmon, know the salmon, say goodbye to the salmon," says Susana Santos, a Tygh artist, fisherwoman, and community organizer. "Now I am looking at the completion of destruction, from the Exxon Valdez to . . . those dams . . . Seventeen fish came down the river last year. None this year. The people are the salmon, and the salmon are the people. How do you quantify that?"

Native American teachings describe the relations all around—animals, fish, trees, and rocks—as our brothers, sisters, uncles, and grandpas. Our relations to each other, our prayers whispered across generations to our relatives, are what bind our cultures together. The protection, teachings, and gifts of our relatives have for generations preserved our families. These relations are honored in ceremony, song, story, and life that keep relations close—to buffalo, sturgeon, salmon, turtles, bears, wolves, and panthers. These are our older relatives—the ones who came before and taught us how to live. Their obliteration by dams, guns, and bounties is an immense loss to Native families and cultures. Their absence may mean that people sing to a barren river, a caged bear, or buffalo far away. It is the struggle to preserve that which remains and the struggle to recover that characterizes much of Native environmentalism. It is these relationships that industrialism seeks to disrupt. Native communities will resist with great determination.

> Salmon was presented to me and my family through our religion as our brother. The same with the deer. And our sisters are roots and berries.

And you would treat them as such. Their life to you is just as valuable as another person's would be.

—MARGARET SALUSKIN, Yakama

[. . .]

In our communities, Native environmentalists sing centuries-old songs to renew life, to give thanks for the strawberries, to call home fish, and to thank Mother Earth for her blessings. We are the descendants of Little Thunder, who witnessed the massacre that cleared out the Great Plains to make way for the cowboys, cattle, and industrial farms. We have seen the great trees felled, the wolves taken for bounty, and the fish stacked rotting like cordwood. Those memories compel us, and the return of the descendants of these predators provoke us to stand again, stronger, and hopefully with more allies. We are the ones who stand up to the land eaters, the tree eaters, the destroyers and culture eaters.

[. . .]

I live on an Anishinaabeg reservation called White Earth in northern Minnesota. [. . .] We, the Anishinaabeg, are a forest culture. Our creation stories, culture, and way of life are entirely based on the forest, source of our medicinal plants and food, forest animals, and birch-bark baskets. [. . .] Virtually my entire reservation was clearcut at the turn of the century. [. . .] Our trees provided the foundation for major lumber companies, including Weyerhauser, and their destruction continued for ten decades.

[. . .] There is a direct link in our community between the loss of biodiversity—and the loss of the material and cultural wealth of the White Earth people. But we have resisted and are restoring. Today we are in litigation against logging expansion, and the White Earth Land Recovery Project works to restore the forests, recover the land, and restore our traditional forest culture. Our experience of survival and resistance is shared with many others. But it is not only about Native people.

In the final analysis, the survival of Native America is fundamentally about the collective survival of all human beings. The question of who gets to determine the destiny of the land, and of the people who live on it—those with the money or those who pray on the land—is a question that is alive throughout society. The question is posed eloquently by Lil'wat grandmother Loretta Pascal:

> This is my reason for standing up. To protect all around us, to continue our way of life, our culture. I ask them, "Where did you get your right

to destroy these forests? How does your right supersede my rights?" These are our forests, these are our ancestors.

[. . .] As Columbia River Tribes activist Ted Strong tells us,

> If this nation has a long way to go before all of our people are truly created equally without regard to race, religion, or national origin, it has even further to go before achieving anything that remotely resembles equal treatment for other creatures who called this land home before humans ever set foot upon it. . . . While the species themselves—fish, fowl, game, and the habitat they live in—have given us unparalleled wealth, they live crippled in their ability to persist and in conditions of captive squalor. . . . This enslavement and impoverishment of nature is no more tolerable or sensible than enslavement and impoverishment of other human beings. . . .

DOCUMENT 5.13

FROM JADE SASSER, "FROM DARKNESS INTO LIGHT: RACE, POPULATION, AND ENVIRONMENTAL ADVOCACY" (2014)

ENVIRONMENTALIST POPULATION ADVOCACY IS CENTRALLY CONcerned with constructing narratives about the relationships between particular populations and natural resource use, and devising interventions to change those relationships by reducing the number of people in the population. Whether voluntary or coercive, these interventions have historically been based on identifying rapidly growing populations in the global South as productive of environmental problems and resource shortages, a process in which racialization is central. As such, populations are marked for intervention not solely on the basis of what they do in the world in terms of resource use and consumption, but also what they represent in terms of sheer numbers and their ability to invoke racialized anxieties.

[...] I argue [...] in the context of population-environment-narratives, [...] that the development and circulation of ideas of racialized populations as environmentally problematic and in need of intervention is reflective of a

---

Jade Sasser, "From Darkness into Light: Race, Population, and Environmental Advocacy," *Antipode* 46, no. 5 (2014): 1240–57. Reproduced by permission of Wiley.

particular kind of power possessed by development actors. This power—the power to develop and circulate construct narratives about marginalized global South others, and to have that knowledge serve as the basis of international policy and program interventions—is predicated both on the prestige of development institutions, as well as the social marginalization of the people who are the objects of knowledge.

[R]acial narratives are deeply embedded in American environmentalist approaches to international population policy advocacy—but that these efforts invoke race in complex and contradictory ways. While population discourses have historically marked racialized bodies and populations as environmental threats, racialized and gendered bodies occupy a key role in new efforts to reframe advocacy projects as socially progressive. As such, those marked in population–environment discourse as racial "others" simultaneously represent both population "problems" as well as strategic solutions for ENGOs[1] engaged in population work, even as race is no longer explicitly invoked. In an ironic moment in which scientists are increasingly returning to discussions of the biological and genetic basis of race, these framings mark the reproductive bodies of women of color in the global South as both global burden and potential salvation.

Exploring race in this context is a challenging undertaking, as it usually operates as an unmarked category in environmentalist discussions of demographic difference.

At the heart of the policy-oriented "degradation narratives" promoted by Ehrlich, Vogt, Osborn and Hardin is a logic that identifies both poverty and natural resource shortages as the result of a surplus of bodies. But which bodies were they talking about? Bandarage's analysis of population crisis rhetoric demonstrates that struggles for independence from colonization across the global South gave rise to a reframing of the significance of colonial populations in the North. While a range of policies were introduced across colonial nations to boost the size of colonial labor forces, after independence, the resulting population booms were recharacterized as threatening, dangerous, and potential drivers of neo-Malthusian food shortages.

[...]

While population–environment advocacy does not call for the killing of racially different populations, it can be understood as calling for the selective suppression of life through restrictive food aid policies, withholding medical care to rapidly growing populations, and forced restrictions on fertility—views that found their way into more mainstream environmentalist approaches over the twentieth century.

[...] [There is] a longstanding practice in the development community: that of using visual imagery to stand in as a representation of population growth and poverty in the global South. Ranging from pictures of large, teeming crowds, mothers surrounded by babies, cartoon drawings of hordes of people hanging from the edges of a beleaguered earth, and masses of dark bodies swarming around food aid packages, these images have become well recognized icons that represent the "population problem." In the 1960s and 1970s, these images were often seen on the covers of popular magazines and full-page spreads in newspapers; today, the image of the anonymous, teeming crowd continues to serve as the iconic focal point of advocacy materials and special issues of environmental magazines. Yet the basic message of the images remains unchanged over the course of time: populations are still growing, but they are only certain populations: people of color, often overwhelmingly poor and foreign.

[...] Depictions of "the masses" also preclude any understanding of poverty, gender inequality, and power. This is particularly salient in the context of pictures depicting "population," "population growth," or "the population problem." When "population growth" is reduced to a flat, two-dimensional image, it is abstracted from any context within histories of colonization, or contemporary webs of relations in which global capitalism and patriarchy give rise to conditions that maintain population trends. At the same time, race and gender remain unproblematized in these images: population growth is the domain of the poor, the racially coded, the environmentally problematic actor. Images of black and brown bodies, proliferating rapidly and filling up crowded images of urban chaos, mark a striking absence—that of white bodies. In the racial politics of population imagery, the "crisis" on display is one of a world which is rapidly filling with people of color. [...]

The 2009 book entitled *A Pivotal Moment: Population, Environmental, and the Justice Challenge* outlined a new concept known as population justice. Described by its author as both an "ethical compass," and a framework for "understanding—and acting upon" population growth, climate change, and global scale social and economic inequality, population justice is defined as drawing on environmental and reproductive justice frameworks to focus attention on the "inequalities—both gender and economic—that underlie both rapid population growth and the destruction of the natural environment" (Mazur 2009:17).[2] [. . .] The model draws on environmental justice and reproductive justice for inspiration, in an attempt to articulate a response to perceived injustice—in this case, the injustice of inadequate access to contraceptives for women in the global South. At the same time, population justice eschews addressing the specific forms of social inequality that the environmental and reproductive justice frameworks were mobilized to undermine, specifically racial inequality. [. . .] Alternatively, some US-based RJ[3] activists have worked to reframe the link between reproductive health and environment by positioning the bodies of poor women of color at the nexus of exposure to environmental harms and their reproductive health effects. This approach allows for a critical intersectional analysis of structural violence along the lines of race, class, and gender, as well as marking women's fertility and reproduction a productive space for understanding the workings of environmental power and privilege. If social justice is framed as a link between women's racialized bodies and environments, this is a good place to begin.

NOTES

1. Environmental non-governmental organizations.
2. Laurie Mazur, ed., *A Pivotal Moment: Population, Justice, and the Environmental Challenge* (Washington, DC: Island Press, 2009).
3. Racial justice.

INDEX

Africa, 46, 67, 80, 84, 90, 132, 152–54, 193–94, 198, 206–8, 209–12, 237–38
Amazon, 231
America. *See* United States of America
Americas. *See* New World
Anthropocene, x, 200, 228–29, 230–32
Arab Spring, 198
Armstrong, William, 114
Asia, 46, 84, 90, 152–54, 198

Bakewell, Robert, 57, 105
Bangladesh, 182, 212
Beddington, John, 217–21
Bengal famine, 183
Besant, Annie, 98, 128–30, 199
Beveridge, William, 100
birth control, 98, 143, 147, 149, 152, 154–55, 156, 159–60, 167–68, 176–77, 199–200, 233–34
birth rate, 5, 129, 136, 160, 178–79, 237
Blade Runner, 4
Borlaug, Norman, 145, 184–88
Botero, Giovanni, 13, 20–22, 57
Boyd Orr, John, 142, 156–58, 185
Boyle, Robert, 4
Bradlaugh, Charles, 128
Brazil, 100–101, 138–40, 207
breeding. *See* eugenics
Burundi, 210

carrying capacity, 5, 159
Castro, Josué de, 100–101, 138–40, 142
census, 2, 59

Certayne Causes, 13, 17–19
Charlemagne, 30
checks to population growth. *See* limits to population growth
China, 7, 29, 35, 83–84, 89, 218, 219, 227
Christopher, Warren, 238
Cincotta, Richard, 214
cities. *See* urbanization
climate change, 4, 10, 15, 162, 171, 200–201, 203–5, 219–21, 222–24, 225–27, 228–29, 230–32, 236–40
coal, 3, 98–99, 112–15, 118–19
Cobbett, William, 58
Cohen, Joel, 222–24
Coke, Thomas, 86
Cold War, 142, 158, 197–98, 207–8, 215, 236–37
collapse hypothesis, 198–99, 209–12
colonies. *See* imperialism
Commoner, Barry, 144, 174–77
Communism, 107–11, 128–30, 142, 158
Condorcet, Marquis de, 2, 8, 55–58, 66–71, 73
conservation of nature, 3, 6, 119–20, 122, 126–27, 136, 166, 187–88
Crutzen, Paul, 228–29

Darwin, Charles, 6, 96–98, 102–6, 107–9
Darwinism, xi, 96–98; social, 97
David, King, 21
De Candolle, Augustin, 102
democracy, 146, 148, 198, 208, 235
depopulation, 31–32, 33–38, 39–43, 135–36
demographic transition theory, 56

249

developing world, 2, 7, 142, 144, 176, 182, 185–87, 194–95, 198, 213–15, 218–20, 226, 237
Diamond, Jared, 198–200, 209–12
Diodorus Siculus, 37
Dionysius Halicarnassus, 20
D'Orbigny, Alcide, 109
Du Bos, Jean-Baptiste, 36
Duvalier, François, 204, 237
Duvalier, Jean-Claude, 204, 237

Earth Day, 144, 174
East, Edward, 6
Easter Island, 212
ecology, 4, 141, 147–49, 150, 171
ecosystem, 4, 161–62, 200–201, 217–21, 232
Ehrlich, Paul, 3, 4, 5, 10, 143, 145, 159–63, 174–76, 194, 197, 199, 200, 213–14, 246
Einstein, Albert, 205
England, 85–86
Enlightenment debate about population size, 15, 28, 32, 33–38, 39–43, 56, 80
environment, 1, 3–4, 141–42, 143, 160–63, 207–8, 230–32, 241–44
environmental determinism, 14, 15, 28–31, 34, 39–40, 41, 48–50, 210–12
environmental history, 7–9
evolution. *See* Darwinism
eugenics, xi, 5–6, 46, 70–71, 97, 134–37, 167–68
Europe, 30–32, 80, 131–32, 152–55

famine, 30–31, 39, 43, 142–44, 156, 159, 181–83, 184–85, 194
feminism, and population, 5–7, 98, 129–30, 199–200, 233–35, 236–40, 245–48
food, 2, 56; availability and entitlement, 181–83, 217–19; triage, 5, 144, 156, 170
Food and Agriculture Organization, 100, 142
Forster-Lloyd, William, 165
France, 30–31, 67, 136–37
Franklin, Benjamin, 13, 14, 16, 44–47, 62, 141
free trade and capitalism, 99–100, 116–18, 145, 158, 165
French Revolution, 58, 72, 96
Fuller, Buckminster, 142

Galton, Francis, 6, 97
Germany, 29, 46, 132–33, 136–37, 151
ghost acres, 2
Glacken, Clarence, 7–9
global South, 7, 143, 233, 245–48
Godwin, William, 2, 55–60, 61–65, 73, 74, 82–88, 96, 142, 199
Goldstone, Jack A., 213–16

Graunt, John, 14, 25–27
Greece, 29, 31, 35
Green Revolution, 145, 184–88

Haiti, 204, 237
Hardin, Garrett, 3, 4, 5–6, 10, 143–44, 164–68, 170, 174, 190, 246
Hartmann, Betsy, 236–40
Hazlitt, William, 58, 199
Henry VIII, 13, 14
Holdren, John, 144, 175–76
Holland, 29, 31, 210, 212
Holocene, 228
Homer-Dixon, Thomas, 208, 237
Hume, David, 8, 13, 14–15, 33–38
Huxley, Aldous, 134–37
Huxley, Thomas, 97, 109–10

imperialism, 22, 30, 35, 37–38, 44–47, 53–54, 59, 125, 148, 179
India, 5, 7, 142, 160, 178–80, 183, 198, 207, 218, 238
Indigenous peoples, 59–60, 90, 200, 241–44
industrial economies, 13, 60, 114, 117–18, 132–33
International Conference on Population and Development, 7, 145, 199, 238
IPAT equation, 144, 146, 175
Italy, 34–37

Japan, 89, 151
Jevons, William, 3, 98, 112–15

Kaplan, Robert, 197, 206–8, 237
Keynes, John, 3, 99–100, 131–33
Kropotkin, Petr, 97–98, 107–11

LaDuke, Winona, 241–44
land, uncultivated, 55–57, 59, 61–62, 83–85, 86–87, 118, 122, 125, 151–52, 231–32
Lebensraum, 151, 154–55
limits to population growth, 21, 34, 45–46, 62–63, 68–69, 74–75, 77–79, 82, 102–4, 165–66, 195–96
London, 14, 25–27, 35–36, 51–53, 93
luxury, 14–16, 17–19, 36, 39, 48–50, 51–54, 68

Malthus, Thomas, 56–60, 72–81, 82–88, 89–90, 91–92, 96, 102, 104, 112, 132, 156, 157, 170, 172, 176, 187, 195, 200, 207, 220
Malthusianism, 108, 178, 199–200, 211–12; Green, xii, 142; moment of, ix, 4–5, 9, 141–46, 202; reverse, xii; sooty, 98

Mamdani, Mahood, 143, 178–80
Martineau, Harriet, 58
Mathews, Jessica, 203–5
migration, 22, 45–46, 59, 128, 131, 136, 152, 154–55, 221, 238
Mill, John Stuart, 3, 99, 121–23, 126
Montesquieu, Charles de, 8, 14, 15–16, 28–32
mortality, 14, 16, 21, 48–49, 54, 135
Mukerjee, Radhakamal, 142, 150–55

nature, 3–4, 56–58, 60, 67, 74, 75, 92, 102, 103–4, 124–25, 179, 199–200
Nile, 161, 207

O'Neill, Brian, 225–27
OPEC oil crisis, 3, 144, 172
organic. *See* industrial economies
Osborn, Fairfield, 6, 246
Ostrom, Elinor, 143, 189–92

Paddock, Paul, 143
Paddock, William, 143
pandemic, 94, 229
Petty, William, 195
plague, 20, 21, 25, 94
Plattes, Gabriel, 13, 15–16, 23–24
political arithmetic, 2, 12, 14, 25–27, 51–54
political economy, 58, 112, 125, 132
population: bomb, 7, 142–43, 159–63, 194, 197–98, 213–16; concept of, 1–2, 146, 200–201, 228; density, 2, 36, 122; optimum, 99–100, 122, 125–26, 136, 150–52, 155; problem, 2, 13, 57, 136, 141, 145, 160, 164, 169, 176, 178–80, 247; quality, 6, 100, 134–37; and rate of growth, 2, 34, 45–46, 153, 187, 218, 233–34. *See also* overpopulation
Price, Richard, 14, 16, 51–54, 85
progress, 66–71, 114
Puffendorf, Samuel, 30

quantification of population, 14–15, 25–27

race and population, 5–6, 46, 150–55, 200, 233–35, 245–48
Reagan, Ronald, 145
resources, 2–3, 56, 146, 195–96; relation to population, 74–77, 82, 85, 88, 89, 93, 103, 112–13, 119, 129, 131–32, 176, 194–95, 201–2; scarcity of, 2–3
Ricardo, David, 58, 125–26
Rockström, Johan, 230–32
Rome, 14, 20–22, 32, 34–37

Roosevelt, Theodore, 3, 6
Rousseau, Jean-Jacques, 109–10
Ruskin, John, 99, 124–27
Russia, 98, 133
Rwanda, 198, 210–12, 237–38

Sanger, Margaret, 199
Sasser, Jade, 245–48
security demographic, 199, 201, 203–5, 207, 213–16, 236–40
Sen, Amartya, 143, 181–83
Shelley, Mary, 58–59, 93–95
Short, Thomas, 14, 48–50
Sierra Leone, 198, 206–7
Simon, Julian, 7, 145, 193–96, 199
Smith, Adam, 73, 164–65
Socialism, 107–11, 128–30, 142, 158
Soviet Union. *See* Russia
Spencer, Herbert, 97, 109
stadial theory of society, 29–30, 41–42, 53–54, 67–68, 75–76, 79–80, 119
Stopes, Marie, 199
struggle for survival, 97, 100, 104–6, 107–12, 121

technology, 23–24, 29, 56–57, 59, 67–69, 76, 84–85, 113–14, 122, 142, 145, 156–58, 168, 174–77, 185–88, 194–96, 221, 229
territory, 2, 26, 30, 45, 151
tragedy of the commons, 164–68, 189–92

uncultivated land. *See* land, uncultivated
United Nations, 141–42, 148–49, 167, 193–94, 235. *See also* Food and Agriculture Organization; International Conference on Population and Development
United States of America, 24, 35, 37–38, 44–47, 51, 53–54, 76, 79–80, 84, 89–90, 128, 133, 136, 141, 144, 145, 148, 161, 174–77, 233, 236–40, 241–44
urbanization, 20–22, 35–36, 48–50, 51–54, 136, 138–39, 214, 218, 220–21, 226–27

Versailles, Treaty of, 100, 132–33, 153
Vogt, William, 3, 147–49, 156, 246

Wallace, Alfred Russel, 3, 96–98, 107, 116–20
Wallace, Robert, 8, 14, 15, 39–43, 55, 73
Wordsworth, William, 3, 99
World Bank, 211, 234
World War I, 99–100, 132–33, 136

youth bulge, 198, 214

INDEX | 251

ROBERT J. MAYHEW is Fellow and Senior Tutor at Pembroke College, Cambridge and Honorary Professor of Historical Geography at the University of Bristol. He has published extensively on the history of Malthusian thought, including *Malthus: The Life and Legacies of an Untimely Prophet* (2014) and *New Perspectives on Malthus* (editor, 2016). He has also edited Malthus's selected works for Penguin Classics. He is a Fellow of the British Academy.

WEYERHAEUSER ENVIRONMENTAL BOOKS

Charged: A History of Batteries and Lessons for a Clean Energy Future, by James Morton Turner

Wetlands in a Dry Land: More-Than-Human Histories of Australia's Murray-Darling Basin, by Emily O'Gorman

Seeds of Control: Japan's Empire of Forestry in Colonial Korea, by David Fedman

Fir and Empire: The Transformation of Forests in Early Modern China, by Ian M. Miller

Communist Pigs: An Animal History of East Germany's Rise and Fall, by Thomas Fleischman

Footprints of War: Militarized Landscapes in Vietnam, by David Biggs

Cultivating Nature: The Conservation of a Valencian Working Landscape, by Sarah R. Hamilton

Bringing Whales Ashore: Oceans and the Environment of Early Modern Japan, by Jakobina K. Arch

The Organic Profit: Rodale and the Making of Marketplace Environmentalism, by Andrew N. Case

Seismic City: An Environmental History of San Francisco's 1906 Earthquake, by Joanna L. Dyl

Smell Detectives: An Olfactory History of Nineteenth-Century Urban America, by Melanie A. Kiechle

Defending Giants: The Redwood Wars and the Transformation of American Environmental Politics, by Darren Frederick Speece

The City Is More Than Human: An Animal History of Seattle, by Frederick L. Brown

Wilderburbs: Communities on Nature's Edge, by Lincoln Bramwell

How to Read the American West: A Field Guide, by William Wyckoff

Behind the Curve: Science and the Politics of Global Warming, by Joshua P. Howe

Whales and Nations: Environmental Diplomacy on the High Seas, by Kurkpatrick Dorsey

Loving Nature, Fearing the State: Environmentalism and Antigovernment Politics before Reagan, by Brian Allen Drake

Pests in the City: Flies, Bedbugs, Cockroaches, and Rats, by Dawn Day Biehler

Tangled Roots: The Appalachian Trail and American Environmental Politics, by Sarah Mittlefehldt

Vacationland: Tourism and Environment in the Colorado High Country, by William Philpott

Car Country: An Environmental History, by Christopher W. Wells

Nature Next Door: Cities and Trees in the American Northeast, by Ellen Stroud

Pumpkin: The Curious History of an American Icon, by Cindy Ott

The Promise of Wilderness: American Environmental Politics since 1964, by James Morton Turner

The Republic of Nature: An Environmental History of the United States, by Mark Fiege

A Storied Wilderness: Rewilding the Apostle Islands, by James W. Feldman

Iceland Imagined: Nature, Culture, and Storytelling in the North Atlantic, by Karen Oslund

Quagmire: Nation-Building and Nature in the Mekong Delta, by David Biggs

Seeking Refuge: Birds and Landscapes of the Pacific Flyway, by Robert M. Wilson

Toxic Archipelago: A History of Industrial Disease in Japan, by Brett L. Walker

Dreaming of Sheep in Navajo Country, by Marsha L. Weisiger

Shaping the Shoreline: Fisheries and Tourism on the Monterey Coast, by Connie Y. Chiang

The Fishermen's Frontier: People and Salmon in Southeast Alaska, by David F. Arnold

Making Mountains: New York City and the Catskills, by David Stradling

Plowed Under: Agriculture and Environment in the Palouse, by Andrew P. Duffin

The Country in the City: The Greening of the San Francisco Bay Area, by Richard A. Walker

Native Seattle: Histories from the Crossing-Over Place, by Coll Thrush

Drawing Lines in the Forest: Creating Wilderness Areas in the Pacific Northwest, by Kevin R. Marsh

Public Power, Private Dams: The Hells Canyon High Dam Controversy, by Karl Boyd Brooks

Windshield Wilderness: Cars, Roads, and Nature in Washington's National Parks, by David Louter

On the Road Again: Montana's Changing Landscape, by William Wyckoff

Wilderness Forever: Howard Zahniser and the Path to the Wilderness Act, by Mark Harvey

The Lost Wolves of Japan, by Brett L. Walker

Landscapes of Conflict: The Oregon Story, 1940–2000, by William G. Robbins

Faith in Nature: Environmentalism as Religious Quest, by Thomas R. Dunlap

The Nature of Gold: An Environmental History of the Klondike Gold Rush, by Kathryn Morse

Where Land and Water Meet: A Western Landscape Transformed, by Nancy Langston

The Rhine: An Eco-Biography, 1815–2000, by Mark Cioc

Driven Wild: How the Fight against Automobiles Launched the Modern Wilderness Movement, by Paul S. Sutter

George Perkins Marsh: Prophet of Conservation, by David Lowenthal

Making Salmon: An Environmental History of the Northwest Fisheries Crisis, by Joseph E. Taylor III

Irrigated Eden: The Making of an Agricultural Landscape in the American West, by Mark Fiege

The Dawn of Conservation Diplomacy: U.S.-Canadian Wildlife Protection Treaties in the Progressive Era, by Kirkpatrick Dorsey

Landscapes of Promise: The Oregon Story, 1800–1940, by William G. Robbins

Forest Dreams, Forest Nightmares: The Paradox of Old Growth in the Inland West, by Nancy Langston

The Natural History of Puget Sound Country, by Arthur R. Kruckeberg

WEYERHAEUSER ENVIRONMENTAL CLASSICS

Debating Malthus: A Documentary Reader on Population, Resources, and the Environment, edited by Robert J. Mayhew

Environmental Justice in Postwar America: A Documentary Reader, edited by Christopher W. Wells

Making Climate Change History: Documents from Global Warming's Past, edited by Joshua P. Howe

Nuclear Reactions: Documenting American Encounters with Nuclear Energy, edited by James W. Feldman

The Wilderness Writings of Howard Zahniser, edited by Mark Harvey

The Environmental Moment: 1968–1972, edited by David Stradling

Reel Nature: America's Romance with Wildlife on Film, by Gregg Mitman

DDT, Silent Spring, and the Rise of Environmentalism, edited by Thomas R. Dunlap

Conservation in the Progressive Era: Classic Texts, edited by David Stradling

Man and Nature: Or, Physical Geography as Modified by Human Action, by George Perkins Marsh

A Symbol of Wilderness: Echo Park and the American Conservation Movement, by Mark W. T. Harvey

Tutira: The Story of a New Zealand Sheep Station, by Herbert Guthrie-Smith

Mountain Gloom and Mountain Glory: The Development of the Aesthetics of the Infinite, by Marjorie Hope Nicolson

The Great Columbia Plain: A Historical Geography, 1805–1910, by Donald W. Meinig

CYCLE OF FIRE

Fire: A Brief History, second edition, by Stephen J. Pyne

The Ice: A Journey to Antarctica, by Stephen J. Pyne

Burning Bush: A Fire History of Australia, by Stephen J. Pyne

Fire in America: A Cultural History of Wildland and Rural Fire, by Stephen J. Pyne

Vestal Fire: An Environmental History, Told through Fire, of Europe and Europe's Encounter with the World, by Stephen J. Pyne

World Fire: The Culture of Fire on Earth, by Stephen J. Pyne

ALSO AVAILABLE:

Awful Splendour: A Fire History of Canada, by Stephen J. Pyne

CPSIA information can be obtained
at www.ICGtesting.com
Printed in the USA
BVHW061453200322
631481BV00002B/9